AMERICAN LIBRARY PHILOSOPHY

An Anthology

CONTRIBUTIONS TO LIBRARY LITERATURE SERIES

John David Marshall, *General Editor*

American Library Philosophy

AN ANTHOLOGY

Selected and introduced by
BARBARA McCRIMMON

THE SHOE STRING PRESS, INC.

HAMDEN, CONNECTICUT

1975

Library of Congress Cataloging in Publication Data

Main entry under title:

American library philosophy.

(Contributions to library literature series)
Bibliography: p.
Includes index.
1. Library science—Philosophy—Addresses, essays,
lectures. 2. Libraries—United States—Addresses,
essays, lectures. I. McCrimmon, Barbara.
Z665.A544   020'.8   75-9544
ISBN 0-208-01503-5

Printed in the United States of America

CONTENTS

American librarians are reputed to think and write almost
exclusively about their activities in the library—about what
they do, not why it should be done. In this they could be
said to exemplify the pioneering spirit of the American environment in which experimentation and self-reliance have
replaced Old World traditions. Yet during the past hundred
years enough has been written about the objectives, purposes,
and uses of libraries, and about the aims and obligations of
librarianship, to provide an overview of the development of
the professional consciousness. As librarians have sought a
theoretical foundation for their calling, two factors have been
basic to all their thinking: faith in democracy and belief in
the power of education to promote the general welfare. These
tenets have constituted the solid understructure of American
librarianship. Therefore, where statements of purpose occur
in American library literature, they generally reflect contemporary social ideals and the objectives of the educational
process in American life. The library has been established by
the people for their use, and it must be responsive to their
demands: their philosophy must to a large extent be the
library's philosophy.

The tenets that underlie American librarianship find
another expression in the two points of view toward the profession that have existed from the first among librarians. One
of these is oriented to the people and advocates the businesslike provision of useful reading matter for the electorate at
large; the other is book-oriented and devoted to the perpetua-
tion of the deepest meaning and the best taste. One is

concerned with the informational and recreational needs of
the mass public; the other with the personal development of
individuals through reading. Both have ardent advocates, but
since public librarians have dominated the profession in
America, and since the bookmen's values are fundamentally
European, the broader sociological viewpoint has had the
majority of adherents in the United States.

Today both types are being challenged by those who are
committed to the methods of the sciences and who bid fair
to revolutionize traditional ideas of the purpose and function
of the library. While the ascendency of this new view is as yet
incomplete, it is instructive to look back over library literature of the past to see what has been said whenever an ideo-
logical statement was called for. From the writings of American librarians who have answered that call, this anthology has
been selected. The aim has been to choose articles that
demonstrate the successive stages of library development in
this country and that represent the thought of outstanding
members of the profession. All are reprinted as originally
published except for the correction of typographical errors.
The words of the authors often reflect the varying cultural,
political, and economic conditions of the time in which they
wrote, as well as the constant tension between the library's
two responsibilities in a democracy, for individual freedom
and for social stability. But there is also evident a considerable area of agreement in which the nucleus of an American
library philosophy may be found.

The first six selections come from men of the nineteenth
century who represent the founders of American librarianship: Dewey, Dana, Foss, Bostwick, Putnam, and Richardson.
The first three of these conceive of the library as an extension
of the public educational system and are chiefly concerned
about its administration as a public institution. The last three
are interested in the librarian as the agent of the book, in his
qualifications and his duty to his patrons.

Next are three articles by men who were shaped professionally by the Graduate Library School at the University of
Chicago in the 1930's and '40's: Danton, Martin, and Goldhor.

They belong to the strongest current in mid-century American librarianship, the attempt to find the true place of the
library in society through sociological research, and they deal
with reading as an object of controlled investigation. In contrast to them we have four bibliophiles—Sayers, Haines,
Butler, and Powell—whose writings have helped to balance
those of the pragmatists in the literature. Their concern is
with the contents of good books as they affect the character
of the individual and the cultural tone of society.

Shera, Nitecki, and Marco are also Chicago men. They
join with Harlow to bring us to the newer philosophic
thought of the 1960's, Shera taking account of the impact of
post-war electronics on library science, and Harlow giving us
a glimpse of the current attempts to apply concepts from the
scientific world to the philosophy of the library, while
Nitecki analyzes the profession in philosophic terms. Their
contemporary, Marco, on the other hand, proves the strength
of the traditional humanistic outlook in the face of wide-
spread changes in library practice. Shores and MacLeish
round out our survey with their idealistic respect for the
graphic expression of knowledge as the best hope of civilization and for the library's potential share in the fulfilling of
that hope.

Thus we have a fair representation of the various views
of the profession that have put their stamp on its first century: the educators and the book-lovers, the sociologists and
the humanists, the businessmen and the esthetes, all have
stated their convictions throughout the years. When their
beliefs are blended the resulting formulation comes close to
that of an American library philosophy.

My thanks go to the authors and publishers who have
allowed their publications to be used in this volume, and to
John David Marshall, a most sympathetic and helpful editor.

—BARBARA McCRIMMON

At the end of the nineteenth century librarians in America were somewhat unsure of their role among the other professions, but looked to their leaders for sound advice. They were often told by those leaders that they had a mission—to make knowledge available through bibliographic devices, to encourage reading, and to promote the Puritan standard of values that had made their country a world power. They did not call these aims a philosophy, for they were too well occupied with practical affairs to feel the need of one. Instead they imagined the best possible librarians bringing their profession to the highest possible estate and described the scene they envisioned for the inspiration of their fellows.

In 1897 Melvil Dewey went to England for the International Conference of Librarians and addressed them on the library in its relationship to government. He began by announcing that the "Library Age" had dawned, meaning that the development of libraries had reached a point of refinement where the chief task before librarians was "excluding the pernicious" from their collections for the protection of both "the individual and the State." While acknowledging the value of good newspapers, Dewey expressed great distaste for sensational journalism, and exhorted librarians to militate against it. They should also, he said, convince the State of its obligation to support the continuing education of citizens after they leave the public school system. "Home education" was the responsibility of the library, which should act as a community center for cultural activities. Good reading, according to Dewey, had helped make the Anglo-Saxon civilizations supreme in the world, and the next step was to see that knowledge was free to all. If government support and protection for libraries were universal, Dewey thought, and there were a "strong man" in each State to lead library development, as he himself did in his own state of New York, the world would undoubtedly be a better place.

The details for Dewey's outline of professional ideals were filled in by John Cotton Dana in his article of 1906 on the obligation of the library to act as a cultural force in its community. Dana gave specific examples of ways to take the library to the people and give them incentives to read. In Dana's view "the library must allure to knowledge," and it could also aid social cooperation by promoting mutual sympathy among citizens of different national backgrounds. He believed that books contained so much wisdom that those who regularly used them could not help but be more wise themselves. But the library must first "make itself known," by using every device—the newspaper, the telephone, the mails—in order to advertise its potential for study, information, and stimulation. This frankly commercial approach carried to its logical conclusion Dewey's claim that the library had become "aggressive" as an educational force. In his article Dana also presaged the growth of specialized information services, a development he himself later helped to promote. To him the library was both for scholars and for the people; it was an "index" of all the facts, theories, and fancies of life and its object was to stimulate and satisfy every kind of reading interest.

In contrast to Dana's pragmatism was the idealistic attitude of Arthur E. Bostwick. His graceful tribute to the book as an object of affection, delivered in 1906 to the New York Library Association, compared the love of books to that for human beings. Some men, he said, may cherish books for their outward appearance, for their binding or their decoration, but the true lover would be attracted by their content, or "soul." It was not just a desire for knowledge, which might be shared by savages, but reverence for the book itself as a vehicle for transmitting ideas, claimed Bostwick, that had impelled civilized men to establish libraries. Librarians, therefore, should be lovers of books. A mere fondness for reading, shallow and without emotional commitment, would not be the same, though to Bostwick even journalistic writing had at least temporary value for an extensive readership. It should be realized, however, that there were many people who had no desire whatever to read, who might have developed in school an antagonism to books which would have to be overcome if they were to be drawn into the library. This, said Bostwick, was the duty of the librarian; he could encourage such people to read good literature by being sympathetic and helpful to them. If he himself loved books, he would, in Bostwick's opinion, find this easy to do, and he would then be practicing "true librarianship."

A point of view closer to that of Dewey and Dana was expressed by Sam Walter Foss, author of the humorous *Song of the Library Staff.* The deceptively informal words of his speech to the Massachusetts Library Club in 1908 convey a deep concern for the best in library service. Foss considered the librarian as a person, saying that his "great cardinal virtues" should be enthusiasm for his work with books and tolerance for all types of people and every kind of literature. An intolerant librarian could hold his community back in the march of progress, whereas a "good mixer" could infect others with the "measles of enthusiasm" for books and reading. Foss gave advice as to how the librarian could influence his city government and board of trustees in order to get "liberal appropriations" and support for his "broad general scheme." Then, admitting that the librarian's first task was to acquire a good collection, he stressed the second task, which was getting the books read, especially by men. The foremost goal for the librarian, to Foss, was increased circulation, not only of his books, but of himself. In this way he could assume the intellectual leadership for which his profession fitted him and which constituted his "modern opportunity."

In contrast to Foss's benign attitude is the argumentative one which Herbert Putnam expressed to his colleagues in the American Library Association at their annual meeting at

Berkeley in 1915. In order to answer some critics of libraries who had been cited by ALA President Hiller C. Wellman, Putnam made a legalistic defense of the public ownership of books. The basic principles of the public library, he pointed out, had been set forth as long ago as 1850, and its foundations were so firmly established that they should not be reconsidered in the face of criticism by outsiders. One common assertion was that libraries contained too much ephemeral matter, and this Putnam denied out of respect for the contemporary needs of contemporary lives. He found nothing to fear in the "age of print," deeming it impossible for people to be harmed by the luxury of too much reading. By a series of rich analogies he stated the case for the widest indulgence in books, defending the typically casual American attitude toward them. Since the entire population, rather than an elite, was to be served, the library must, Putnam said, accept all levels of taste; but an opportunity for raising the lower levels existed in "freer direct contact with the books themselves," and the "mediation" of the librarian well versed both in books and in the characteristics of readers.

Twelve years later, in 1927, Ernest Cushing Richardson addressed himself to the question whether librarianship in America had overemphasized the commercial attitude to the neglect of the furthering of knowledge. He recognized that the profession was in part a business and that "the philosophy of business is a part, therefore, of the philosophy of librarianship." But he also saw that knowledge, in books or in people, had to be the chief preoccupation of the librarian. In an attempt to reconcile these two emphases, the material and the spiritual, Richardson inquired into the "real nature and meaning" of the profession, calling this a search for a philosophy. He conceived of the library as a repository for a multitude of fragments of knowledge which, when classified, constituted a microcosm of the universe. It contained, he said, the recorded cooperative knowledge of all men and was, therefore, the "memory of the race." In modern terms, the library, to Richardson, was a source of energy to be tapped in order to make people "more alive." The librarian, however,

must provide the spark, and this he could do only by virtue
of a thorough knowledge of books. The best way Richardson
could see to avoid the dominance of the commercial mental-
ity in the profession was to accentuate learning by the development of higher education for librarians.

The greatest impetus in the direction Richardson anticipated came when the Graduate Library School was founded
at the University of Chicago in the following year. From it
emanated the most influential library thought, writing, and
research of the ensuing decades. In accordance with its
strongly sociological emphasis, the faculty soon launched a
series of studies intended to provide a factual basis for the
study of library science. At the same time the school encouraged consideration of the philosophy of librarianship and its
implications for the future development of library service in
the United States.

One of the outstanding doctoral students who tackled
these problems at the Chicago school was J. Periam Danton,
whose "Plea for a Philosophy of Librarianship," 1934, attempted to present a foundation for discussion of the subject.
Danton differentiated library philosophy from library science,
cited evidence that there was no "adequate" library philosophy, told what a philosophy should do and what the results
of the lack of one were, and gave a framework for thinking
on the subject. He suggested that a series of articles, each one
dealing definitively with the philosophical basis of one area
of the profession, when taken together, might "serve as a professional philosophy." This is one of his best insights; yet he
despaired of his ideal ever being achieved, for he found no
such writing in library literature. The statistical research then
being conducted at Chicago, he said, did not cover whether
or why the library should be involved in the matters under
investigation. To Danton's mind, if purpose could be put
first—if it could be said, "the library is aiming to do thus and
so and to do it adequately we need these data"—then the collection of the information would be "validated" by its having
sprung from a declared purpose, a philosophy. Danton envisioned "an entirely new social order" in which such elements

as national planning for libraries would need to be based on clear objectives. Although only a "social philosophy" was possible to libraries at their current stage of development, said Danton, a metaphysical one might eventually be elaborated if librarians could agree on a library world view.

Lowell Martin, in his article of 1937, considered the library as an example of a social institution, giving his own definition of the latter term to stress the pattern of cooperative relationships involved and the "vital human need" each institution was intended to serve. The library's social function, said Martin, was "the transmission of the cultural heritage," and here "social control," or the inculcation of values, entered into the purpose of the library. But the main object must always be freedom of opportunity for self-fulfillment of the individual. By analyzing the factors relating the library to society and by tracing the conditions under which libraries had developed in the United States, Martin found the library to have been "the expression of its age," at first educating people for democracy and then providing recreation for an already-educated populace. Because it was "a sanctioned rather than a basic institution," it was bound to change with the times; this had kept it flexible and healthy. Its greatest challenge came from the competition of other recreational facilities with their tendency toward standardization. But there was promise, Martin felt, in analytical studies of libraries on the basis of which leaders in the profession could bring the institution to "a higher plane of effectiveness," constantly adjusting it to new conditions.

Another proponent of sociological analysis, Herbert Goldhor, writing in 1942 on book selection, contributed a possible segment for a general philosophy written in parts by different authors, according to Danton's prescription. Setting out to clarify and elaborate current book selection theory, Goldhor introduced his discussion with the remark that the exclusive use of literary criteria, traditional in the past, was no longer sufficient for the selection of useful library materials because reading situations were "to be understood only in sociological and psychological terms." From analyzing readership into its component parts and considering the library as a "distributing mechanism" for print, he deduced that the meshing of the reader's purpose with "the effect produced upon him by his reading" was the ideal of successful book selection. Goldhor devoted his attention to "institutional" rather than individual selection, convinced that investigation of the "nature of the reading situations" to be satisfied would provide a reasonable basis for the standards to be adhered to. Most library patrons seemed to be seeking "reinforcement" of their beliefs, not the "purposively guided change" of education, recent studies showed. In the light of such information, said Goldhor, the library's goals should be limited to those which it might most effectively and uniquely meet. Then librarians could devote their energies to achieving real "reading satisfaction" in their communities.

France Clarke Sayers has taken a different stance: that of dedication to good books as a cultural force, a force that must not be dissipated by diversion onto side issues. In a 1949 lecture honoring William Warner Bishop she praised the "belligerency" of his professional commitment, recommending that quality to her audience. Let them, she said, be infused with "a fierce and beautiful love of books." In actuality, however, she found that American librarians, having begun with an inspired purpose, "the joyous obligation to read and to induce others to read," had retreated from it before the onslaught of mechanization and advanced educational theory. She regretted that, instead of maintaining independence, the profession had adopted the trappings and language of schools of education, "whose function is not our function." This, in Mrs. Sayers' view, had lowered librarians' original lofty sights and caused them to neglect the insides of books to concentrate on techniques. Then, after World War II, these same librarians had cut their educational ties and joined the sociologists and psychologists, who, she claimed, had promptly set about surveying librarianship in a meaningless way. To Mrs. Sayers, reading should be considered an art, involving sensitivity and imagination, which cannot be measured by scientific means. The librarian dedicated to it should "assail people with books" to try to lead them away from the prevalent commercial mass standards.

Helen E. Haines, too, had an esthetic vision of librarianship. To her, book selection was an art, and her own experience with reading was evidence enough for her of the personal and cultural value of books. For knowledge to be truly absorbed, said Miss Haines, the stimulation books can give needs to be added to the direction given by education. It is through books that we "receive and enlarge the heritage of the human mind," making ourselves stronger and the world more interesting. Miss Haines' reverence for the inspirational power of literature extended, however, only to works of imagination and right purpose: she had little use for magazines and newspapers, which constituted "deterrents" to her kind of reading. Good books, she said, help to form character, to mature judgment, and to deepen understanding. Her definition of "good reading" involved personal needs and taste, but in order to carry the intellect beyond the familiar, she urged exploration of a wide range of literature. If, as she believed, the object of librarianship was to bring books "into the common life of the world," then the ownership of books should be acknowledged as a necessary complement to the use of the library, though the librarian's relationship to readers seemed to her more rewarding than that of publishers or booksellers. The best attributes of the library profession— belief in books, receptivity, and broad-mindedness—when framed by social consciousness, confidence, and purpose, can, said Miss Haines, make librarians worthy intellectual leaders for a better world.

Pierce Butler, as teacher at the Chicago Graduate Library School, appreciated the sociological viewpoint toward librarianship, but also, by his interest in philosophy, largely set the philosophical tone of the school. In a speech delivered in the last year of his life, Butler took his audience into his study for a philosophical discourse on the book. To him, as to Dana, books were "alive," having escaped from their authors to come into independent existence. Other man-made objects, such as machines, might exhibit this "nonbiological life," but they were fashioned on a pattern taken from nature. The book, on the other hand, was "wholly original," actually transcending nature. The text of a book, as the reduction to print of the conscious mind, was to Butler "probably the most remarkable achievement of culture," partaking of the attributes of a miracle. He believed that his own books, when opened, took a friendly interest in him: some tried to educate him, some to amuse him, some to move him. All affected his conduct. And they spoke to him as books, not as authors. For these reasons, Butler felt that bibliographical history was essential to the training of librarians in order for them to comprehend their professional goals. Librarians also needed to be aware, he said, that the movement of books through space was essential to scholarship, and that, when some of those books were "captured by a library," they became the charge of the librarian and were thenceforth dependent on him, not only for their preservation, but for the dissemination of their living messages.

Lawrence Clark Powell came to librarianship after experience in the commercial world of books, as did Bostwick and Miss Haines. Yet far from being businesslike in philosophy, all three have been among the most eloquent spokesmen for the book in its esthetic and moral dimension. Powell, in his "A Bookman's Credo" of 1954, reported on an argument he had precipitated by insisting that the prime qualification for an academic library administrator was "a passion for books." Some in his audience had considered bibliomania a deterrent to good service to the scholastic community. But, contended Powell, the administrator sets the tone of his library, and if he is not bookish himself, he is not likely to make sure that he has a bookman on his staff to provide balance. Admitting that service and conservation were in actuality equally important, Powell said that to be too businesslike would be as fatal to the library's purpose as to be too immersed in print. Librarians were obligated, in his view, to past heritage, present support, and future creativity, and they would neglect any one of these at the peril of their mission. To Powell, the ideal librarian would revere books as the "truest immortality" and the greatest teachers of Man; he would take advantage of techniques for efficiency in library management, in the "humble desire" to assist his patrons; and he would fight censorship of ideas. Thus he would have all the qualities necessary to promote learning, liberty, understanding, and tolerance.

Jesse H. Shera bridges the gap between the older attitudes and the recent developments in the profession. He has long pondered the deeper questions of librarianship and is known as one of its philosophers, while at the same time he has been in the forefront of research on the applications of communications theory to library science. Speaking to the Louisiana Library Association in 1961, Shera gave a succinct account of his concept of his profession. American librarians, he stated, had been too indiscriminately concerned with service to develop a philosophy, but the coming of automation to libraries made a review of their objectives necessary. Information, or sensory stimulation, had been shown, he said, to be essential to the sanity and health of Man. Therefore the librarian, as "mediator between reader and book, between society and its graphic records," had a high responsibility. As we discover more about the way in which learning takes place, Shera predicted, we will become more aware of the way the brain, "the library of the individual," processes information. A special value of the computer is its ability to show "the relation between the mind and the printed page," and what we know about computers can be applied to the investigation of human thought processes. According to Shera, if librarianship is "the management of knowledge," then its handling of the social transcript is crucial to the development of the culture of which it is a part. Librarians must keep pace with new knowledge and new technology in order to fulfill their social obligation.

Joseph Z. Nitecki's approach to the philosophy of librarianship is enriched by the logical and analytical bent of his mind. In the chapter of his master's paper included here, Nitecki looked upon the library from the point of view of its political and social environment. He based his analysis on the theory of the influence of groups in a democracy, with their competition for acceptance of their group objectives. The library, he said, is subject to group pressures to provide service, education, and mediation on controversial matters. As an institution representing the whole community, the library must "neither ignore nor succumb to" these pressures; but its response to them "constitutes the basis for the theory of librarianship," and also becomes, when put into action, a new set of pressures on society. Nitecki would formulate his philosophy by arranging library activities into procedural (technological), conceptual (planning), and contextual (administrative) aspects, and these can be directly related to similar interpretations of the public interest. To create a unified theory of the role, goals, and decision-making process of librarianship, Nitecki said, the distinctive postulates of the discipline must be stated so as to include "subtheories" to account for the separate objectives of specializations within the field. This would enable the librarian to see in perspective the pressures he exerts on society, as well as those he receives from it.

Guy A Marco argued from two different sides in his address to an Ohio Library Association meeting in 1966. Assuming that the essence of a philosophy is "a clear set of objectives," he explored possible answers to professional questions beginning with "why" and "what is," rather than "how." The answers will vary, said Marco, according to the conception of library objectives held by the individual. The great "whys" of American librarianship were raised at the New York conference of librarians in 1853, but they "remain as disturbing as ever." Charles Coffin Jewett at that time proposed for libraries a direct implementation of the distinctive aspects of American democracy. In two more recent philosophers of library science Marco found representatives of the social sciences and the humanities: Pierce Butler thought that libraries should make good citizens, while A. Broadfield of England recommended that they promote complete freedom of thought. Butler would condone some censorship of library collections in the interest of societal harmony; Broadfield would allow none. These opposing intellectual schools, the one centered on groups, the other on individuals, were mutually exclusive, said Marco, but together they contained all the possibilities for a complete philosophical theory. He himself found merit in studying socially "useless" subjects, and saw the library as possessing the same potential for "shaping our mind, taste and judgment," for enlarging our understanding, as a work of art. He invited his audience to choose between the two philosophies, each for himself, and to frame library objectives accordingly.

Neal Harlow, in a paper prepared for a seminar at Rutgers in 1969 on the topic of possible changes in the curricula of library schools, advocated the application of the physicists' "field theory" as a means of broadening and modernizing the structure of the curriculum. His suggestions began with a historical review of library education which left him with the conviction that course offerings had to a certain extent become fossilized as separate entities, whereas a look at them through a scientist's eyes might reveal many affinities that were not otherwise apparent. Field theory, dealing with larger areas of phenomena, accentuates the interaction of elements as organic wholes. All the activities of the system are considered as "special instances of the same underlying continuity," a way of thinking about library activities that would seem to have useful philosophical possibilities. Harlow did not claim to give a "valid general theory of librarianship," for no one has yet ventured that far, but he was able to posit a "field" of librarianship with structure, particles, and waves, divided into sub-systems, and with room for irrational elements. He could see librarianship as a process, which must be in harmony with other parts of the wider intellectual field in which it exists. To educate for such a profession, to incorporate into the curriculum "leadership, motivation, and inspiration," might require a "clean break" with the past; if this were to be undertaken, said Harlow, "field theory" could be the catalyst for reconstituting the fragmented curriculum into a unified whole.

When he spoke to library school students in Japan in

1971, Louis Shores expressed his personal philosophy of librarianship. He denied that his fellow-librarians were deficient in deeply-held beliefs regarding their profession and cited individuals all around the world who had discussed with him their philosophies. Shores pronounced his own definition of the profession to show its concern with "the knowledge most significant to mankind," which is contained in what he called the "generic book," consisting of all kinds and formats of learning materials. Communication seemed to him to be the essence of human life. The vehicle by which knowledge was transmitted, said Shores, was important to comprehension and should be given as much attention as other criteria in such library activities as book selection. He opposed the contemporary tendency to elevate science and repress the influence of the humanities, preferring the middle path of mediation among all the "specialisms" of other disciplines. He expressed a desire to see a narrowing of the focus of human intelligence toward a deep center, an "implosion" to combat the diffuseness that results from the "information explosion." He also dreamed of reconciling the aims of information science with those of traditional librarianship, a process he called "modulation," and of furthering world peace through comparative librarianship.

In his address at the opening of the Scott Library at York University, Toronto, in the fall of 1971, former Librarian of Congress Archibald MacLeish explored the fundamental nature of a library and of the books it contains. He considered the messages in all kinds of books as reports on what men know of life, reports which speak to us over centuries and across space. The reporters not only record facts, but also interpret what they have learned from existence, and their reports constitute "true" books. A library consisting of such books appeared to MacLeish as "one of the greatest of human achievements," because the individual reports, when taken as a whole, implied a meaning behind the universal mystery, a meaning which held the possibility of being understood. The very fact of the existence of such an institution as the library reassured MacLeish. Although contemporary philosophers seemed to him to have given up trying to find the ultimate answers which in an earlier day had been eagerly sought, and although contemporary intellectuals seemed to have deserted meaning and taken refuge in the absurd, still there was affirmation in the opening of a new library. There was hope and promise in a new edifice filled with reports on life and the world from which a synthesis might at any time be drawn. MacLeish, dwelling in the poet's universe of cause and relationship and, above all, meaning, saw a reality beyond the self which made the cult of despair seem ridiculous. To him, the meanings Man has put into his reports down through the ages are the essence of a living library.

To the reader of these essays, be his reading intensive or casual, the total effect is bound to be one of unity in diversity. From Dewey to MacLeish, the fundamental message is similar, but with differing surface accents. The consensus appears to be that the library plays a distinctive role in American civilization, encouraging reading both for good citizenship and for the pure pleasure of knowing. Its purpose is to conserve and make available the record of Man's mind for any who seek it. The librarian is obligated to try to stimulate a desire for the meaning contained in this record, but must also tolerate all points of view and all kinds and forms of expression, while at the same time favoring the highest, truest, best, and most useful. By a thorough knowledge of books, by enthusiasm for his calling, and by sympathetic interest in individuals, the librarian should attempt to attract people to the library and should provide for them there a congenial atmosphere in which to find materials selected to give information, knowledge, recreation, reinforcement, and emotional satisfaction. To achieve this objective he should make an effort to know his patrons and to ascertain their reading needs, being sure to subordinate library techniques to the human element in library service. He should see that the library becomes an integral part of the social structure of the community it serves and that the public interest is well represented in library activities. To prepare himself for his varied responsibilities, he should read widely and should seek the broadest possible education. He should think about the implications of his professional commitment and keep his mind attuned to developments in library science. His activity should be consciously aimed at enriching the life of the individual, enhancing the values of society, and strengtheing the fiber of the nation.

Once all this is accomplished, the librarian's actions will spring from a rounded concept of his part in the communications network of American society and in the storage and distribution of the world's knowledge. That concept will then constitute his philosophy. It seems apparent that the American librarians represented in this anthology understand that role and actually have such a philosophy; they differ only in their ways of expressing it. □

THE RELATION OF THE STATE
TO THE PUBLIC LIBRARY

Melvil Dewey

We have been listening to an admirable account of the development of the library movement from earliest times to the present day, and I venture to believe that when the history of the age in which we live is written, and is looked back upon by those who shall come after, it will be known distinctively as the "Library Age."

Libraries of one sort or another have existed from the beginning of human history, and we are now well into the fifth century since the invention of printing; so that it would seem as if there had been abundant time for library development. But so great an institution as the modern library is of slow growth. It has taken a thousand years to develop our school system from university down to kindergarten. The public library is much more rapidly going through corresponding stages in order to come to its own. The original library was a reservoir, getting in and keeping safely, a storehouse for posterity. That was and is a great function, for which I have profound respect. Then, after many centuries, came another library epoch, for which we all feel still greater

Reprinted from the *Transactions and Proceedings of the Second International Library Conference*, 1898, by permission of the Library Association, and from *The Library and Society: Reprints of Papers and Addresses* (New York: H. W. Wilson Co., 1921; Freeport, N.Y.: Books for Libraries Press, Inc., 1968), pp. 185-192, by permission of the H. W. Wilson Company.

respect. The cistern was made a fountain; giving out was seen to be more important than getting in. The library is no longer merely a passive receptacle, but becomes an aggressive educational force in every community. The reservoir will not become a stagnant pool, for, in its branches and deliveries, the public library has mains and pipes laid through every street, and reaching almost to the door of every householder. And we live now not in the age of the reservoir, but in the age of the fountain. In our zeal and admiration, however, we are apt to forget that there is yet another and even more important stage to reach. In my own city, some time ago, we spent half a million dollars in providing an ample supply of water. But we found that we had really opened convenient communication with the cemetery by water, for the quality of the new and abundant beverage was such that our death-rate steadily rose. The burning question became qualitative, not quantitative, and we are now spending our money on efficient filtration. Of course no library intends to circulate injurious books, but equally no town intends to distribute harmful water. We are concerned more with the results than with the intention. The mortality tables make plain the physical defect, but alas! science has as yet devised no instruments delicate enough to record the greater danger to the individual and the State from poison in the great current, which has come to be a mighty flood, of modern reading matter. The most hopeful, and perhaps the only practicable, method of guarding against this serious danger is through the public library, which must now in the last days of this eventful century recognise the gravity of the new responsibility which it cannot shirk. Before another audience I might dwell at length on what this problem of selection means, but the representative librarians of the world will understand my claim that, wonderful as was the development from the cistern to the fountain, its importance is overshadowed by this great question of excluding the pernicious, which I sum up in the world filtration. This is the great problem of the modern library, and its solution must depend largely on the State.

It is often said that the modern periodicals and

newspapers are our greatest danger; but this, of course, is true only of the sensational and other objectionable types. I yield to none in my high appreciation of what the best kind of newspaper may do in its capacity as the strongest ally of the public library and of the public school. I am confident that early in the next century such journals will be recognised as a distinct part of our educational machinery, but I am equally clear that the worst journals, conducted merely as money-making enterprises, and catering to the worst instead of to the best elements of both society and individuals, are the most potent factors for evil, and the greatest enemy which the ideal librarian has to combat in carrying forward his best work. They leave their habitual readers with neither time nor taste for anything above their own low plane. The mind will inevitably rise or fall to the level of its habitual reading, and we apostles and missionaries of the book have no more disheartening outlook than on the readers whose literary atmosphere is limited to the modern sensational newspapers. But the apologists for such reading say that the history of their own times is of more importance to them than any other history; should they not, therefore, become as familiar as possible with it? But when a man, on account of "pressure of business," never looks inside any good book, yet has time to read everything in the newspapers, he is—well, specializing too much in "history." How many men and women there are, who, from year's end to year's end, read nothing but the so-called history of their own times, and who can tell you nothing better than which dog won the last fight! It is a good thing to know the history of our own times; so is a pinch of salt a good thing on one's breakfast potato, but it is not necessary to drink a barrel of sea water each morning in order to get it.

It is highly desirable that I should know the geology and topography of my own State, but I can learn all that is worth knowing without creeping on hands and knees with nose close to the ground over the barnyards and dump heaps of our commonwealth, under the vain delusion that I am exhaustively studying its geology. We must join this battle squarely. The eternal conflict of good and the best with bad and the worst is on. The librarian must be the librarian militant before he can be the librarian triumphant. At the end of another century, when a conference like this is held, our descendants will look back with wonder to find that we have so long been satisfied to leave the control of the all-pervading, all-influencing newspaper in the hands of people who have behind them no motive better than the "almighty dollar." The solution of our difficulties lies in recognition by the State that public libraries are not only good things, but that they are an absolutely necessary part of our educational system. We started with the university, but found that we had to put under it the college. Then we went a step further, and had the academy and high school to prepare for the college; the primary and grammar schools to prepare for the high school; and now we have the kindergarten under the primary school. I am not giving a chronology, but simply pointing out that during these centuries educators have constantly been facing the question of adequate provision for meeting completely the public wants. We have at last reached step by step from the university to the nursery, and have provided a series of schools covering the entire field. Yet, with all this, we have not attained the full system of education that we ought to attain, and every thoughtful person is now asking, "What next?"

Huxley has well said that a system of education which in the early years trains boys and girls to read and then makes no provision for what they shall read during all the rest of their lives, would be as senseless as to teach our children the expert use of the knife, fork, and spoon, and then make no provision for their daily food. The whole history of education has been a series of broadening conceptions. I can recall no case in which the ideal has narrowed, but step by step we have come to a general recognition that education is for poor as well as rich, for plebeian as well as prince, for black and white, for native and foreigner, for brilliant or backward, for women as well as men, for deaf, dumb, and blind, and all defectives and delinquents, who in the old conception were left without the pale. It is almost within our memory that we have come to substantial agreement that the State owes an elementary education to every boy and girl born within its limits, not alone as a right to the child, but as a matter of safety and practical wisdom on the part of the State; and this broader conception is followed closely by a second and still broader one, that every boy and girl is entitled not only to an elementary, but to something also of higher education. I have met no competent student of this subject who dares deny that hereafter the State must recognize that education is not alone for the young, for limited courses, in schools which take all the time of their pupils, but that it must regard adults as well; and not alone for short courses, but all through life—not in our recognized teaching institutions alone, but in that study outside of office or working hours that may be carried on at home. I may sum it up in the one sentence, "Higher education, for adults, at home, through life."

In this home education, which must hereafter be recognized side by side with school education, the library is the great central agent round which study clubs, reading circles, extension teaching, museums, and the other allied agencies must cluster. A statesman solicitous for the future welfare of his country will find his most fruitful field in protecting and guiding the reading of the people. It is what a man reads that shapes his future, which depends, not at once upon the rostrum and the pulpit, but on the book and the newspaper. In education we recognize that the supreme end is the building of character, but many of us have never thought clearly how directly this character-building rests upon the public library. It is reading that begets reflection, reflection begets motive, motive begets action, and action begets habit, and habit begets character; and who here dares question this, that it is not the air nor the water, nor yet the "roast beef of Old England," not its history nor traditions nor laws nor geographic location, but *character,* that has made the Anglo-Saxons, England and her daughters across the seas, the most wonderful people of the earth. It is not brawn, but brain. The dogs and horses might have the physical qualities, but it is the

MANY-SIDED INTEREST:
HOW THE LIBRARY PROMOTES IT

John Cotton Dana

I believe that libraries are for scholars; that they should supply the material which studious and thoughtful men need in pursuing their studies and ripening their thoughts. In libraries the lamp of learning should be kept always lighted, that here men of study and reflection—the guides we must always come to at the last—may relight if need be their several torches.

I believe that libraries are for delights, and should contribute directly to the happiness of their people.

I believe that libraries are for other purposes also. I wish now to set forth my belief that libraries should serve as incentives and stimulants; that they should try by all proper methods to increase the interest their constituents take in the world they live in, to the end that those constituents, the people, may find that the library they have set up has helped them to become broader, more generous-minded, better balanced and more able and willing to work for the common welfare with their neighbors—with their neighbors who are both their fellow-countrymen and their fellows of other countries. The library should be a mental irritant in the community; it should help to make the old fresh, the strange

Reprinted from *School Journal*, December 22, 1906, by permission of *Intellect: The Magazine of Educational and Social Affairs*, and from John Cotton Dana, *Libraries: Addresses and Essays* (New York: H. W. Wilson Co., 1916; Freeport, N. Y.: Books for Libraries Press, 1966), pp. 135-146, by permission of the H. W. Wilson Company.

tolerable, the new questionable, and all things wonderful. I believe this because I think most people are too well satisfied with their own narrow lives, and do not take interest enough in the life about them; if they took more interest in it they would understand each other better, would work together better, and would make this a more peaceful, more effective and happier world.

Let me restate this ancient creed in another way.

A secret of happiness is accomplishment. This is as true of a people as of a person. A people's power of accomplishment is their social efficiency.

The secret of social efficiency is voluntary organization: not governmental organization, which is compulsory, but the free organization to which we chiefly owe our industrial development, our esthetic, our social, and our religious life.

This voluntary organization is voluntary cooperation—to restate it in terms which make prominent its essential points of skill, free choice, and mutual aid.

The secret of cooperation is enlightened sympathy. Not pity, not condescension, but kinship of thought through feeling, through the good will which accompanies a clear understanding of the views of life, the prejudices, the creeds, and the aims of others.

The secret of sympathy is likeness in custom, ideal, and aim. How and why sympathy springs from similarity in manners, morals, and purpose is still a secret; but we know that we work gladly and well with those whose manners, though they differ from our own, we are wonted to; whose ideals, though they differ from our own, we know are not bad; whose ambitions, though not ours, we find lead to no harm.

The public library, like the public school is the product of mutual aid, of a cooperation primarily voluntary. It is in turn itself a factor, and as such adds to social efficiency not by teaching directly how effectively to organize and cooperate, but by promoting sympathy. It exposes to many the similarities between manners, ideals, and aims which seem at first quite dissimilar. Government, diplomacy, war—these are on the surface in our relations with other nations, for

example, the Orientals. These superficial international relations point to a substratum of individual ignorance, narrow-
ness, and selfishness. We first ignore, then despise, then fear,
then hate the alien. But contact opens our eyes. We soon find
that though his manners are strange they are harmless; that
though his ideals are curiously expressed, they are high; that
though his aims are not what we inherit, they are worthy.
Then we applaud, we sympathize, we cooperate—and peace
is here.

The native antagonism of races is as I have said, an exaggerated form of the personal antagonism which is at large
among us, and among all other peoples, and always will be,
until knowledge begets sympathy and diversity of forms in
manners, ideals, and aims is no longer taken for diversity in
substance.

The library, in its efforts to expose to its constituents
the likeness of their aims, customs, and morals, finds that as
the secret of ignorance is indifference, so the secret of knowledge is interest. This secret is more important to library than
to school. The school can compel to knowledge; the library
must allure to knowledge. The schools are for educible
young; the libraries are for persuadable old. The child is in
the age of observation, acquisition, and change; the old are in
the age of knowledge, conviction, and creed.

How then—and this is the library's question which is
always waiting for more fullness of answer—how can the library arouse in its people an interest in the wide world? How
can it prove itself the proper inheritor of the efficiency of the
Athenian Gadfly? How make its supporters feel that this
world is full of the permanent possibilities of pleasure? How
make them realize that though wisdom linger when knowledge comes, without knowledge wisdom will not stir abroad?
How show them that to be interested is to be laying up
knowledge? that to have a many-sided interest is to have
sympathy and willingness to cooperate? and that skill will
follow? and that he who has power and will to cooperate has
acquired a social education?

The good book is alive. A gathering of good books is an

organization of the wise. Any library may stand idle, but every library has infinite capacity for good work. The library can hold its books to the simple task of giving strength, incentive, and guidance to the few who spontaneously seek them; just as the school can wait upon the call of the student who comes and asks its aid. But the library may also awaken interest and stimulate inquiry; just as the school summons the indifferent to its tasks by making plain the pleasures and profits of the knowledge it can give. But the school can also command attendance and compel study; while the library can invite and attract, but no more.

It is in the wide range of its powers, the variety of its profferings, and the number of its constituents that the library finds its advantages over school and college; and these same advantages assure the success of its efforts to add to the interest of life.

But first it must make known its powers. It is under the burden of misapprehension. Books were formerly for the bookish only. The bookish formed a class apart. They were literary in the old sense of the word. From those days comes the feeling that a public collection of books is a collection of literary books useful chiefly to the professed student of books and to the reader of *belles-lettres*. In my town a library can openly follow its mission for seventeen full years, and an active man of affairs in the town can still express surprise when he learns that his library will gladly answer his inquiries, to the full of its abilities, about the price of books, the choice of books, or the tests of wood-block paving. The instance is typical. The fact is told a thousand times yet it is still known to but few, that while the library is for students and readers it is not for them only, but is also for the daily use of every citizen. Just what this will mean in the life of our towns and cities, when all are awake to its possibilities, it is impossible to say. I am sure the librarian will then look on its figures of books lent as even less important than he considers them today.

First, then, I repeat, the library must make itself known, and it must make itself known, not so much as a library in the conventional sense of the word, as an index, easy to reach and easy to use, of all the facts of life, all the best theories of life, and all the skilfully woven fancies of life.

The newspapers, many of them at least, understand the library better than the librarian. They note that to its shelves come reports of all that the world is doing, saying, and dreaming, and they may well wonder that so little comes from them. The news is a little belated for morning scare-heads, it is true; but in fullness, accuracy, and depth it excels. The librarian cannot retail this world-news through the daily press; but he can bring it nearer to his people than do a few figures of circulation and a bibliography of earthworms. The daily record of the library's additions to the possibilities of profit, pleasure, and wisdom on its shelves should fill a corner of the paper and be found of interest by many. Librarians will know that I am not speaking from experience. Rather, I am prophesying.

The library should be a commonplace to every one. To use it should be as natural when one needs news or knowl-edge, fiction or fact, as it is to use the trolley when one needs transportation.

The telephone is the mutual friend of all. It is a great leveler, and it adds a million strong-threads to that great social fabric which we are all trying to weave. It brings the li-brary, in a sense, to every fireside. That its use between the people and their books has been so little is another indication of the academic remoteness of the library. Having found by telephone that the book, pamphlet, journal, catalog, quota-tion or what not is in the library, the inquirer should be able to have it quickly brought to him. Private enterprise delivers its goods; a public institution can well imitate this example as far as means permit.

The newspaper and the telephone bring the library into the every-day world. The newspaper—I am repeating my prophecy—shows from day to day how the library gathers the best that is done and thought and said in the world in every field. The morning paper says that Peary failed; the library soon will have in its books the story of the successes of his failure. Santos-Dumont flies; Herculaneum is to be excavated; the English soap trust dissolves; Japan floats a ship of war;— these are the morning's notes. Later the library offers the same, in book or journal, carefully considered and set in proper relations. Of each of these and ten thousand other things a few wish to know the full truth. So far as the library gets full and careful chronicles it should let their coming be known. To do this requires scholarship, of which our libraries have not enough. But parenthetically let me say that they never did have enough. Many of the old librarians were readers, few of them were students. They cultivated the muses; but the muses did not respond. Their admirers mistook a cheerful literary geniality for high converse and apt reference to the learned for learning itself.

Often it is possible for the library, by note, or postal, or brief list, to send to the one or the few in its city that word about book or journal which is just what he needs. In time the organized special information work of a public library will be very great. Many will ask for what they need when they need it. Many will ask, also, to be told when that which they need comes to the library shelf. Private enterprises can clip you the notes you wish from a thousand journals as they appear. Surely a public institution, for a moderate fee, if need be, can furnish notes of books and articles on special subjects.

If you say all this is informing the library's constituents and not interesting them, then I have not made my chief point plain. The library contains information, more or less full and recent according to its resources, on every subject that every person in its city finds it interesting and profitable to know about. And if there is any subject which would interest any of its people did they chance to hear of it—about that subject also the library has information. Now, given a storehouse like this, if it make itself widely known for what it is, present interests will be fed, new interests will be aroused.

I am aware that these remarks smell more of commerce than of the lamp. The old-fashioned student, if he heard them, might well ask where he can find, under the conditions I suggest, that old-fashioned library with its penetralia

perfumed with emanations from ancient volumes in which
the old-fashioned librarian pores over books that are books
and joins with inquiring spirits in peaceful dialog. Let me say
to this that I began with the axiom that libraries are for
scholars. Then let me add that every library, even though the
rumor get abroad that the active motion within it has pene-
trated the places some would wish reserved for the spirits of
the dead and the meditations of quietists—every library, I
say, no matter how grievously awake and sinfully modern it
may be, can furnish a quiet corner for rumination. Every librarian delights in its readers. If to any the old books and a
place apart are of the essence of library enjoyment, these the
librarian can provide and will with pleasure.

Then let me add that the disturbance of that fine quie-
tude which old folios, disintegrating leathers, ancient dust,
and venerable readers typify, by change, newness and restless
use, is not a new thing. Had Caesar perfected for Rome the
great public library he planned it would not have been an
abode simply for the ancient browsers of the day—unless we
are quite mistaken in our Caesar. When all the libraries of
Rome rejected Ovid's books as not fit for their readers, the
wits surely had their joke about silly and presumptious cen-
sors of morals and the passing of the good old times when
libraries let the wise choose their own reading. The latter-day
librarian, one says, is too commercial and talks too much of
methods of persuasion and conducts his place as if readers
were not born, but made by advertising. Well, the Ptolemies
ransacked the world for books and then that these might not
uselessly lie idle provided food and lodgings for the readers
they invited! To this, with all its modernity, the American
free public library has not yet come. Lipsius asked, three centuries ago, why gather books if they are not to be freely
used? Mazarin, fifty years later, was proud to open his library
to all the world without excepting a living soul. These, mind
you, are ancient ideas, not new ones. And it is cheering to
feel that the librarian of to-day is awakening at last to their
full import.

The library, then, should be accumulative of books;

hospitable to students; a sedative for quietists, and provocative of interests—and the last is not least. To be stimulating it must be known, easily reached, and by post and telephone easily bespoken.

The rest of my argument is not so easily set down. I wish to touch in a few words on some of the activities which, in harmony with the thought that a people's books should broaden and multiply that people's interest, emanate from or find their first movements within our modern libraries. Again I do not speak from experience or from the history of any one library. I say simply that things like these are done in this, that, and the other village, town, or city; not all in any one.

A lecturer of note is coming; a famous opera is revived; the art of printing is discussed; the river front is to be redeemed; the smoke nuisance is to be abated; the library sets forth in newspaper or special list the best and latest writings on each and every one of these topics.

The town needs a museum of art, of science, of local history; the library is among the first to note the fact; by letters, lectures, and references to appropriate books and pamphlets it brings the need home to the few best fitted to consider their advantages and opens a corner in the library to the humble beginnings of one or all of them.

Foreigners, knowing no English, flock to the factories. The library calls in the children, and gives them the English books they ask for; through them it attracts the parents; learns that the latter wish to read of their new country in their own tongue; finds that there are no books in foreign languages which simply and briefly describe us and our ways, and sets to work to have them written.

Posters about the library go up in railway stations, trolley cars, and other public places.

Lecture courses are given in library halls and at them the library's appropriate books and lists thereof are shown and distributed.

Children whose homes are without books, ideas, or reading habits are taught the pleasures of literature by wise story-tellers and skilful readers.

Branches are set up here and there in cities; books are sent by the basketful from the village library to country cross roads; open cases full of books are put in stores; tiny libraries are sent to homes in remote corners of the city and to lone farmhouses among the hills; a library agent tours a state, enlightens, interests, instructs, and exhorts by turns in every village and town—all to the end that more may find pleasure and profit from books and through them multiply their interests, moderate their prejudices, and broaden their sympathies.

In due course every school-room becomes a library, every teacher a librarian, and every pupil is encouraged to form the habit of reading good things and collecting ideas.

The library displays collections of beautiful things. The sciences and the trades also are shown, and the library becomes now a miniature museum of some industry, now of some art.

The story could go on through many other details; and you may think it strange that one ventures to say it is not enough. In answer let me say that, for all our eighty million, we publish few of the best books, we do not maintain properly a single weekly or monthly journal of high scholarship, we are self-centered, unduly prejudiced in our judgments, and are thoughtless and clamant hero-worshippers. Our published utterances are what we should expect. Out of the conflict between them come many sparks of wit, but these rarely flame up into the clear light of sound learning. We need to feel that others also think, and think with care and with background of more learning than is given to many of our people to acquire. In the libraries are the books of the wise; the very souls of the wise. We are all learning to read; perhaps the library will in time learn how to induce more to read the best. If many read the best, interests will multiply and deepen and, if Herbart was not mistaken, broader views will be taken and wiser councils will more often prevail.

Our Lindsay Swift laments the day "when the cry went forth that the librarian must be a business man and not a scholar." The edge of his kindly wit is turned a bit when we recall that he is himself in the library business; and we feel that so long as libraries find his like useful, scholarship is not forbidden among us! Also we may take his humor with better grace, if we remember that while many may refine subtly on the violin, flute, and other tender instruments, for a complete orchestra one at least must beat the drum. And, once more, it had been a sad day indeed if the cry had gone forth "that the librarian must be a scholar and not a business man."

Through all this paper I have assumed, what librarians know quite well, that in a library's books are found all the interests of life; I point my story once more by saying that it is one of the library's duties to make known to its people that this is true; and that in their books are all the thoughts and deeds and dreams of all men, and that through these their books they may get the broad and wholesome view of things.

If I speak too much of the art of making things known to others, of helping others to find that this is an entrancing world of wonderful deeds and charming fancies and humorous contrasts, and if I say too little about our own shortcomings, I do not regret it, for I confess I am just now beating the drum. A sentence of Pater's, which I paraphrase, may help you to see my point of view. "To his pious recognition of that one orderly spirit—scholarship—which diffuses itself through the world and animates it, the librarian adds a warm personal devotion towards the whole multitude of the old gods—the good books—and one new one besides—utility— by him we hope not ignobly conceived."   □

THE LOVE OF BOOKS
AS A BASIS FOR LIBRARIANSHIP

Arthur E. Bostwick

Is the love of books a proper or necessary qualification for one who is to care for books and to see that they do the work for which they were made? First, let us ask a question or two. What is the love of books; and what is there in books that one may love? The same question might be asked and answered of the love of human beings; for between it and the love of books there are curious analogies. Of what, then, do man and book severally consist as objects of interest and affection?

First of all there is the man himself, the ego, the soul—which cannot indeed exist on this earth without its material embodiment, but which most of us realize is in some way distinct from that embodiment. So the book has its soul. The ideas or facts that it sets forth, though dependent for their influence on the printed page, exist independently of that page and make the book what it is. Next we have the material embodiment; that without which the man or the book could not exist for us; which is a necessary part of him or it, but necessary only because it is the vehicle through which man or book may be known by the senses. The body of the book is thus so much, and only so much, of its material part, its paper and its ink, as is necessary to present the contents properly to the eye. Lastly, we have the clothing of man and

Reprinted from *Library Journal* 32 (February, 1907):51-55, with permission of the publisher.

of book, having the function of protection or of decoration, or both; in the case of the book the protective cover, often highly decorated, and so much of interior elaboration as cannot be said to be strictly necessary to the presentation of the idea. The "body" and the clothing of the book, let it be noted, are not strictly separable as are those of the man. The line between them may be drawn in different places by different people. The same illustration, we will say, may be considered by one reader an absolutely necessary part of the book—an organ of its body—while to another it is but an ornamental embellishment—a decorative gewgaw. In spite of this vagueness, however, there is here an undeniable distinction between those material parts of the book that are necessary to its existence and those that merely embellish it or protect it.

The book therefore, like the man, is made up of soul, body and clothes. Which of these is the entity that may be loved? Now there are many kinds of lovers and many kinds of love. The belle of the ball may be surrounded with admirers, but if clad in rags and seated in a gutter she might excite no favorable notice. Still more may a pretty face be loved when it has no mental or spiritual qualities behind it. Yet these types of affection are inferior—no one would deny it. In like manner those who love the book merely for its fine clothes, who rejoice in luxurious binding and artistic illumination, and even those who dwell chiefly on its fine paper and careful typography, are but inferior lovers of books. The one loves his book for its clothes, and the other for its bodily perfection; neither cares primarily for its contents, its soul.

Now the true lover is he who loves the soul—who sees beyond clothes and bodily attributes, and cherishes nobility of character, strength of intellect, loftiness of purpose, sweetness of disposition, steadfastness of attachment—those thousand qualities that go to make up personality. All these the book has, like the man or the woman—for is it not the essence of its writer? Your true book-lover would rather have a little old dog's-eared copy of his favorite author, soiled and torn by use, with binding gone, and printed on bad paper with poorer type and worse ink, than a mediocre production that is a typographic and artistic masterpiece.

And yet we call the collector of fine bindings and rare editions a "book-lover," to the exclusion of the one who loves truly and devotedly. The true book-lover wants to get at the soul of his book; the false one may never see it. He may even refrain from cutting the leaves of the rare first edition that he has just bought, in doing which he is like the ignorant mother who sews her child up in his clothes for the winter—nay, worse; for you cannot sew up the child's soul.

Now let there be no misunderstanding. As the true lover would have his mistress beautiful—nay, as she *is* beautiful to his eyes, whatever she may be to others, and as he would, if he could, clothe her in silks and adorn her with gems, so the true book-lover need not be and is not averse to having his favorite author sumptuously set forth; he would rather than not see his books properly and strongly printed and bound; his love for the soul need not interfere with proper regard for the body and its raiment. And here is where the love of the book has an advantage over the affection whose object is a person. In spite of the advertisements of the beauty doctors, a homely face can rarely be made beautiful; but the book may be embodied and clothed as we will; it is the same, however printed and bound, to him who loves it for its contents.

Thus it will be seen that when I speak in general of "a love of books" I mean not a love of their typography, their illustration, or their bindings, but of their contents; a love of the universal mind of humanity as enshrined in print; a love of the method of recording ideas in written speech, as contrasted with their presentation in the spoken tongue—a love of ideas and ideals as so recorded. Such a love of books is pre-eminently a characteristic of civilized man. It is not synonymous with a love of knowledge—the savage who never saw a book may have that; it is not even the same as a love of *recorded* knowledge, for knowledge may be recorded in other ways—in the brain by oral repetition, in sculptured memorials, in mere piles of stone. It is a love of the ideas of men recorded in a particular way, in *the* particular way that has commended itself to civilized man as best.

The very existence of a library presupposes such a love of books. No one who had not an affection for the printed records of his race would care to possess them, much less to collect and preserve them. It would seem, then, that a love of books should be not only a qualification but an absolute prerequisite for entrance upon librarianship. By inquiring how and why it has come to be regarded as a non-essential or as of secondary importance, we may perhaps learn something.

A young woman comes to me to ask for library work; and when I demand sternly, "Have you training or experience?" she timidly answers, "No; but I'm very fond of books." I smile; you all smile in like case. Why do we smile? What business have we to underrate such a fundamental qualification and exalt above it mere technicalities? The ability to acquire these technicalities exists in ten persons where the ability to love books as they should be loved is found in one. If the love so avowed is real, even if it is only potential, not actual, our feeling in its presence should be one of reverence, not amusement. It should prove the candidate fit, perhaps not for immediate appointment, but for preliminary training with a view to appointment in the future.

If it is real! Candor compels me to confess that, like some other avowals of love, that of a love for books does not always ring true. "What have you read?" I once asked one of these self-styled book-lovers. She fixed me with her eye and after a moment's impressive pause she replied "Deep thought!" I mentally marked her as a false lover. Proud parents relate how their progeny in childhood would rather peruse E. S. Ellis than play and pore over Alger than eat—this as irrefragable proof of fitness for a library career. Consideration of cases like these makes us wonder whether the smile is so much out of the way after all. Does the true book-lover publicly announce her affection in the hope of gain? Does she not rather, like Shakespeare's maid, "never tell her love?" It is to be feared that some of these people are confusing a love of books with a love of reading. They are not the same thing. Some persons enjoy the gentle mental exercise of letting a stream of more or less harmless ideas flow through their brains—continuously in and continuously out again—apprehending them one after another in lazy fashion, and then dismissing them. The result is a degree of mental friction, but no permanent intellectual acquisition. How much of our own reading is of this kind I shudder to contemplate. Far be it from me to condemn it; it has its uses; it is an excellent cure for wakefulness after a busy day; but it no more indicates or stimulates a love for books than shaking hands with a thousand callers makes it possible for the Governor or the President to claim them all as intimate friends.

A real love for books, after all, is betrayed rather than announced; it shows itself in the chance remark, the careless action, just as another kind of love may show itself in a glance or a word.

I believe this to be the reason why a love for books is so little considered among the modern qualifications of librarianship; it appears in acts, not in words; it cannot be ascertained by asking questions. He who protests that he has it must needs be an object of suspicion. And yet I venture to say that if any librarian has made a conspicuous success of his work, apart from the mere mechanics of it, he has achieved that success primarily and notably through love of books. This I assert to be the case down to the assistant of lowest grade.

To be good, work must be ungrudging. And though other things than love for one's task may make one willing to do it and able to do it well, intelligent interest is always a prime factor in securing the best results.

And love of one's work becomes a very simple matter when there is love of the subject matter of that work. Those who lament that they are doomed to drudgery should remember that drudgery is subjective. All work consists of a series of acts which taken apart from their relationships are unimportant and uninteresting, but which acquire importance and interest from those relationships. It is so also with sports. Think how childish are the mere acts of striking a ball with a racket or of kicking an inflated leather sphere over a crossbar! Yet in their proper sequence with other acts they may be the object of the breathless interest or enthusiasm of thousands of spectators. And if this may be the case with a mere game, how much more so with an occupation that is part of the world's life! To dip a brush in color and draw it across a canvas is a simple act, yet such acts in their sequence may produce a work of art. Here the workman understands the position and value of each act in the sequence; hence he is not apt to feel it as drudgery. Drudgery is work in which the elementary acts are performed unintelligently, with little or no appreciation of their position in the scheme of things, as when a day laborer toils at digging a hole in the ground without the slightest knowledge of its purpose, not caring, indeed, whether it is to be a post-hole or a grave. But to the man who is searching for buried treasure the digging ceases to be drudgery; he knows what he is about, and every shovelful as it is lifted brings him nearer to possible gold and gems. To change drudgery into interested labor, therefore, realize what you are doing; know its relation to what has gone before and what is to come; understand what it is you are working on and what you are working for. Learn to love that something; and all that you can do to shape it, to increase its usefulness and to bring it into new relationships will have a vivid interest to you.

What could be duller than the act of writing in a book, hour after hour, certain particulars regarding other books, the author's name, the title, the publisher, the size, the price? But if you love those volumes, individually or generically, and if you realize that what you are doing is a necessary step in the work of making their contents accessible and useful—of leading others to love them as you have learned to do—then and only then, it seems to me, does such a task as accessioning become full of interest. And so it is with every one of the thousand acts that make up the daily work of a library assistant. I am saying nothing new; you know and we all know that the laborer who does his work well is he who does it *con amore*. The wage-earner may labor primarily to support himself and his family, but he will never really *earn* his living unless his work is of a kind that can command his whole-hearted interest—unless he likes it and takes pride in doing it well. This is why the love of books—an intelligent interest in literature and in the world's written records—is so fundamental a necessity for a librarian.

It should be emphasized that one may love books even if some of the great masterpeices leave him cold, just as one may love humanity though Alexander and Caesar, we will say, do not happen to stir his enthusiasm. One may even in a way, love books when that love is expended on what is by nature ephemeral, so long as it is lovable and excellent. Perishability and excellence are not contraries by any means. Indeed, I heard a painter once, indignant because his art had been characterized as less permanent than sculpture, with implied derogation, assert that all beauty is of its nature perishable. If this be so, a thing of beauty, instead of being a joy forever, is a passing pleasure and the more evanescent as it nears perfection. This thesis could hardly be successfully maintained, and yet I conceive that it has in it an element of truth. There are critics who refuse to admire anything in art that has not in it the elements of permanency. A sunset they will acknowledge to be beautiful, though fleeting, but its artistic portrayal, they say, must be lasting. An idea, a passion, may be fine, even when forgotten in a moment, but if enshrined in literary form it must be worth preserving forever or they regard it as without value. These people are confusing mere durability with beauty. "Is anything that doesn't last three years a book?" asks Mr. Carnegie. We might as well refuse to admire a flower because it fades over night, or turn from our daily food because it is incapable of retaining indefinitely its savor and nutritious qualities. It cannot be too strongly emphasized that a thing may possess beauty and usefulness in a high degree to-day and lose them both tomorrow. That is an excellent reason for discarding it then, but not for spurning it now. What is cast into the oven of oblivion to-morrow may to-day be arrayed, beyond all the glories of Solomon, in aptness of allusion and in fitness of application.

Much of the best that appears in the daily press is of this kind. Along with a good deal that is worthy of long life, there

is a host of admirable material in the ephemeral paragraphs·
that we are accustomed to despise. We may despise them, but
still we read; and nothing that is read with interested attention by fifty millions of people is really despicable. The
average newspaper writer may well be content to toss off
paragraphs for us; he need not care who constructs our leading editorials. The influence of the paragraph is incomparably
the greater; it has the raciness of the soil, shrewd wit driven
home with our native exaggeration, and the sting of the
epigram. And much of that which is bound between covers
has this peculiar aroma of journalism—its fitness to-day, its
staleness to-morrow. This sort of thing may be badly done or
it may be well done—inconceivably apt, dainty and well-
flavored. If it is of the best, why may we not love it, though
it be to-morrow as flat as the sparkling wine without its
gaseous brilliancy?

To those who have been accustomed to books from
childhood, who have lived with them and among them, who
constantly read them and read about them, they seem to be a
part of the natural order of things. It is something of a shock
then when we awake, as we all must occasionally, to the
realization that to a very large proportion of our population,
supposedly educated, they are a thing apart—pedantic, useless, silly; to be borne with during a few years of schooling
and then cast aside; to be studied perfunctorily but never to
be read. When the statistics of reading are analyzed I believe
we shall be startled, not by the great increase in it, notable
and indubitable as this is, but at the enormous amount of
progress that still remains to be made before the use of books
by our people indicates any real general interest in them and
appreciation of them. An attitude toward books that is very
general is indicated by a series of cartoons which has now
been running for several years in a New York evening paper—
a proof that its subject must strike a responsive chord, for the
execution of the pictures is beneath contempt. It is entitled
"Book-Taught Bilkins," and it sets forth how on one occasion
after another Bilkins relies on the information that he finds in
a book—and meets with a disaster. This is a trifle, but it is one

of those straws that tell which way the wind blows. A presumably intelligent man, a graduate of the public schools, occupying a position under the city, recently remarked to one of our library people that he spent his holidays usually at one of the nearby recreation parks. "Why don't you go sometimes to one of the branches of the public library?" he was asked. He laughed and said, "I've never read a book yet, and I don't think I'll start now." How many are there like him? We are educating them by thousands. They leave school with no interest in books, without the slightest appreciation of what books mean—certainly with no love for them. To these people books are but the vehicles and symbols of a hateful servitude. Perhaps this is inevitable; if it is, all that we can say is that far from "continuing the work of the schools," as we are often told is our function, we may often have to undo a part of it, which consists in creating an attitude of hostility toward books and reading. Can this be done by those who do not appreciate and care for literature?

I do not want to be considered pessimistic. This lack of interest in books I believe to be noticeable largely because we have changed our whole attitude toward the relationship of literature to the people. Love for books used to be regarded as properly confined to a class; that the bulk of people did not care for literature was no more significant than the fact that they had never tasted *paté de foie gras.* Now we consider that every one ought to love books—and the fact that vast numbers of people do not, no longer seems natural to us. That these people are beginning to show an interest, and that the ranks of the indifferent are growing slowly less, I firmly believe; and it is my opinion that the public library is no inconsiderable factor in the change. Some, it is true, are beginning to care for books by caring for poor and trashy books. These, however, are on the right road: they are on their way up; it is our business not to despise them, but to help them up further. Can we do it without having ourselves a proper appreciation of what is good in books?

But can a love for books be taught? To those who have the aptitude for it, it certainly can. In other cases it cannot.

To those who have it in them, however, appreciation for the beautiful may certainly be awakened by precept and example. I have in mind a farmer in the Virginia mountains, dwelling in a lovely region, but among a rural population without the slightest appreciation of the beauties of nature. This particular man had worked for years in and about a summer camp and had thus associated with people from the city whose appreciation of the fine prospects from cliff and summit was unusually keen. In time he actually came to feel such appreciation himself, and he would spend the whole of his rare holidays on a rocky peak 4,000 feet above the sea, drinking in the beauties of the scene and eagerly pointing them out to his tousle-headed children, all of whom he took with him. None of that brood will cease to love nature, I am sure, and their lives will be sweeter and better for it. In like fashion, association with people who appreciate good books will awaken a similar love in many an unpromising mind. Mere contact with the books themselves may do it, and so our open shelves have brought it to thousands, but the additional influence of a sympathetic human mind will hasten it wonderfully. The busy assistant at the desk may have a chance to say but a single word. Shall that word relate to the mechanics of librarianship—the charging system, the application form, the shelf-arrangement—or shall it convey in some indefinable way the fact that here is a body of workers, personally interested in books and eager to arouse or foster such an interest in others?

But how may one tell whether the true love of books is in him? To detect it in another, as already noted, requires more than a brief acquaintance. But to test oneself is easier. What would the world be to you without books? Could you go on living your life, physically and mentally, even as you do now, if the whole great series, from big to little, from old to new, from the Bible and Shakespeare down to the latest novel, were utterly wiped away? If you can truthfully say that such a cataclysm would make no difference to you, then you certainly do not love books. If the loss of them, or of some part of them—even the least—would leave a void in your life, then you have that love in greater or less degree, in finer or coarser quality. Let us pity those who have it not. And as for you who have it, you surely have not only a fundamental qualification for librarianship, but that which will make, and does make, of you better men and women. Let us perfect ourselves in all the minutiæ of our profession, let us study how to elevate it and make it more effective, but let us not forget the book, without which it would have no existence. Possibly the librarian who reads is lost, but the librarian who has never read, or who, having read, has imbibed from reading no feeling toward books but those of dislike or indifference, is surely worse than lost—he has, so far as true librarianship goes, never existed.   □

SOME CARDINAL PRINCIPLES OF A LIBRARIAN'S WORK

Sam Walter Foss

The first great cardinal virtues of a librarian should be toleration and enthusiasm. These are qualities that are not easily combined, for a man who is tolerant is usually not enthusiastic, and a man who is enthusiastic is seldom tolerant. A man who combines these two qualities must be lymphatic and nervous at the same time—a kind of hot cake of ice. But we put lemons into lemonade to make it sour and put sugar into the same lemonade to make it sweet. So we put toleration into a librarian to make him judicial, and we put enthusiasm into him to make him human.

As a librarian a man should be as tolerant as charity, which "beareth all things, believeth all things, hopeth all things, endureth all things." As a man, and outside his library building, he may have his own beliefs, his own tastes, his own fads and his own orthodoxes and heterodoxes. He may be a Baptist with Quaker antecedents and an Episcopal temperament; he may inwardly despise the old masters and see nothing in Shakespeare and know nothing of Kant. But as a librarian he says nothing of these things, out loud. As a librarian he is both Greek and Barbarian, Jew and Gentile, realist and romanticist, aristocrat and democrat, theosophist, secularist, orthodox, liberal, populist and patrician. He is all things to all men—and all men are the same thing to him. He

Reprinted from *Public Libraries* 14 (March, 1909):77-81, by permission of the American Library Association.

is, as it were, the janitor of an amphitheater where warring creeds, beliefs and tastes contend like gladiators. He champions none and antagonizes none, but simply keeps his amphitheater in good repair and takes a sportsman's delight in seeing the fight go on. He loves all ideas—even when he despises them and disbelieves in them—for he knows that the ferments and chemic reactions of ideas keep the old world from growing moldy and mildewed and effete. Let him attain to absolute intellectual hospitality—if he can. A narrow man in a library—a bigot, a partisan or a crank—is a positive curse to any community that hires him. He keeps his town behind in the great intellectual procession that is moving on with a swinging stride toward something better. He is a discord in the world-tune. He is out of step with the new music—the music that is going to make the twentieth century resonant among the centuries; the music of the march of men all stubbornly holding to their own ideas and persistently developing their own personalities, but marching together in brotherhood, harmony and toleration. Let us not tolerate an intolerant man as a librarian. If such a man should become a librarian it would be money in the pocket of his community to double his salary on condition that he resign.

The librarian today should be a good mixer. The reason why Shakespeare interests all men is because all men interested Shakespeare. The tolerant librarian I am trying to portray will circulate with the long-heads and the pundits, and also with the flatheads and the triflers. All human interests are his interests. The canals on Mars and the fall style of bonnets both supply food for his omnivorous hunger. He is a man who supplies men with intellectual victuals; and he doesn't know his trade if he doesn't know the taste of all kinds of victuals himself. The supple intellect that sympathizes with all tastes; the rubberneck that stretches itself with ease into all the hubbub of affairs about it; the elastic taste that finds some satisfaction and sanction in all the schools of thought; these are what the modern-spirited librarian will at least affect, if he cannot obtain. If the man is tolerant at the inner core he has the first prime requisite of librarianship. He is ready to stand in his library, as at the threshold of a way-side inn, and welcome all his guests with an equal smile. And when he has welcomed them he should break out with the measles of enthusiasm and give them all his disease. By the exercise of his toleration he should get them all in, and then by the contagion of his enthusiasm he should make it welcome and pleasant for them. Enthusiasm in a library would once have been considered as much out of place as a stove in an icehouse. But the modern library is not a refrigerator. It is not enough to hand out books, we should let out a heart-throb with each book.

Well, now that we have our librarian perfectly tolerant and perfectly enthusiastic, what does he need next? He needs a larger appropriation. It is easier for a librarian to be perfect himself than it is for him to get an adequate appropriation from an imperfect and unappreciative city government. Yet the librarian should set himself the task of getting a large appropriation. He should make this a part of his personal business. As a rule the majority of the city government know nothing about the public library, and, in their hearts within their hearts, they care nothing about it. The librarian should learn to love the mayor and all the members of the board of aldermen. If he is in a town, let him or her love the select-men. But shall he become a politician and use the politician's arts? No, indeed. But let him become as wise as a serpent and as harmless as a dove. Any man, especially the supremely tolerant man we are describing, can get acquainted with any other man. Any librarian ought to be able to get acquainted with any alderman, and after he is acquainted he can behave prettily and be agreeable; and it is much more easy to give liberal appropriations to an agreeable librarian than to a disagreeable one, to a visible rather than to an invisible one. Let the librarian see to it that he is not an absentee among the city officials. Let not the pathway between the city hall and the library become overgrown with grass. After this tolerant librarian has become acquainted with all the members of his city government, let him be agreeable. This will be easy. In fact, it will be a thing he cannot help—because he is absolutely tolerant. He should never pester the city fathers with reiterated requests for more funds, but he should happen about at critical times when the financial budget is under discussion and look anxious. "Do not marry for money, but go where money is." Do not ask the official holders of the public purse for cash, but keep near them in every time of trouble. An adequate appropriation is an indispensable requisite in running a library, and a librarian should make it the paramount object of his life to get it.

A librarian's attitude toward his trustees should be much the same as his attitude toward the city officials. The trustee system is not the best system in the world, as all good trustees know themselves. In most instances the trustees are the governing board of the library. But nine men cannot govern a library. They cannot govern anything. It is good arithmetic to assert that nine governors can do nine times less governing than one governor. A public library to be managed efficiently must be managed by a one-man-power—and that one man ought to be the librarian. This view prevails in all boards of public library trustees in proportion to their efficiency; and one of the cardinal principles of a good librarian should be to make this view prevail in his own board. This will involve a delicacy of management that will test our tolerant librarian to the utmost. I have heard it maintained that the ability to manage a board of trustees is the first requisite of librarianship. Rules for managing trustees have not as yet been set down in any book, for the reason that the only men who are capable of formulating these rules have, for obvious reasons, been afraid to publish them. Perhaps, however, my official life may be spared if I throw out one vague and suggestive idea: Let the librarian in his relation to his trustees yield his personal preferences on many minor points of management for the sake of carrying out his own broad general scheme. Most disagreements between men are over little things so infinitesimal that if they were not magnified they would be invisible. But do not get into a quarrel over either a big or a little thing. In any fight both sides always get the worst of it. Do not argue overmuch with a trustee. Agree with him while he is in the way as frequently as your conscience will permit, and, if he is found hopeless and unmalleable, put in missionary work among the other trustees and they will outvote him.

Our tolerant librarian now having brought the city government and his own trustees under subjection, may perhaps find time to attend to his legitimate duties. What is his first great work? To get good books and then get them read. Now most librarians get good books, and that part of our subject may be dismissed. But most librarians do not get them read. The masculine half of the population in most localities, as a body, does not use the public library. There has been a fear expressed in some quarters that the public library is becoming feminized. This usually means that there is danger that the masculine element does not predominate sufficiently upon library staffs. But the masculine element is woefully small among library patrons. I am tempted to infer that the males of this epoch are relatively non-intellectual. The intellectual wife and the practical husband are a much more frequent phenomenon than the intellectual husband and the practical wife. More women go to church than men; more go to concerts and lectures; more go to clubs; more go to symphonies and more go to public libraries. I am told that the only gathering where men predominate over women is at a prize fight. At any rate man is in as small a ratio to woman in a public library as he is in a Monday bargain sale. His lack has indeed begun to be lamented in public libraries almost as vociferously as it is lamented at summer resorts. We have piped unto him, but he will not dance; we have bobbed for him with all kinds of bait, but he is an indifferent fish who will not bite. Now it is not the masculine weaklings and mollycoddles who are absentees from the public library. It is the hard-headed, dynamic, successful men—men with red corpuscles in their blood, and phosphorus in their brains, and money in their clothes. This kind of man, I fear, has become a newspaper drunkard and no other intellectual tipple appeals to his taste. I am something of a newspaper tippler myself and profoundly believe in newspapers; but a man who gives up books entirely for daily newspapers is not wise. Man is

rapidly becoming a bookless animal; but if the librarian only
knew how to do it, he might introduce him to a wise intellectual domain of which he has never dreamed. We need man
in the public library to take away our reproach. We need him
to take away the reproach of excessive novel reading—a
reproach to which the taxpayers, who are largely masculine, are beginning to make us sensitive. Women come to
public libraries much more than men, and children come
much more than women, but nobody comes enough. The
general public does not patronize the library except to
a very limited extent. My own library, in a city of
70,000 inhabitants, gives out something above 400,000
books a year. This is an average of about five and five-
sevenths of a book to each member of our population.
There was a time that I rather exulted in this record. But
after a little examination my exultation has been modified.
Each member of the population in our city reads five and
five-sevenths of a book from the public library during the
entire year—say, two books in the spring, two books in the
summer, three books in the fall and five-sevenths of a book in
the winter. Really is this a record to be proud of? And of
course I know that it is only a small proportion of our population that takes out all the 400,000 books. Our registration
number at present is 24,201. Certainly not over 20,000 of
these are actual borrowers. That means that at least 50,000 of
our 70,000 population do not visit the library at all. Only
two-sevenths of our people use the library. Assuredly this is a
bad showing—and it is a good deal worse in some places; it is
far worse in most places. It has long seemed to me that the
great imperative, overtopping problem that confronts the
public library today is a larger circulation. Get your people to
read the books they have paid for, is the librarian's first and
great commandment.

   But how shall we do it? Shall we make it compulsory to
go to the public library as it is compulsory to go to the public
schools? We cannot under the constitution make it compulsory, but there is nothing in our public statutes that forbids
us making it pleasant. I have seen libraries where it looked as

if the librarian was under heavy bonds to make his library just
as disagreeable to his patrons as possible. It is the tendency of
the small-minded man, when placed in a position of authority, to grow into a tyrant. We read about the tyrants of the
Roman Empire and regard them as monsters unspeakable.
But they were simply carrying out, on a large and extensive
scale, the same tendencies that abide in all thin and vacuous
men. They made themselves monsters through the operation
of the same law that makes librarians martinets. The martinet
and the fuddy-duddy librarian, if he had been a Roman
emperor, might have been a Caligula or a Domitian; and Nero
and Commodus, if they had been librarians, would have been
martinets and fuddy-duddies. Shakespeare, as usual, knew his
business when he said:

> Man, proud man
> Clothed in a little brief authority,
> Plays such fantastic tricks before high heaven
> As makes the angels weep.

So one of the cardinal principles that should govern the
librarian should be the determination to keep down the cardinal tendency to tyranny that asserts itself more or less in all
men placed in authority. Why not plainly show men and
women that you love them rather than that you despise
them. Take as much pains to be pleasant to people as you do
to catalog your books correctly and to keep your account
straight. Get acquainted with as many people as you can, and
every one you get acquainted with like—if it breaks your
heart. Count each acquaintance as worth a dollar to you, and
then try to become a millionaire. Get everybody that comes
to the library so pleased with himself that he will become a
missionary and bring in all his neighbors.

Don't stay in the library all the time yourself and stag-
nate in the musty atmosphere of your dead books. Be a public and not a private man. Get out and feel the dynamic thrill
that comes from contact with live men. The club, the exchange, the street, the philanthropic and economic organizations that are feeling out for the betterment of mankind are
the places where the librarian should be found frequently. He

should be the best known man or woman in the city. A dollar bill that never circulates is not worth as much as a copper cent that keeps moving. Nearly every librarian ought to double the circulation of his books and treble the circulation of himself. In other words, the librarian ought to meekly and modestly assume the intellectual leadership in his community. He is certainly the logical man for the intellectual leader. He is the custodian of the intellectual treasures of his town; he is the adviser of its scholars, the teacher of its teachers and the keeper of the keys of the vaults of knowledge. The intellectual leadership has passed away, to some extent, from the clergy. The other learned professions—doctors, lawyers and teachers—are so circumscribed by their specialties that they cannot, unless they are very great, become the tolerant and catholic intellectual latitudinarians that we look for in the truly unbiased, educated man. This is the librarian's modern opportunity. Let him be the intellectual file-leader of his community. Let him grow big enough to fill the great place it is his duty to assume.   ☐

"PER CONTRA"

Herbert Putnam

There is an exposition across the bay. A feature of it is an attempt upon the part of various agencies for education, for culture, for comfort and for human welfare generally, to show what they are, to illustrate what they are doing, and in a measure to justify themselves. It is a sort of justification—of ourselves—that has been assigned to me to-day. For our president seems to think that the service we represent is not yet beyond cavil; that there are those who still question it, or who question it on new grounds. "More people are reading books," he remarks; "more books are in libraries and covering more subjects; more people are registered as users; more money is appropriated; new departments and new activities are being entered upon. Yet some critics cry out for the good old times when readers, though few, did not dilute their minds with so many ephemeral books, etc."

Noe the argument of such critics is in the nature of a demurrer. Admit the increase in libraries, in books, in facilities, in readers: what of it? What does it prove? That more people are reading more books. Yes; but what of *that?*

Well, I am "not so sure." I am not sure of the answer. I am not absolutely sure that we are required to give it. A demurrer—in court—is to be decided by the judge, not by the jury. It involves a question of law, not of fact; a question,

Reprinted from *Library Journal* 40 (July, 1915):471-476, with permission of the publisher.

therefore, to be determined by principles and precedents, not by the unprofessional, inexpert and undisciplined impression of a group of men representing merely the average in experience and opinion, and without a permanent relation with the subject matter.

In the case of books, and of libraries to supply them freely at the public expense, the principles were enunciated, the precedents established, sixty-five years ago. Is there to be no statute of limitations? If under them there has been this continuing and prodigious development, doesn't that fact in itself create a presumption very nearly conclusive? Doesn't it mean that we are at least an institution?—with foundations cemented by the general judgment of the community?

If so, we ought not to be called upon to dig up those foundations and reset them whenever anyone questions their soundness. The upper structure is a different matter, and the annexes. These may have to be modified as the developing needs of the community may require. But the modifications will be of detail or of emphasis, or of relative accommodation. They should leave the fundaments unchanged.

For one fling at our libraries there are, I suppose, a half-dozen at our universities. What of them? Does anybody seriously propose to discard our universities? Does anybody really doubt that the fundamental reason of them is sound; or deny that, taken by and large, they are supplying something which the community needs and must have? And does anybody really think attention is to be paid to the complaints against them, save as they concern mere systems or methods?

Complaints of system and of method are always to be expected, and are always in order, whatever the institution. They leave untouched the organs which are essential, and the *raison d'être* of the service itself.

When, therefore, a critic declares a college training "useless," we are apt to be amused or tolerant, or tolerantly amused. We fancy that he is arguing from one or two results under his personal observation: of a youth who was a born fool, and remained so in spite of a college course; of another who was born a genius, and came into his own in spite of the lack of it. And whenever another critic declares a public library "useless" because books are nowadays plentiful and cheap, and the people who really need them will buy them, why not be contentedly amused at him?

But this latter critic goes further: he declares that the free supply of books may be actually injurious; that it deprives the ambitious of an incentive which is valuable—to save, and buy them himself. It also deprives the book itself of that added relish which comes of its acquisition through painful abstinence in some other direction. And finally, that the supply of books by our public libraries, as actually operated, means the supply predominately of books that are educationally or culturally worthless, yet by their very profusion tend to enfeeble the mind, as an incessant diet of sweets may enfeeble the palate. Particularly the ephemeræ. They are like the true ephemeræ in nature which at certain seasons fall like snow upon the river. The fish gorge upon them till they become easy prey to the king-fisher. Or perhaps like the little book on Patmos: "And I took the little book out of the angel's hand and ate it up, and it was in my mouth sweet as honey: and as soon as I had eaten it my belly was bitter."

The physiology on which this latter complaint rests is doubtless sound. We do not deny it. What we question is the facts upon which the complaint is based, or the possibility of the alternative which a deference to it would involve. That our libraries are buying much of the "ephemera" of the day is true; are they, however, spending an excessive proportion of their funds in the acquisition of it? And is the tendency to spend more rather than less? Granting both—the fact and the tendency—what of the alternative? Shall they ignore wholly the predominant interest of the public in the literature which is "current"?

Our lives are contemporary. Our thoughts are the thoughts of to-day. Our actions are to affect the affairs of to-day. Our motives are the motives of to-day. Our contacts are contacts with the men of to-day and with the things of to-day. We are indeed subject still to influences which are hereditary; but the influences of which we are conscious are the

influences about us *now:* the facts, the people, the books, all
that which constitutes our environment. It is these with
which we take our start. They are the impulse, an ambition to
influence them is the incentive; and it is the hope of influencing them more potently that is our chief motive in looking
to the past at all.

The aid in this which the past can render is of great concern. It is the office of a library to make it available. No
doubt it is, as President Wellman has pointed out, the prime
and most important office. But a public library deals not
merely with students preparing for life, but with men and
women leading lives. It cannot go to them. What brings them
to it is either some condition in their own lives, or some condition about them, which they hope to improve, or to benefit
by. These conditions are reflected or dealt with in the literature of to-day. If the library refuses to supply this, it fails to
meet its readers on their own ground. And the distance between this ground and the past is a considerable one. It is
difficult to bridge. If not bridged by the books themselves
continuing into the present, the task falls upon the interpreting staff. But it will be a staff lacking apparatus.

I take it, therefore, as unavoidable that a public library
shall include literature of the day. The question is only: how
much? And in what proportion? I do not see how it can avoid
supplying many books and periodicals that will prove merely
"ephemeral." It will certainly supply many far inferior to the
"standards": inferior in literary form, in intellectual power,
in moral tone. It need not supply those admittedly debasing.
But consciously it does not. This we assert and insist upon.
And as to the other values, it does draw a line. What the critic
complains of is that this line is not drawn high enough. What
we answer is that it is being drawn higher with each developing year. And we point out that this effort is made possible
by two developing features in administration: the prevalence
of the system of "open access," ensuring to the reader the
direct contacts which enable the better books to make their
own appeal; and the increased personal attention given to the
reader by the staff, which recognizes him as a human being

alive, in a living present, and meets and differentiates him accordingly.

The criticisms are always in general terms, and therefore vague. I have yet to see one based on statistics, one that named a single book supplied which ought not to be supplied. An excess of current *fiction* has always been alleged. And as to this, statistics are quoted. They are always, however, statistics of circulation; and they overlook, what has frequently been pointed out, that the current novels are the small change of literature, and, therefore, being issued, read, and returned more rapidly, count more in the total than the so-called "serious," which is also the more deliberate, literature.

The detail of the complaint—that they serve no useful purpose to the reader himself—we can afford to ignore. I think it time that we did. The fair reason for reducing the number of them that we provide, or of eliminating them altogether, is a more practical one. It is, that the endeavor to supply them in adequate quantities to meet the interest of the moment, is futile; and that the mere profession of supplying them invites demands which are an expense to deal with even in the negative by answering that the book is "out"; and that the cost of administering the volumes which are actually acquired and supplied, is in itself excessive. For we must not forget that the cost of issuing a volume of fiction is as great as that of issuing a volume of history or philosophy; and if, as happens, the volume of fiction is issued a hundred times in a year to the other's one, the cost will be multiplied accordingly.

It is on this ground and on this particularly that I am personally in favor of leaving the "current fiction"—that is, all novels within one year after publication—to the subscription libraries. I have frequently said so; and have not changed my opinion. Such a course would alone, I believe, dispose of nine-tenths of the critics.*

-----

*It was recommended by Mr. Dana at the Niagara Conference a dozen years ago. His paper there states the case tersely and with complete good sense.

That is, however, a mere detail. The omission would still leave a wide range of literature neither definitely instructive, nor in any way beneficial save to the judicious. But are we to regard solely the injudicious? Let us take courage from the Areopagitica: "If it be true that a wise man, like a good refiner, can gather gold out of the drossiest volume, and that a fool will be a fool with the best book, yea or without book, there is no reason that we should deprive a wise man of any advantage to his wisdome, while we seek to restrain from a fool that which, being restrained, will be no hindrance to his folly."

But people read too much! Particularly they read too many of the books that signify nothing because they require no effort on the part of the reader.

Certainly, they do. This is an age of print; and the schools—and the oculists—have given us the ability to take advantage of it. We are gregarious; it makes us citizens of the world. We are curious: it brings to us all the facts and phenomena of our time. We are self-conscious: it reflects us. We love gossip: it provides it, and food for it. We are—still—romantic. It supplies the romance. And we court excitement: it supplies that also. In some moods and states of exhaustion, of petulance or of despair, we crave mere distraction. To some among us this may be achieved by means of a master book, a classic. They are fortunate. To the common run, if it can be achieved by a book at all, it will be only by a book contemporary with the reader; which takes the phenomena of life familiar to him and recomposes them so that they become dramatic; or sheds intelligence upon them so that they represent to him something significant which he had not before seen in them; or it changes his angle of vision; or it relates them in some sympathetic way to himself. Perhaps it may relate them also to that which is permanent in all literature. If so, the author has himself bridged over the gulf between the reader and the classics. He has interpreted the classics; but he has done so in a language which is intelligible, because it is the language of the reader himself.

For such an author the reader is the point of departure, and the present day. Equally must it be for the library.

But a profusion of books is so "enervating." So in a sense is a profusion of any other good thing. Civilization itself is enervating: it deprives us of the discipline of privation and hardship. Every luxury made available, every necessity made easy, means one less opportunity for the exercise of hardening virtues. I heard a physician remark that the tests and the instruments of precision which had made for the safety of modern surgery were ruining the faculties of observation in the medical profession. He meant, because they render the exercise of those faculties less necessary. Very likely. But the answer is that they *have* rendered modern surgery possible. As for the faculties of observation: other faculties—of reasoning, for instance, which deals with the results—have still their opportunity and their exercise.

"We value only what we have to work for." To be sure. To the toiler in a city sweatshop who secures his annual week in the country only by penurious self-denial during the remaining fifty-one, the woods, the fields, the birds, the very air are paradise. To the country boy who lives among them they are commonplaces of which he is unconscious. But this does not prove that they do not benefit him. The book secured by self-denial has an added value; but it is a value added only in relation to the circumstances of the possessor. Its essential quality remains the same, and its potency, as if it came to him without effort.

The man of few friends sets a special store by each disproportionate to his merit. But the man of many friends may be more capable of valuing the few whom he makes his intimates; for the possession of the many enlarges and diversifies his *sense* of values.

The man limited to a narrow area may profit by the very necessity of making the most of his opportunities in an intensive way. But the man who can travel, and through travel secure varied contacts and experiences, is enlarging and diversifying not merely his sense of values, but other elements in himself, very useful to him individually and as a citizen.

In mere power the man who keeps his thoughts, his passions, and his purposes within narrow confines, and conforms rigorously to them his acquaintance, his reading and his experience, surpasses; just as in mere power the stream confined between the narrow limits of a gorge excels an equivalent body of water spread out over wide and shallow areas. But the service of the latter may be the more benignant. There are times when the narrow and intense, rather than the broad and sympathetic, qualities are necessary to society. But those times—requiring the Puritan, one may even say, the fanatic—are times of stress and crisis. They are not the normal times of modern society.

So this very profusion of opportunity which modern civilization affords, has its compensations. It is relaxing—undoubtedly. It affects the mind as a Turkish bath affects the body. It opens all the pores. And the risk is the risk of open pores; which is that they will let something in injurious to the system. To be more exact physiologically, it is that they will let something out which the system cannot spare. In the case of the body, this is a certain vital warmth. In the case of the mind it may, I suppose, be either warmth—of energy and conviction, or that conscious power which comes of tense and sustained effort against a specific obstacle.

But Civilization has still its obstacles. There are plenty of them; it is only their character which has changed, and the direction of the effort required. We may no longer have to fell the trees or uproot the stumps; but there will still be the soil to enrich, and the crops to diversify, and the question of markets, and the ultimate consumer.

The awe in which book-learning was once held extended to the books themselves. It has passed. We are now on easy terms with them. We treat them casually as we do mere acquaintances upon the street. We approach them for a word, a laugh, a mere nothing, and then pass on. We do not exhaust the opportunity. Others will occur. Still less do we "make up for it" as for a formal occasion.

Awe has its values; the loss of it is a loss of certain values. On the other hand, the easy familiarities which displace it may bring some efficiencies very desirable. They may be merely social; but social efficiency is not to be disparaged, nor even social facility. To relax is also to expand.

So far as books are concerned, the present confusion goes along with other perilous profusions, of which most nearly analogous are the performed play, and the moving picture. Neither requires effort in the spectator—intellectual effort, that is to say. They are, however, facts. Vaudeville is a fact; and so is the "movie." Philosophizing, one would find much to deplore in them. It would not be their morality; for the most popular of them are those whose moral is unimpeachable. The worst that can be charged against them is vulgarity; and this charge lies against only a fraction of them.

But we must not forget that a large portion of each audience lives in an atmosphere even more "vulgar," and that in earlier times that portion would have had no experience at all outside of their particular environment. The play or the "movie" gives them such an experience. It may be merely emotional. If it appeals to their sense of humor it is also, in a measure, intellectual. It may at least widen their sympathies and quicken their imagination.

It requires no effort; it involves no discipline. This is a pity. Plays and pictures which would be intelligible and could be enjoyed only by the active exercise of the reasoning powers would certainly be more "educational." If we had only such plays, and only such examples in art, in music, and in literature; and the public would flock to them as they do to those actually provided, our republic might become an amplified Athens. But the others exist and appeal, and the vast majority of the public to whom they appeal and who by supporting render them possible, is of people who in Athens would have formed no part of the audiences; for we must not forget that of that entire community it was but ten thousand —the "upper classes"—alone who were privileged to such experiences.

The participation in them of the rest of the community —of the community as a whole—is a phenomenon only of our day. That is true of the plays and the pictures. It is true of the books. With this difference—of moment to us: that where the books are to be supplied by an agency acting as we do in behalf of the community as a whole, and at its expense, there are certain responsibilities. They involve certain standards—variable, but progressive. The moral standard is already, I think, amply recognized. The intellectual is recognized as far as contemporary conditions permit. There remains the question of taste. And it is as to this in books, as in the play and the moving picture, that the opportunity for improvement chiefly lies.

Taste isn't something which may be handed a man. Knowledge may be; but not taste. It isn't something which, having got, he merely possesses. Rather it possesses him. It is the man himself: a unit, in the sum total of his sensibilities.

It is subjective; it cannot be dictated to. But it may be influenced. The sure influence is association and a progressive experience; for the improvement cannot be abrupt, it can only be gradual.

In our reading public the hope of improvement lies, I believe, in the two influences I have mentioned: the freer direct contact with the books themselves, attracting to new experiences; and increasing mediation between them and the reader by the librarian who, knowing them, relates them to the needs of the reader as a present-day human being. It is in efficiency in this human relation rather than in catalogs and classification, and the other instruments of precision, that our distinctive opportunity as librarians now lies. It is this which is now having our attention as never before. Concern for it has taken the place of the concern for mere system and apparatus that excited us forty years ago, in that second stage of our development, when mere expansion of the opportunity for the reader having become assured, our zeal turned to the perfection of systems and apparatus, and we were in danger of losing sight of the religion in the mere ritual. We recognize now that those mechanical devices, while necessary, are merely devices. They are to be utilized; but they are to lead the reader to the book, not to be consciously interposed between him and the book. They are to be a gateway, not a barrier. They are also, in a way, a guide. But the main guide must be the librarian himself, herself. The first contact should be with him, and so far as practicable,

this should continue, until the final contact with the author
has been assured. The qualities that it demands include
some not characteristic of the librarian of the older school.
The qualities he had were in some respects admirable. But
the readers he had to meet were a limited, a select class.
They approached him endowed already with appreciations.
The impulses he responded to were already existing; he did
not have to create them.

The modern librarian of a public library (and it is the
ordinary public library I am speaking of throughout) has
often to create the impulse as well as to direct it. The old-
time librarian was contemporary with the past. The present-
day librarian must not forget to be contemporary also with
the present. He must be informed not merely as to the
book, but as to the reader. He must understand him and
what actuates him. For this, he must have the widest possible familiarity with the affairs, the interests, the influences of to-day; a familiarity gained not by formal education, but by travel and by varied social contacts. In quite
a new measure, therefore, is it necessary that our librarians
shall secure these; and not merely the librarian-in-chief, but
the entire interpreting staff. With them, with the fundamental education back of them, with the temperament and
the instinct for service; as human beings part of your own
time in thought and feeling, but as librarians infused also
with the thought and feeling of *all* time, you have opportunities for service not surpassed by that of any other profession, and certainly not vouchsafed to former generations of
our own.

And the distinctive opportunity is incident to the very
conditions which the critics deplore. For if this present age
is profuse, and superficial, it is also alert, eager and impres-
sionable. You can aid it to exact knowledge, clear and
discriminate thinking, and the choice of the better reason.
That is the prime office of books and of libraries. In the
promotion of morality and of taste, however, their service
is chiefly auxiliary; and you must refuse to admit them
accountable as if the only responsible agency. The prime

agencies are clean and comely homes, decent standards in business and civics and whatever is refining in art, architecture, music and the drama. Let the community see to those and it may count upon the public library for its due share in co-operation with them.   □

THE BOOK AND THE PERSON
WHO KNOWS THE BOOK

Ernest Cushing Richardson

At the recent meeting of the American Council on Education,
the paper which most arrested the attention of the three
A.L.A. delegates present was by Mr. Dietz of the Western
Electric Company—a business man, speaking for business education. It contained several matters highly suggestive to librarians on the business and educational sides of their profession.
The most suggestive was his diffident presentation of the
simple fact that business men are now working out a philosophy of business.

The special interest of this fact lies of course in the
circumstance that librarianship is from one point of view a
business occupation. The philosophy of business is a part,
therefore, of the philosophy of librarianship.

It is true that from another point of view librarianship is
a learned occupation, and that learning is indeed its dominant factor. The goods in which librarianship as a business
deals is knowledge. It buys and sells, stores and delivers
quantities of knowledge, done up in concrete parcels called
books, to be used in the factories of the human mind as
materials to produce living knowledge, wrought into that
living, organized parcel of knowledge which is called a person. The preoccupation of librarianship is with knowledge;

Reprinted from *ALA Bulletin* 21 (October, 1927):289-295, by permission of the American Library Association.

knowledge contained in books and knowledge contained in persons. It is therefore typically a learned occupation.

Nevertheless librarianship is in fact at the same time a business occupation. It is, like the men and books with which it deals, a double something with a material and a spiritual side. It has a business side and a knowledge side, both real.

As a business, librarianship is a service corporation, producing units of service. It deals with concrete books and concrete persons. Its object is to connect the reader and the book. The unit of service is a connection: one reader, one book, once.

The business involves buying, storage and transportation problems, personnel management, waste elimination, simplification of practices, job analysis, budgets, accounting, etc., in these days, even salesmanship.

In the prosecution of this business, librarianship has made many contributions to or developments of business method. It invented the cumulative file used in every business office as card file, loose leaf, or vertical file. It standardized the index card used by the billion in American offices and now recognized as an international standard. It was early in the field of cooperation by standardization and the methods of simplified practice. Hundreds of millions of cards and books, standardized to D. C. and L. C. classifications and to the so-called international rules for printed cards, save untold time as well as effort to users and to administration. The publication of printed cards alone saves perhaps a million dollars a year to library administration and a vastly greater amount in the valuable time of users of libraries.

Altogether, librarianship as a business occupation is an honorable and strenuous vocation. It is a real business which calls for business aptitude, business experience, knowledge of business method, and whatever belongs to business. Any neglect of its business side is fatal to usefulness.

Nevertheless, the main thing about librarianship, even as a business, is not business but learning or knowledge. What distinguishes the library business from all other kinds of business is the fact that the goods in which it deals is knowledge.

As the steel man deals in steel, so the librarian deals in knowledge, and as the main thing for a steel manufacturer is to know steel, so the main thing for librarianship is to know knowledge.

The main aspect of librarianship is therefore not business but learning, and the neglect of this aspect is even more fatal than the neglect of the business side.

It is feared, however, by many, and alleged by some that there is precisely such a trend in librarianship at the present day. There is a tendency, it is alleged, in library education, in the selection of library personnel and in the operation of the library to emphasize the method of efficiency, aptitude for action, the methods of modern salesmanship so-called, general stir and bustle, over reflection, knowledge, learning, tact, sympathy, humane development, and the other factors which go to set up a connection between the knowledge which is in books and the knowledge which lives in personality. There have been times in the history of librarianship, it is said, when the pendulum swung the other way, and the sole qualification required of a librarian was knowledge, when men were made librarians simply because they were learned, but today, so it is said, the pendulum has swung to the business extreme. Men are chosen as librarians because of business energy, not intellectual energy, efficiency in directing persons, not efficiency in directing ideas.

That is the point of this paper. It was just before this Council on Education meeting that the Children's Librarians Section of the A.L.A. suggested the presentation of this paper on the *Book and The Person Who Knows The Book,* and the idea was precisely this. It was thought that in library training and practice today there is a real danger of emphasizing the business aspect of librarianship at the cost of the knowledge aspect.

Whether or not there is real danger, the mere suggestion challenges inquiry as to the nature of the library business. It calls for a philosophy of librarianship.

A philosophy in this sense is simply a thorough inquiry into the real nature and meaning of things. What then is the real nature of librarianship?

It has already been remarked that it is a human occupation with a business side and a learning side. It has also been suggested that its object is to connect the knowledge contained in books with the living knowledge in the person. It involves these two factors: the book and the person who knows the book. As a business, it consists in making connections between these two. The function of librarianship is to help in the process. Its object as an occupation is to help persons to know books. To understand the real nature of this business, it is necessary to understand the nature of the book and of the person who knows the book, of learning and helping. What then is a book? What is a person? What is knowledge? What is it to know? What to help? The answer to these questions is the essence of the philosophy of librarianship.

There are many definitions of each of these matters and all of them right as far as they go. Each adds something to the conception, but all of them alike have now been put a little out of date by the modern method of resolving everything into terms of energy. First then the older definitions.

What is a library? A *library* is a collection of books kept for use. Librarianship is connecting a user and a book, or better, with the knowledge which is in a book.

The twin factors of the problem are books and the persons who use books. Both books and persons are, like librarianship, each a double something with a spiritual and a material side. In both cases the spiritual side is knowledge, learning or information. This is the common factor of the book and the person who knows the book.

What then is a book? A *book* is a quantity of knowledge done up in a parcel to suit the need of the consumer. It consists of a form of words embodied in a volume. It is a word incarnate; recorded knowledge. It may be irreverently spoken of as canned knowledge. Books are reservoirs or storehouses of knowledge.

What again is a person? A *person* is a thinking thing, or a knowing being, who stores the results of his thinking or learning or knowing in memory or self in the form of knowledge or information. He is a knower. He too is a double something with a body, soul and spirit. His soul and spirit are knowledge and words. He is a verbal being. He is knowledge incarnate, a living word, organic knowledge. He is made up of his ideas. What they are he is. He too, like the book, is a reservoir of knowledge.

Knowledge is the common factor of both books and persons. It is the essence of both and the key to both. It is the cornerstone to the philosophy of librarianship. What then is knowledge?

If one should try to gather up all the answers which have been given to this question, it would take whole libraries to contain them. All mythologies and all literatures in all times have given their answers in a thousand forms, and all the great religious and the great philosophies agree on certain main aspects of the idea. Knowledge is personality itself. Knowledge is life. Knowledge is the cosmos, or at least, the image of the cosmos.

The idea that man's personality and his knowledge are one is obviously true as far as it goes. We think, therefore we are, and what we think, recorded by the act of thinking, is what we are. As the Indian philosopher says: "We are our thoughts, we are made up out of our thoughts." For better, for worse, we are our knowledge. We are what we have thought, such as it is, good and evil and mixed. Man is a knower. He takes the consequences of his nature. What he knows he becomes, and he may become in large measure what he chooses to be by choosing what he will know, good or evil, human, sub-human or superhuman.

In the conception of universal religion, the personality of God, like the personality of man, is knowledge. Odin is the All-Knower. His name is Knowledge. Brahma and Buddha, possibly even Zeus in the genitive, bear the same name. In the old Semitic philosophies, the idea that Wisdom is God is a favorite one. In Hellenistic and Old Jewish philosophy the Word is God.

Again the idea that knowledge is life in the sense of vitality, animation, continued existence is also nearly universal. Egyptians, Indians, Persians, Greeks and Scandinavians alike have held that knowledge is the bread of life—the food and drink by which it is sustained and renewed, the nourishment of immortal life, on which even the gods depend for their immortality. Ambrosia and nectar, ritual beer, soma, haoma, Odin's mead, Kvasir's blood, Mimer's fountain, Heidrun's milk, Sutting's mead, and the apples of Iduna, all alike are knowledge, and all alike vitality as well as knowledge.

Life in both its aspects is knowledge. Enduring life is the knowledge of enduring things. Eternal life is knowing God.

Finally, the notion that knowledge and the universe of reality or the cosmos are one is common. The idea takes two paths. One leads into a labyrinth of metaphysics. It holds that there is no reality save in the mind of the thinker. Man's mind or knowledge is the cosmos and the only cosmos there is. The second path leads to the common-sense notion that the universe of knowledge is the image in man of a great universe of outward reality, a microcosm. In the subtleties of mythological philosophy the great universe itself is sometimes identified with knowledge. In the old Northern philosophy, the world, tree, Ygdrasil, symbol of the universe, is sometimes the objective universe itself and sometimes the inward tree of knowledge. Even Ygdrasil, however, is in the main not the outward cosmos, but the image of the universe in the human mind, the microcosm. It is knowledge, nourished from the fountains of memory and reflection, and made dazzling white each day by the water of knowledge poured over it by the wise Norns. It is the abode of Iduna, goddess of immortal youth, and its fruit is knowledge—the apples of Iduna:

> "Whose casket fair
> Held apples rare
> That render gods immortal."

It was the leaves of Ygdrasil which fed the goat, Heidrun, whose milk was knowledge and at the same time the precious mead which gives endless life to the gods.

In short, knowledge is the image of the universe in man.

This idea, of course, rests on the common-sense fact that

every idea is the image of some object and therefore the sum total of all ideas an image of the sum total of things. Whether this image is a model, a photograph, a verbal image, or something else quite different from any of these, is immaterial. Somehow the records exist and these records put together form a miniature universe.

As an image of the whole of things, the knowledge of any one man is a poor, fragmentary, and as a rule, rather confused heap of jumbled impressions and cognitions. The classification of these ideas organizes the confused ideas into the representation of an orderly universe, and gives unity, coherence, and integrity to knowledge and personality. Even if the classification is a rather bare skeleton, it forms a basis onto which each added bit of information can be worked so that with every increase of knowledge a man's inward whole of ideas grows into a nearer and nearer approach to a complete image of the great whole of knowable things.

At best, the detail of one's mental picture of the universe is scanty. Any one man by himself would never get far toward the complete picture, but happily knowledge is co-operative. It grows by each man producing something, recording it in books, and gathering the books into libraries. Each of these boks is the image of some man's idea or idea complex. Libraries are thus the sum total of the recorded ideas of all men. These too, like men's minds, are, if unclassified, a mere jumble of ideas, but classified, they become a true microcosm, the fullest image of the universe that exists. The living microcosms of men's minds are all fragmentary, but they are the real microcosms, and the great function which the microcosm of books, the library, performs, is to serve as a common basis of unity and like-mindedness which tends to aid the process of welding in one all the living microcosms of humanity, to serve as a concrete basis for that unity and like-mindedness which gives reality and stability to human society or civilization.

The library is thus not only the memory of the race, but by the same token the concrete basis of its corporate personality.

A man's knowledge is thus on the one hand a living image of the universe and on the other hand his personality and his vitality—his hope of more life in the life that now is and of immortality in the life to come.

The soundness and usefulness of these older definitions of books, persons, and knowledge are not to be denied, but the modern notion of reducing everything to terms of energy adds something. It provides at least a fresh figure and point of view in stating the old facts as to books, personality and knowledge in their relation to life. Instead of visualizing the book as a storehouse of intellectual food or drink to be transferred into the living storehouse of a man's mind, it becomes a storage battery of intellectual energy, from which a man charges the battery of his own personality.

The idea that "knowledge is power" is nothing new. The notion has long played an active role in the literature of books and librarianship, but more often than not it has here been regarded as a mere figure of speech, indicating that knowledge puts a man in the way of doing things. The modern idea counts intellectual energy as real.

The most ancient idea is, however, very close to the most modern one. Soma and ambrosia, ritual beer and the divine mead, those foods and drinks which are at the same time knowledge, are not merely ideas but the energy which gives courage to heroes, vigor in battle, intensity of wisdom and knowledge, duration of life. They are at the same time energy and idea.

Life, knowledge, books, learning, personality may thus all be expressed as different manifestations of energy. Life is energy itself. Knowledge is energy, potential in a book, dynamic in a person. Personality is energy which may be increased indefinitely by absorbing energy from books or other sources of knowledge. Every item of knowledge gained adds so much to a man's store of spiritual or intellectual or personal energy. Whether this is the same kind as electrical or chemical energy or not, it is real. The person becomes more energetic, able to enjoy and act more intensely.

Of course, mere reading does not increase intellectual

energy any more than running water through a sieve fills reservoirs. There must be storage ability. Learning is a strenuous matter. Odin hung nine days over the abyss learning the runes. The energy stored in knowledge runs close to the amount expended in getting it. The significant thing is that it is stored. As a man by food and exercise stores muscular energy, so by information and intellectual exercises he stores personal energy in the form of ideas or knowledge. This energy is not a figure of speech. It is energy. What then is knowledge? Knowledge is the energy of personal life. It purifies and strengthens personality. Knowledge is the water which daily whitens Ygdrasil, the tree of life. It is the mead which gives inspiration to poets, renews the strength of the gods, sustains immortality in gods and men.

All this adds a good deal to the idea with which we have to deal. The task of librarianship in helping readers to know books is helping them to increase their energy or life, to increase their ideas or knowledge, to be sure, but not so much for information as to increase the energy itself, in short, to make more alive. The object of learning and teaching is thus to increase energy of personality, to make a person more able to do things, able to enjoy more intensely and act more vigorously, in short, to make more alive. This is the significant message of modern science for modern education. The object of education everywhere is not knowledge for knowledge's sake but knowledge to make more alive.

Returning now to the task of the librarian, it has been said that this is to help persons to know books. It is not, on the one hand, to dump down a mass of books and tell readers to help themselves. On the other hand, it is not the forcible feeding of readers on books that we think will do them good. It is to help them, and to help anyone is to cooperate with him in carrying out his own plan or wishes, to help him to help himself. It is one-sided service. Library service is cooperation with persons who wish to know books.

How then do we go about this? So long as it is a problem of connecting the reader with a book that he knows that he wants to use, it is a very simple matter, but as soon as the problem is extended to connecting him with the book that he ought to want to use, or would want to use, if he knew of it, the matter becomes vastly complicated. As soon as one tries to help to the information which is contained in books, the problem begins to widen into what is literally the most complex problem of human learning—the knowledge of all books in their detail and as a whole in such way as to be able to apply the books to the particular needs of users.

The library has been called a pharmacy of medicine for the soul—a place containing a remedy for every mental ill. It has also been called a magazine, storehouse, or treasury, a place where intellectual food and drink and clothing are laid up to be issued when and as needed. Recently the less poetic figure of the department store, which aims to fill every need and suit every taste, has been used. Whatever the figure, this is in fact the aim of the modern library as to knowledge—to meet every demand in every field. It is a task to give plenty of scope for the best business and the best learning that a man has in him. It calls for more than the combined intellectual resources of a Casaubon and a Carnegie. It is a learning demand which, in the infinite complexity of modern scholarship and the rapidly increasing quantity of modern books, librarianship can meet only by highly cooperative intellectual methods and highly trained and organized staffs.

The organized methods so far developed for meeting this insatiable demand for help in finding information, is what we call our standard library practice. For those who know the book that they want to use we serve what we have, buy what we can and borrow the rest from other libraries—if we can locate the book and a lender. This much is a simple matter. It was executed in a simple and inexpensive way by the old librarianship up to the point of books in stock, by the method of passing over the counter. It does not go far however in the modern effort to serve those who only know the information that they want and ask to know the book that will give it. For these we furnish reference books, bibliographical cataloging, classification on the shelves and reference service to show the book that they ought to want and then proceed as before to serve it, or to beg, buy, or borrow it for them. This is what exhausts all the time, energy, learning, ingenuity and money that a librarian can command.

The organized methods for multiplying the librarian's time and learning are happily being developed in the development of library schools. This is the most significant fact in present circumstances. Whatever is to be said about the danger from the exaltation of business, it must also be said that the constructive remedy is already being found in the movement for the higher education of librarians—the higher entrance requirements and higher studies. This is the case too on the side of personnel selection, with the movement for personnel classification and its higher requirements in learning.

On the other hand it is not well to ignore a certain danger in this direction in our practice which we have had recently called sharply to our attention by the unfavorable comparison of our purchase departments with those of foreign libraries in the matter of learning equipment and results. There is a certain danger in the emphasis on business. It is a mistake, e.g. to think that a purely business man can run a library as effectively as a man of considerable learning. It is of course an equal mistake to suppose that a purely learned man can run a library effectively, but the danger is a less modern one. The obsession of certain types of the businss mind that business is the main thing and business can buy with salaries the brains necessary to make the library job the best success is contrary to reason and to experience, in spite of apparent exceptions.

It is contrary to reason that the man who knows all the details about purchasing and storing, organizing, investments, etc., but to whom the real material of the industry is unknown, should be able to analyze all the complex elements of the job and wisely establish the hundreds of routine operations which go to make up the business of connecting a person with the knowledge which he wishes to acquire.

It is equally contrary to library experience. Mr. Winsor is the classic case. He made the Boston Public Library the best working library for scholars in the United States. He left for Harvard because the Boston politicans believed that they could go out on the street and hire as good a man any day. They did hire an extremely good man in Judge Chamberlain, a man of scholarly sympathies, good taste in books and a considerable amateur knowledge in certain classes, a man of good business qualifications and knowledge, but without the scholarship of Winsor, and from the moment of the change the prestige of the Boston Public began to wane and that of Harvard to increase until within a very few years conditions had been reversed and Harvard was the most distinguished working library for scholars in this country. A stream does not rise higher than its source.

It seems to follow from what we have been saying that the man who would help other persons to know books must know books himself—for if the blind guide the blind, both shall fall into a pit.

On the other hand the constructive remedy is being vigorously applied—the remedy for a lack of learning being ovviously education.

The conclusions from this study of the knowledge aspects of librarianship are:

1. The main stress both in the education of librarians and the choice of personnel should be on knowing books not on knowing methods.

2. For effective helping, the librarian must both know books and know about books—know them to increase his own personal energy, know about them in order to fit them to the various aptitudes, deficiencies, moods, diseases, needs or appetites of the persons who wish to know.

Finally it may be recalled that the characteristic mistake of the modern world is to forget that thinking comes before doing, reflection before action, looking before leaping, knowledge before business. What the world needs today is not more practicality but more theory, more philosophy, in short more thinking.   □

PLEA FOR A PHILOSOPHY OF LIBRARIANSHIP:
Philosophia vero omnium mater artium

J. Periam Danton

The purpose of this paper is fourfold: (1) to point out the
lack of any adequate existing philosophy of librarianship;
(2) to consider briefly the place of the philosophical approach to the study of librarianship; (3) to indicate some of
the ways in which the lack of a professional philosophy has
proved a detriment, or, put positively, the ways in which the
creation of a philosophy would prove advantageous; and
(4) to suggest briefly some of the problems and questions
which should be considered in the formulation of such a
philosophy. Because civilizations and national cultures are
what they are, and because they differ so markedly from each
other, the discussion which follows is limited to American
librarianship. The validity of this limitation will be apparent
if one considers how different must of necessity be the organization, administration, functions, aims, and hence philosophical bases of librarianship in, for example, Fascist Italy, Nazi
Germany, and the United States. But the author believes that
much of what follows is applicable to librarianship generally.

I

Twenty-two centuries before Voltaire invited those who
wished to converse with him to define their terms, Confucius

Reprinted from *Library Quarterly* 4 (October, 1934):527-551 by permission of the author and the University of Chicago Press.

enunciated his famous doctrine of the rectification of names, of which one section reads: "If names [i.e., terms] be not correct, language is not in accordance with the truth of things. If language be not in accordance with the truth of things, affairs cannot be carried on to success."[1] In spite of the obvious wisdom of these words, it may be almost as dangerous to attempt a "correct" definition of philosophy in any sense of the word as to leave the term undefined. Still, the meaning which it is here intended to convey should be apparent. With philosophy in the "philosophical" or metaphysical sense this paper is not concerned. Nor is it concerned with that unfortunate concept of the term which denotes a priori reasoning about questions, the solution of which should depend upon inductive techniques. Rather, the present use of the word philosophy implies the "careful, critical, systematic work of the intellect in the formulation of beliefs, with the aim of making them represent the highest degree of probability, in face of the fact that adequate data are not obtainable for strictly demonstrable conclusions."[2] It implies, further, that such beliefs shall have to do with aims, functions, and general objectives, that these last shall be intelligently related—with an eye to the future—to the social order, and that the beliefs, taken together, shall comprise a systematic body of general concepts.

It would probably not be possible to evolve an all-inclusive definition of librarianship which would be, at the same time, succinct. Library science has been defined as "that branch of human knowledge which treats of the production, care and use of the records of human knowledge."[3] Numerous other definitions have been attempted from time to time. The following one, though admittedly imperfect, is sufficiently inclusive and concise for our purpose: Librarianship or library science is that branch of learning which has to do with the recognition, collection, organization, preservation, and utilization of graphic and printed records.[4]

It requires little or no proof to state that the profession has never set forth a complete, inclusive statement of its philosophy; that no such statement exists is well enough

known. This fact would be neither notworthy nor a reproach
provided there had appeared from time to time philosophical
disquisitions on individual types of library work which, taken
as a group, would serve as a professional philosophy—provided, in short, there was evidence to show that librarians had
given ample thought to the philosophical bases of their profession. The lack of any such evidence may be easily demonstrated, the only difficulty in doing so being that of deciding
at which of the several possible fruitful points to begin. A
natural starting point would be the corpus of professional
literature. It is too much to expect a section in Cannons'
Bibliography[5] devoted to this subject, or a heading "library
philosophy," "philosophy," or "philosophy of librarianship"
in *Library literature, 1921-32.*[6] But, though titles may be
deceptive, even the most casual observation of those listed
and the headings under which they are classified will disclose
how preponderantly our professional literature has been concerned with nearly everything under the sun *except* the
philosophical principles which underlie library activities. A
more careful examination, although it brings to light a few
notable exceptions, serves only to strengthen the first impression. There has certainly been no single, comprehensive philosophy of librarianship, and the isolated articles and
addresses of a philosophical nature have been, in the first
place too few, in the second place either too limited or far
too general, and, finally, totally incapable of being co-
ordinated into a unified whole. To be more specific, it is of
interest to analyze the topics discussed at recent American
Library Association conferences and the articles which have
recently appeared in the professional journals. During the last
five annual conferences there were held more than two hundred group meetings and general sessions, excluding business
meetings of boards and committees. Over five hundred papers
and addresses were presented, of which, if one is willing to
stretch a point, it may be said that a dozen or so considered
some aspect of librarianship from a genuinely philosophical
point of view. During the four years, 1930-33, inclusive, the
A.L.A. *Bulletin* published about 180 main articles (in

addition to conference papers considered above). While perhaps eight or ten of these had a philosophical or questioning approach, not one can be said to have considered a "systematic body of general concepts" or to have expounded a definite philosophy of librarianship.

In the *Library journal* during 1931, 1932, and 1933 there appeared 318 contributed articles (this figure includes conference papers). At most, three or four of these belong to the select group which considers in some part the why, wherefore, and whither of the profession. Happily, and quite naturally, the *Library quarterly* can boast a slightly better average. Since the first number of the *Quarterly* in January, 1931, and up to and including the July, 1934, issue, one hundred and five main articles have been published. Four or five of these seem definitely to be philosophical both in approach and objective. But even this showing is surely no cause for unrestrained jubilation or self-congratulation in the ranks. The sad truth of the matter is that the profession has not concerned itself with evolving or even thinking about a philosophy. Whether this is due to lack of interest, irrecognition of the importance of the matter, or the newness of the profession which has up till the present necessarily demanded all of the available time and effort of its members for the handling and solution of practical problems is difficult to say. But there can be no disputing the main fact: of articles, papers, and addresses devoted to criteria and the means for arriving at them, data and methods of compiling them, techniques and ways of applying them the number is legion; of discussions devoted to philosophical fundamentals, the profession, from its whole existence of the past few years, cannot muster a decent handful, and these do not constitute in any sense a comprehensive body of philosophical thought. It should be noted, too, that these years have been admittedly more conducive to serious questioning than most periods of similar length in our recent history—though we may have been too busy saving the ship to have time to wonder about her course and the reason for it. At the risk of laboring the point, it may be said that neither the books which the profession has produced, the articles in other library periodicals, nor the references in the *Readers guide* can be satisfactorily cited in support of the opposite thesis.[7]

However little the activities and functions of the library may have found philosophic expression, and however serious this may be, it will not do to ignore the exceptions. Ernest Cushing Richardson has discussed in a philosophical fashion the meaning of the concepts "library," "book," "knowledge," and "persons" and has considered their relation to each other and the cosmos.[8] He has examined, in a very general way, the nature of librarianship—though without specific application to library problems—and has suggested the need for greater attention to the theory of the profession.

The fields and functions of the national association have been considered from time to time, and have, in one instance at least, been set forth in an inclusive and definite fashion.[9] Such a statement is, however, quite obviously not concerned with the functions of libraries themselves nor with the philosophical bases of library activities.

Parts of William S. Learned's volume are philosophical in their approach and relate the activities of the public library to the people it serves.[10]

As much philosophical discussion about library activities as has appeared anywhere in English print is to be found in a book entitled *The Five laws of library science.*[11] But this treatise, as stimulating and interesting as it undoubtedly is, does not attempt to define the functions of library activity on any other basis than that of present-day good library service; the discussion is not an open-minded enquiry into the validity of functions and activities. Most of it is, furthermore, limited to public-library work.

A few additional references might be cited, but there seems little reason for doing so in view of the fact that they do not offer, either singly or together, a complete creed.

Additional evidence, however subjective, that the basic contention put forward above is correct may be found in the fact that the contention is now a new one—although details to clarify and facts to support it are seldom, if ever, brought

forward. Speaking before the Professional Training Section at
the A.L.A. conference in 1928, J. Christian Bay said:

> Library science thus far·has been touched but lightly by philo-
> sophic inquiry. Highly specialized as its practice is, and wide as is its
> content of special knowledge, its idea has found only a very sporadic
> expression. You may hunt in vain through all our modern literature for
> any expression of the philosophical ideas by which our work should be
> supported.[12]

Dr. Bay's statement is as true today as when he made it.

Carleton B. Joeckel, evidently believing the situation to
be due to the librarian's forced concentration on practical
problems, has expressed the idea thus:

> The librarian himself, always a pragmatist, has been much too
> busy doing things to take time for an objective view of himself and his
> works. The great responsibilities confronting him on every hand have
> left him little leisure for mere contemplation or philosophical specula-
> tion as to the meaning of what he has been doing.[13]

Similarly, Miss June R. Donnelly suggests that there has been
so much for the librarian to do and so many opportunities for
new effort that he has had little time to philosophize over
motives.[14] In somewhat the same vein Douglas Waples com-
ments in a review of *Recent social trends in the United
States:*

> For the public library to have formulated a platform in terms of
> definite social purposes and corresponding activities is, of course, too
> much to expect, since the American public library as a distinctive social
> institution is too young and too much the child of the transitional cul-
> tural stages which produced it to have developed any substantial body
> of critical theory.[15]

The fullest discussion of the question known to the
author is to be found in Pierce Butler's *An Introduction to
library science.*[16] At the very beginning of his book Mr.
Butler says:

> Unlike his colleagues in other fields of social activity the librarian
> is strangely uninterested in the theoretical aspects of his profession. . . .
> The librarian apparently stands alone in the simplicity of his pragma-
> tism: a rationalization of each immediate technical process seems to
> satisfy his intellectual interest. Indeed, any endeavor to generalize these
> rationalizations into a professional philosophy appears to him, not
> merely futile, but positively dangerous.[17]

The crux of the matter is that the librarian has thus far concerned himself amost exclusively with process, achievement, and the immediate objective, and has given little or no thought to function or to justifying that function.[18]

II

Perhaps at this point, if not earlier, the library scientist as well as the library empiricist may be inclined to put the classic question of the modern skeptic, "So what?" The answer to the skeptic's query is writ large in history. But it may be desirable, nonetheless, to consider very briefly the place, function, and value of the philosophical approach to such a field as librarianship.

The philosophical approach to librarianship, as to any phase of human society, is that one above all others which should receive first attention; that approach

.... has been set over against all of the scientific methods as one of the fundamental ways, the most universal of all methods of seeking truth. It has been forerunner and pioneer of the sciences; it has taken up the trail where science found its limitations, and still again has provided .... media and method for the exposition of the validity of science itself.[19]

To the social sciences, especially, philosophy has made tremendous contributions, and in fact in the narrower field of sociology it was, until not so long ago, practically the sole medium of development. In political science most of the earlier theories owe their origin to the philosophical approach. Today, with science making enormous strides in all directions, and with the accumulation on every hand of staggering quantities of factual and statistical data, there is a tendency to belittle philosophy. But, as Ross L. Finney points out, the solution of a very large proportion of the everyday problems of life remains, in spite of the growth of science, partially or wholly dependent upon conjecture.[20] The upbringing of children, the choice of life-interests and pursuits, most questions of politics and finance, and all issues of ethics, behavior, and religion "are still in the twilight of common sense, empirical insight and shrewd guesswork." So long as this continues to

be the case—and it is likely that it will always be the case for
at least some of man's problems—there will be need for the
philosopher. This is particularly true of librarianship as we
know it today—a new branch of learning almost whollly lacking in scientific data. In relatively few instances will our supply of factual information be adequate for a completely
scientific solution; the element of conjecture is being and will
continue to be reduced to a minimum, but that minimum
will seldom be equal to zero.

Even if this were not so, society—and librarianship—
would still be under the necessity of examining their beliefs,
for facts change with changing conditions and yesterday's
truth may not be one today. Whether one looks at medicine,
the practice of democracy, or our system of education, one
cannot escape the realization of this. Further, the more
change there is and the more rapidly it takes place, the more
imperative is it that our philosophy and our objectives be revised accordingly, and the less likely is it that we can turn to
science and factual knowledge for assistance in solving our
problems.

The philosophical approach may be thought of, then, as
having a pre-eminent claim historically, as having contributed
much to the sciences and especially to the social sciences
through methods of logical thought, and as being an important and indispensable concern to society today in all questions of social values, objectives, and aims. Finally, there is
the relation between philosophy and science. There is no
need to enter upon a general discussion of this relationship;
such discussions may be found in most histories of science
and philosophy.[21] But it does seem worth while to consider
an aspect of the relationship which directly concerns the purposes of this paper by indicating the definite, if not sharp,
line of demarcation which exists between the terms "library
science" and "philosophy of librarianship."

The use of these two terms is not always as exact as it
should be, and the result has been an unfortunate confusion
and obscuration of the issues involved. The term "librarianship" may be said to be equivalent to "library science."

Obviously a "philosophy of library science" and "library science" itself cannot be synonymous any more than "medical science" and a "philosophy of medicine" can be. Any science deals fundamentally with the acquisition of facts and data; the description of those data through definition, analysis, and classification; explanation of them by the ascertainment of causes; and, finally, evaluation and the formulation of laws.[22] Science concerns itself directly with concrete phenomena. A philosophy, on the other hand, is interested in aims and functions, in purpose and meaning. To illustrate, consider the subject of reading. When this becomes, as it is slowly doing, a matter for objective, scientific study, when adequate data on reading habits and interests have been gathered and interpreted in accordance with the proved techniques of other sociological fields, and methods and results are borrowed and adapted from other sciences—when, in brief, reading in all its various aspects becomes a field of grounded knowledge, it will have achieved a place in the science of librarianship or library science. In contrast, although a philosophy of librarianship would be vitally interested, indirectly, in the scientifically derived data on reading interests, abilities, etc., it would be primarily concerned with purpose—that is, with finding out whether librarianship should concern itself with the question at all, and if so why, and in saying what use should be made of the data; it would be interested, to speak in general terms, in ends and the reasons for looking toward them.

Of course there is a close relationship between the philosophy of a subject and the practices, experiences, and scientific principles of the subject. Sometimes hypothesis or philosophy precedes experiment or fact, sometimes it follows, very often it does both, and occasionally the two are synchronous, but in all cases the relationship is a close one. Indeed, as John Dewey says, " . . . . if a philosophy starts to reason out its conclusions without definite and constant regard to the concrete experiences that define the problem for thought, it becomes speculative in a way that justifies contempt."[23] Similarly, practices—no matter how scientific and valid the principles upon which they are based may be—are meaningless without a philosophical basis. But the difference between the philosophy and the science of a subject is a definite and not merely an academic one. Dewey has stated it more than once: "It is sometimes said that philosophy is concerned with determining the ends of education while the science of education determines the means to be used."[24] Or, from another writer: "In a philosophy of education the first major problem is that of aim."[25] One may substitute "librarianship" in each instance for "education" without destroying the truth of the statements. And again, in defining science, Dewey says:

> It is of assistance to connect philosophy with thinking in its distinction from knowledge. Knowledge, grounded knowledge, is science; it represents objects which have been settled, ordered, disposed of rationally. Thinking, on the other hand, is prospective in reference.[26]

That there is a distinction between the two concepts should be obvious, but the fact is not always recognized. Mr. Butler, in the volume referred to above, has not always distinguished between the two. He has, in fact, gone so far as to use the terms as synonymous. The most obvious instance occurs in his consideration of the "possible benefits which may be expected to result from the development [of a library science]."[27] Of the four he lists, two are mentioned as benefits which would result from "the development of a library science," a third as an advantage which "a professional philosophy would give to librarianship."[28] Apparently Professor Butler is thinking of the terms "library science" and "professional philosophy" (or "philosophy of librarianship") as synonymous or at least interchangeable, whereas, in point of fact, they are distinct.[29]

The preceding five paragraphs constitute a somewhat long and roundabout way of emphasizing the fact that the present paper deals with a *philosophy* and not with a *science* of librarianship. The pros and cons of a library science, the lack of and need for one, and other ramifications of the subject have received a considerable amount of attention of late in library literature. The observations by Charles C. Williamson,[30] C. Seymour Thompson,[31] Douglas Waples,[32] J. Christian Bay,[33] and finally those by Pierce Butler,[34] in the volume to which reference has already been made, have covered most of what there is to say for the present, at least. And it may be just as well to point out here that there is a small but growing corpus of professional literature that is definitely "scientific." In the *Library quarterly* and elsewhere there are reports of studies which have been carried out in accordance with the canons of scholarly investigation. It should be noted, too, that one phase of library work—in some respects one of the most fundamental phases—is, in a not very different sense, scientific in its approach and techniques. This is enumerative bibliography which, at its best, is the examination, description, and listing of books in accordance with certain well-defined principles and by means of a more or less universally accepted terminology. But, to repeat, little thought has been given to determining in the light of the present (or, indeed, any) social order, policies and functions as a result of which we should be able to state that these studies or these library or bibliographical activities rather than some other ones are of prime importance to the profession or to society. It is, therefore, this general problem with which we are here concerned.

III

Because of the interdependence of a library science and a philosophy of library science, the benefits which would accrue to the profession from the development of the one would also tend to result from the formulation of the other. It would probably not be possible to say with any degree of assurance from which of the two a given benefit would be more likely to result or would more speedily be achieved. The four benefits to be expected from the development of a library science have been listed by Mr. Butler.[35] The realization of all of them will be hastened or aided, also, by the formulation of a professional philosophy. One of them, certainly—number four on the following list—appears more likely to result directly from the formulation of a philosophy than from the development of a library science. These four, then, plus two others constitute the advantages which may reasonably be expected to accrue to the profession as the result of the formulation of a philosophy.

1. First in breadth of implication, and perhaps most important, will be the achievement of a definite and recognized place for the library in the social order and, if there is to be, as seems likely, a new social order, the establishment and recognition of the library as a vital, creative, educative force for the advancement of civilization.

2. Possibly next in importance will be the validation of the library science which is slowly developing. Validation in point of time and present need—not, of course, in point of scientific correctness.

3. A third and almost equally valuable result will be the giving of meaning to technical and mechanical processes.[36] The development of a library science will, of course, contribute here and conceivably in a more marked fashion, through the erection of a sound, scientific framework for practical procedures.

4. Another benefit to be derived from a professional philosophy will be a precision and sureness in action resulting from clear knowledge of purpose.

5. A fifth advantage may be an ability and a means for distinguishing between the duties and the activities of the several types of library workers.

6. Finally, we may expect the creation of what Mr. Butler calls "a sense of professional unity,"[37] that is, the recognition of a definite principle of unified organization within the profession.

These six items merit detailed consideration.

1. THE LIBRARY AND THE SOCIAL COSMOS

It is pretty generally admitted, both within and without the profession, that libraries and librarianship have received little or no attention at the hands of the sociologist and the political scientist even when studies by students in these fields have been of such a nature as to include a more or less complete picture of our civilization or its educational aspects.

Ten years ago William S. Learned commented on the lack of critical attention given to the library as an agency of education and stressed the necessity for a thorough study of the library's functions, organization, management, and support.[38] But it is still true today that: "One looks in vain in histories of culture and education for studies of the modern library as an active force which is making its impress upon the social fabric."[39] This is the more remarkable in view of the fact that it is admitted—even by these same sociologists, historians, and educators—that the library is, along with the school system and the press (perhaps, also, potentially, the radio and the movie?), one of the chief and most powerful educative influences today. In his survey of modern educational tendencies C. H. Judd ignores the place and function of the library. So do the writings of most educators.[40] In Viscount Bryce's deliberate depiction of the American scene libraries are all but disregarded.[41] Similarly, the careful study by the two Beards contains throughout the whole of the more than twelve hundred pages of the revised edition only three brief references to libraries.[42] More recently and more significantly, as most librarians are painfully aware, the President's Committee on Social Trends has seen fit in its exhaustive and searching analysis to dispose of libraries in a few relatively non-significant passages.[43] George F. Bowerman in his review of the two volumes says:

. . . . study disclosed in the report twenty-six references to libraries and librarians, only seven of which appear in the index . . . . . In most cases the references . . . . are very brief and incidental. Nowhere is there a chapter, or if that seems too much to expect, nowhere are there a few pages giving a terse statement of the scope and purpose of the library and the service it renders. The motion picture has three and one-half pages, and the radio ten and one-half pages.[44]

Professor Waples also recognizes this lack of consideration of libraries and library work in his review when he says that whatever attention the report has received from librarians has stressed the infrequency with which the library is noticed.[45] In response to Mr. Bowerman's review, Wesley C. Mitchell, chairman of the Committee, wrote the following:

Though I have not checked up your numerous references to the report, I must say that the general tenor of your remarks seems to me just. I suppose that all of us have fallen into the habit of taking public libraries for granted. They scarcely constitute a "social problem." You probably have observed that we are given to thinking much more about aspects of life which are unsatisfactory than about those whch give us little concern or doubt . . . . . In a genuine sense, the fact that we said so little about libraries is a great tribute to them. But I can also understand that, to the men who are doing library work, this explanation is not wholly satisfactory and I think you are quite justified in protesting.[46]

That is very nice indeed. It is handsome of Mr. Mitchell and it is vastly soothing to the bruised vanity of librarians, but, in the last analysis, it is merely a rationalization *post hoc;* it cannot be accepted at its face value. Would not the public and the Committee be just as likely to "take for granted" the radio, our school system, or our population, as it would our libraries? One is inclined to feel that these and other aspects of our life are more likely to be taken for granted than are libraries, yet the space devoted to them ranges from ten to fifty-nine pages. And are we to assume that the status of "The arts in social life" and "Public welfare activities" on which the Committee reports voluminously is more "unsatisfactory" than that of libraries—that it demands and deserves a critical examination, a placing in the social order which the status of libraries does not? One has the unhappy suspicion that the answers to these questions are in the negative and that Douglas Waples has diagnosed the situation correctly in saying that the reason the Committee did not treat libraries as it did the family, for example, is that "too little is known about the social implications of the public library," and that evidence such as "comparable and reliable data on loans to corresponding social groups of different classes of literature, from a fair sample of libraries of typical sizes and covering a period from 1900 to 1930," was not available.[47] If these and other data had been available and if the Committee had had before it a complete statement of library aims and objectives we should undoubtedly have been rewarded by a criticism of these aims and policies, an analysis of the library as a significant part of the social fabric, and the placing of the library in relation to other social institutions. It would have been immensely helpful, immeasurably stimulating to have had our activities thus presented in a dispassionate, coordinated fashion, to have been able to read, for instance, the Committee's opinion as to the extent to which the library should cater to the non-educational interests of its readers

and the justification for any given stand on this point. That
we do not now reap these and other equally rich harvests is
because we have not sown. Carl H. Milam blames the profession, in part at least:

> The omission from *Recent social trends* of any adequate state-
> ment of the library's place in modern society is one more evidence that
> most of the specialists in the social sciences, including education, have
> not yet discovered the library as an agency for social advancement. This
> may be partly the specialists' fault. That it is also partly the fault of
> librarians no one can doubt, for as individuals the social scientists
> readily admit, and even become enthusiastic about, the potentialities of
> library service when they are told what the best libraries now do.[48]

Elsewhere he says:

> If the public library is to find a permanent place in our state and
> local governmental organization it is desirable that its place and the
> functions of the various governmental units with regard to it be defined
> in a way that will be satisfactory both to librarians and to public
> administrators.[49]

He might well have substituted "imperative" or "essential"
for "desirable." So far as any direct benefit to librarianship
as such is concerned, *Recent social trends* might just as well
never have been written. And the library will continue to be
left out of the social picture, it will continue to be denied the
advantages of sociological analysis and concomitant recognition until it sets forth its objectives, its reasons for them, and
its proposed methods for arriving at them; until, in brief, it
proves itself an organism capable of something more than the
pragmatic—or even the scientific—application of separate
processes and techniques to individual problems.

If the profession should achieve this type of recognition
it is almost inevitable that it will also benefit materially. In
that case, the percentage of public monies given to public libraries may more nearly approximate that received by our
schools; the budgets of college and university libraries may be
witness that they are in fact, as well as in name, the "heart of
the institution."

2 and 3. LIBRARY PHILOSOPHY, LIBRARY SCIENCE, AND LIBRARY TECHNIQUES

At several points throughout our discussion thus far, the interrelation of philosophy and science has been suggested. Neither can, as a matter of fact, do without the other; philosophy which is blind to experiments and practice will be speculative only and of little or no value. This will be all the more true as these practices become scientific and as the profession moves away from the purely pragmatic. Similarly, practices which are carried out without a clear knowledge of their purpose are meaningless—if not actually dangerous—for anything except the activity immediately at hand. And this, likewise, will be all the more true as the practices are given scientific validity and become, accordingly, more depended upon and more authoritative. It therefore behooves science to do everything within its power to assist in the formulation of a philosophy. In our case, at least, science has preceded philosophy to some extent, for while we have already made some progress toward putting practices on a scientific basis, we have not as yet a glimmering of a complete philosophy. By way of being concrete, suppose a hypothetical study on the reading interests of children between the ages of twelve and sixteen. Immediately we are faced with two important questions. In the first place, why make this study at all; why wouldn't some other study better serve the immediate needs of the profession? In the second place, assuming that we can determine accurately just what those reading interests are, what shall we do with our results? If the children display interest in reading matter which we believe to be of too low a standard, shall we cease buying and circulating such books? Or shall we leave the elevating, educative influence to the school and cater to the children's expressed desires? Or, again, shall we try to do some education on our own account by substituting worth-while for worthless literature whenever possible? Numerous other equally interesting questions would arise, but the example need not be further complicated. The important thing is that a philosophy would give to this or any other library study a certain validity, first as to relative value and importance, and second as to the results obtained. We should be able to say, "We are making this study because the library is aiming to do thus and so and to do it adequately we need these data; when we have obtained these data we shall act in accordance with our knowledge of the aims of the library, its relation to education, etc." That is the sort of statement that no research worker in the library field can now make with authority. To quote John Dewey again: "It is for the sciences to say what generalizations are tenable . . . . and what they specifically are. But when we ask what *sort* of permanent disposition of action . . . . the scientific disclosures exact of us we are raising a philosophic question."[50]

This giving of meaning to scientific studies and especially to technical or practical processes is one of the most important benefits which the formulation of a professional philosophy would bring. There is, to be sure, far too much hit-or-miss, trial-and-error library practice, but even this, which will slowly be altered by the development of a library science, is not so pernicious as the carrying out of procedures without a clear consciousness of their purpose and a synoptic understanding of ends and aims.

4. THE CONSCIOUSNESS OF PURPOSE

When the library profession becomes thoroughly conscious of precisely what it is trying to do and why it is doing it, we may hope to see a very significant change affecting not only libraries and librarians but also the society which they serve. The bewildered groping which characterizes so much of our activity is largely the result of lack of a definite conception of our purposes. Not only that, but we can scarcely expect society to think of the library in terms of its own constituent elements until we have made some progress in defining what the library's ends are or should be. The effects of the change, if it comes, will be far-reaching, and will touch every aspect of the profession from recruiting and training to adult education, library extension, the position of the librarian, and the attitude of government to libraries.

5. LIBRARY PERSONNEL

Pierce Butler has presented the case for the fifth benefit so
fully that another detailed exposition would be pointless. The
principal factors are, however, these: (1) The almost complete disregard, which has persisted nearly to the present
time, of any distinction between the several types of library
worker and their activities. (2) The more or less complete distinction in other professions between various types of
workers. (3) The need for such a distinction between technical library workers and clerical workers—that is, between
"professional" and "non-professional" workers. Even at some
of our more enlightened colleges and universities, members of
the faculty consider everyone in the library, except possibly
the librarian himself, much as they do the janitor who brings
a new box of chalk to their classroom. (4) The distinction
must be based upon ability and talent plus education. A certain number of years of training alone are not necessarily any
more adequate than are years of experience without corresponding ability and education. (5) Society as well as the
profession will gain because library work will be more efficiently done: (*a*) people of clerical level will not be doing
work for which they are not fitted, and professional workers
will not be permitted to waste their time on operations which
less expensive employees can do equally well; (*b*) there will
be less incompetence in the higher positions, many of which
are filled today by persons whose chief qualification is length
of service.

6. "A SENSE OF PROFESSIONAL UNITY"

What is meant here needs only brief explanation. At present
the libraries of the country are much like isolated, indepen-
pendent organizations each existing for and unto itself.
Ample proof of this may be found in the obstacles which
have been faced by those who have attempted to set up plans
for unified library service, co-operative buying, cataloging,
selection, etc. Happily the day of co-operation seems finally
to be dawning, but national programs are still retarded by the
consideration of individual interests. They will continue to be

so retarded until the profession thinks of itself in the large and not as service to individual readers by means of certain practical processes; until, in short, there is a philosophy of librarianship.

To remove any possible doubt let it be said here, parenthetically, that the writer does not for a moment believe that the development of a comprehensive professional philosophy will be the panacea for all library ills. It will not, nor will the accompanying, but still inchoate, library science. Neither philosophy nor science is sufficient, nor do the two together comprise everything that the profession needs. The purely humanistic and practical aspects of librarianship must always be taken into account. But the development of a library philosophy will relieve the profession of much of its sterility in respect to social problems, and in doing so it should bring with it the specific benefits mentioned above.

IV

During the course of this paper many of the questions which apparently should be taken into account in the formulation of a library philosophy have, of necessity, been suggested, at least by inference. What is, perhaps, the most fundamental of such questions has not been mentioned and, while it is not within the scope of this presentation or the ability of the writer to offer anything approaching a complete outline for a library philosophy, this point and some of the other more important ones not already given consideration may be profitably noted.

The major aims and objectives of librarianship, as of any constituent of human society, must be derived from the predominating ideals of that society. Consequently, before a library philosophy can be formulated, there must be an understanding and recognition of the ideals and purposes of the society into which that philosophy must fit. This is another way of stating what is, perhaps, axiomatic—namely, that before a library philosophy can be formulated there must be a philosophy of life for the world today. This is easily said, but the answers to problems of values have been sought by man, more or less in vain, down all the ages. However, the idea of value implies value to some one and the spirit of our age decrees that some one to be the individual. Hence our philosophy of life or librarianship or anything else must spring from the assumption that the needs and welfare of the individual impose paramount obligations upon society and its constituent parts. The determination of those needs is, then, the heart of the problem which can probably be solved only through a study of human activities. The individual lives a full life—that is, in so far as these needs are concerned—only when he participates to the greatest possible degree in the institutions of society. The library is such an institution and here, in the writer's opinion, the philosophy of librarianship must begin. But wherever it begins, it must be based upon a philosophy of modern life.

The keystone to the whole problem of the purpose and value of library service is certainly the question of its social responsibility, and, in fact, if the word "social" be used in its broadest sense to include economics, education, government, etc., not only the keystone but the arch itself may have been determined.

The social responsibility of the library will depend to a large extent upon the type of library—whether public, school, college or university. Government and education have an undoubted interest in all three, but that interest is most apparent in the public library, which reaches all classes and ages of people as no other educational activity of government does. Most of our discussion here, though perhaps especially concerned with the public library, is equally applicable, with some obvious reservations and modifications, to libraries generally.

The library is one of the principal democratic institutions created, developed, and supported by our civilization. But can we assume from that fact that libraries are essential in a democracy? If the answer to this question can be proved to be in the affirmative, it still does not follow that libraries are "essential governmental functions." If they are essential *to* a democracy or to government (as, for instance, public health is assumed to be), they would no doubt have to be considered essential governmental functions, but that contention is difficult to prove. If it were proved and definitely written into the law some services which libraries now render —such as, for example, the supplying of cheap fiction—might be endangered.

Granted that the library holds a pre-eminent place among democratic institutions, one might ask, further, whether the library is one of democracy's principal agencies for insuring an enlightened citizenry through the promotion of intelligent understanding of economic, governmental, and other social problems. Most educated persons would immediately answer in the affirmative, but neither they nor the librarian could cite, except in the form of isolated experiences, tangible proof nor a valid, recognized theory in support of the statement. If the library is such an agency what are its duties and how do we know that these duties and not certain other ones will best achieve the end in view? Where does the library belong in relation to other social institutions, particularly educational ones, as depicted in *Recent social trends?*

The whole relation of the library to education is one of appalling medievalism in so far as any effort at real understanding or solution of the problems involved is concerned. It is maintained, and undoubtedly with justice, that libraries are educational institutions. This is far from saying, however, that libraries are essential to our educational system. Most librarians have been brought up, professionally, to believe that libraries are thus essential. But so eminent a librarian as Harry M. Lydenberg recently wrote:

> It is no wonder . . . . that occasionally we should think of ourselves as educators; no wonder that we should sometimes assume that the librarian and his books are an essential part of the educational scheme.
>
> Essential? Nothing of the sort! Libraries are useful but by no means essential . . . . . I feel that if we library workers view ourselves and our work in proper perspective we must realize that we are not educators but rather the caretakers of important instruments of education.[51]

What seems to be the opposite position is taken by the
Secretary of the American Library Association in discussing
the place of library work: "But if the profession has as yet no
brief platform, it has at least the conviction that books and
library service are an essential part of an intelligent existence
under any conditions. . . . ."[52] An "intelligent existence" is
certainly pretty closely related to education in the social system. These two quotations are cited, among many, merely as
an indication of the controversial nature of and the wide
divergence of opinion on even the most basic questions concerned with the library's place and function. Should libraries
attempt to be educational institutions or should the education, even of adults, be put in the hands of a more formal and
less haphazard agency, and the education of children and
adolescents be left strictly to the schools? If it be granted
that libraries should carry out certain educational functions—
how far should they penetrate into the field of adult education? More important still, how can we justify the use of taxpayers' money by public libraries for the duplication of, or
encroachment upon, some of the activities of the public
schools? Just how far can and should the library go in serving
children and adolescents?

Such general problems as these are continuously present
ones. It becomes more imperative to find satisfactory answers
to them by means of a determination of the library's functions when, as now, we are confronted with the possibility of
an entirely new social order. The needs of this new order may
demand a complete change, at least in the external relations
of the library. So also may the new philosophy of education,
with its renewal of emphasis on independent study and adult
education. National planning for libraries, about which a
good deal has been heard recently, is perhaps a beginning. But
if such planning is to be worth very much, it must be based
eventually upon a sound philosophy entailing a clarification
of library objectives and aims. Thus far, library planning "is
not an effort to decide now *exactly what* libraries should be
and do . . . . ."[53]

What has been written above concerns itself, probably

naturally enough, almost exclusively with a social philosophy. It is certainly too early in library history, as we know it, for the writing of a metaphysical or *geistesgeschichtliche* philosophy of the library. Sooner or later, however, if the purely pragmatic aspects of our professional thought are to be raised, it must be placed in its complete relations to the history of human thought. The library as a social institution is, after all, but one phase of its philosophical implications. Does the library have a *Wesen* of its own and does it have metaphysical implications? That is, is the library an institution merely or does it contain within itself the germs of a philosophical relation to epistemological progress? The radio and the movie are, for example, like the library, agencies for the dissemination of ideas. But there are at least two great differences between them and the library in that they have in themselves a unity of sense and emotional appeal which the library lacks, and the library has certain intellectual fundamentals which, in general, do not apply to them, since they are now at least primarily aesthetic.

But these aspects, however important for the history of human thought in the year 2500 A.D., are far beyond the scope of this paper and its purpose, which is to plead for a professional philosophy—a social one—and perhaps also for a philosophical *Weltanschauung* throughout the library world.   □

[1] *Analects,* Book XIII, chap. 3, verses 1-7.

[2] Ross L. Finney, *A Sociological philosophy of education* (New York: Macmillan, 1929), p. 3

[3] H. H. B. Meyer in the *Library journal,* L (February 15, 1925), 177-78.

[4] Modification and elaboration of a definition suggested in an address, "The Sciences in the training of the librarian," by J. Christian Bay. See A.L.A. *Bulletin,* XXII (September, 1928), 449. Also, privately printed, 1928.

[5] H. G. T. Cannons, *Bibliography of library economy . . . .* (Chicago: American Library Association, 1927).

[6] Chicago: American Library Association, 1934.

[7] Cf. also Douglas Waples, "Graduate theses accepted by library schools in the United States from June, 1928, to June, 1932," *Library quarterly,* III (July, 1933), 267-91.

[8] "The Book and the person who knows the book," *Bulletin of the American Library Association*, XXI (October, 1927), 289-95.

[9] "A Program for the American Library Association," *ibid.*, XXVI (February, 1932), 57-62.

[10] *The American public library and the diffusion of knowledge* (New York: Harcourt, Brace [c. 1924]).

[11] S. R. Ranganathan (Madras: Madras Library Association, 1931).

[12] *The Sciences in the training of the librarian* (privately printed, Holstebro, Denmark, 1928), p. 7.

[13] "Supply and demand in the library profession," *Library journal*, LVII (February 1, 1932), 103.

[14] "Library education more abundant," *Bulletin of the American Library Association*, XXII (September, 1928), 361.

[15] *Library quarterly*, III (July, 1933), 312.

[16] Chicago: University of Chicago Press, 1933.

[17] *Ibid.*, pp. xi-xii.

[18] Cf. Leon Carnovsky and E. W. McDiarmid, Jr., "Suggested program for Junior Members," *Library journal*, LIX (January 1, 1934), 32-33, wherein the authors propose that the A.L.A. "Junior Members adopt as their aim the formulation of a philosophy of librarianship"; also Arthur Berthold, "The Science of librarianship," *Wilson bulletin*, VIII (October, 1933), 120-21.

[19] Howard W. Odum and Katharine Jocher, *An Introduction to social research* (New York: Holt [c. 1929]), p. 91.

[20] *Op. cit.*, p. 4. The writer is under obligation to Mr. Finney for several of the ideas which follow; they may be read in greater detail in chapter I, entitled "A Brief for the philosophy of education," of the volume cited.

[21] A brief résumé is given in the work by Odum and Jocher already referred to, pp. 91-102.

[22] Cf., for example, G. T. W. Patrick, *Introduction to philosophy* (Boston: Houghton, 1924), p. 13.

[23] *The Sources of a science of education* (New York: Liveright, 1929), p. 56.

[24] *Ibid.*, p. 55.

[25] Ross L. Finney, *op. cit.*, p. 29

[26] *Democracy and education* (New York: Macmillan, 1920), p. 380.

[27] *Op. cit.*, p. 102.

[28] *Ibid.*, pp. 103, 107, 110.

[29] Professor Butler, after reading these paragraphs, indicated that his use of the phrase "philosophy of librarianship" was something of a *lapsus calami* and that his meaning in each instance, as is amply demonstrated throughout his volume, had to do with a science of librarianship. The criticism noted has not been pointed out in any spirit of cavil but simply to show the dangers inherent in the non-precise use of terms and the necessity for clarity.

[30] "The Place of research in library service," *Library quarterly*, I (January, 1931), 1-17.

[31] "Do we want a library science?" *Library journal*, LVI (July, 1931), 581-87.

[32] "The Graduate library school at the University of Chicago," *Library quarterly*, I (January, 1931), 26-34. "Do we want a library science? A reply," *Library journal*, LVI (September 15, 1931), 743-46.

[33] "Every serious voice deserves a hearing," *ibid.*, pp. 748-50.

[34] *Op. cit.*

[35] *Op. cit.*, pp. 102-15.

[36] Cf. Arnold K. Borden, "We need a philosophy," *Libraries*, XXXVI (April, 1931), 175-76.

[37] *Op. cit.*, p. 114.

[38] *Op. cit.*, pp. 76-77.

[39] Grace O. Kelley, "The Democratic function of public libraries," *Library quarterly*, IV (January, 1934), 10.

[40] C. H. Judd, *Problems of education in the United States* (New York: McGraw-Hill, 1933). Cf. also, for example, *The Educational frontier*, ed. by W. H. Kilpatrick (New York: Century, 1933).

[41] *The American commonwealth* (rev. ed.; New York: Macmillan, 1924).

[42] Charles A. and Mary R. Beard, *The Rise of American civilization* (New York: Macmillan, 1933).

[43] *Recent social trends in the United States. Report of the President's Committee on Social Trends* (New York: McGraw Hill, 1933).

[44] "Library representation in *Recent Social Trends*," *Library journal*, LVIII (March 15, 1933), 260.

[45] *Recent social trends . . . . a review*," *Library quarterly*, III (July, 1933), 311.

[46] *Bulletin of the American Library Association*, XXVII (April, 1933), 184 f.

[47] "*Recent social trends . . . . a review*," *Library quarterly*, III (July, 1933), pp. 311, 313.

[48] "Secretary's report," *Bulletin of the American Library Association*, XXVII (October, 1933), 420.

[49] *Ibid.*, p. 419.

[50] *Democracy and education* (New York: Macmillan, 1920), p. 379.

[51] "Librarians and educators," *Journal of adult education*, V (June, 1933), 260.

[52] Carl H. Milam, "Secretary's report," *Bulletin of the American Library Association*, XXVII (October, 1933), 421.

[53] *Ibid.*, XXVIII (June, 1934), 283. See also American Library Association, *Notes or a national plan for libraries* (Chicago: A.L.A., June 15, 1934).

THE AMERICAN PUBLIC LIBRARY
AS A SOCIAL INSTITUTION

Lowell Martin

The public library has long been referred to as a "social institution." Josiah P. Quincy,[1] in a book of essays published in
1875, refers to it as such. The 1875 report of the federal
government[2] speaks of " . . . . the one secular institution
which encourages self-development as an aim." And the term
is used today, both in general practice and in relation to the
library, in a context only slightly less glib and ill-defined. The
basis for this ambiguity is not far to seek. The character of a
"social institution" is difficult to ascertain when the name is
applied at once to an abstract economic system and a corpo-
real church, to a subjective code of etiquette and an objective
government. Nor are sociologists agreed in their use of the
phrase. There are as many definitions of social institutions as
there are social scientists, and this difference is not only one
of phraseology but actually one of meaning.

Social institutions, says Allport,[3] an opponent of what
he has termed the "group fallacy," are really individual relationships and nothing more. "These habits (which are termed
institutions) are plural and discrete . . . . and therefore devoid
of the synthesis or unity implied by a single term such as an
'institution.' " This is an atomistic view, psychologic rather
than sociologic, reducing institutions to the unit of which
they are composed, and denying scientific validity to any

Reprinted from *Library Quarterly* 7 (October, 1937):546-563, by permission of the author and the University of Chicago Press.

abstraction of a common way from their multitudinous manifestations. On the other side, we can note a statement of Judd,[4] "There is a breadth and scope in the psychology of social institutions which is entirely lacking in any system of individual psychology." It is possible to interpret this as assigning an objective entity to social institutions, making them something more than a sum of individuals, and endowing them with a structure and a control process of their own.

On analysis, however, these two conceptions are in opposition only in so far as they find a dichotomy where none exists. Undoubtedly social institutions have an existence objective to any particular individual. They define his relation to his fellowmen; his personality and his behavior are the product largely of the social forces to which he is subjected. Without the culture which exists separate from him, and which is transferred to him in social contacts, the individual could hardly become human. Conversely, the individual obviously modifies his institutions; using an older terminology, he is at once cause and effect, the creator and the created. Social invention, social leadership—these are the substance of social change, and they are essentially individual products, although they would be impossible without the background and the opportunity which the group provides.

We must seek, therefore, a definition that treats these two elements as the identity which they actually are, elements identified in a relationship just as two individuals may be identified in the relation of the handshake. Such a combination is attained in the following definition. A social institution is an integrated pattern of human relationships established by the common will and serving some vital human need. Both the objective and the subjective phases of the institutional argument are represented in the phrase "integrated pattern of human relationships"; the psychologic unit is there in human relationships; and the sociologic force in an integrated pattern. Further aspects of institutions are indicated in "establishment by the common will," for this it is that distinguishes them from customs, and in the "serving of some vital human need," which relates them dynamically to social value. It is in terms of this definition that we will analyze the American public library as a social institution.

SOCIAL NATURE OF THE PUBLIC LIBRARY

An institution, as we have seen, is a relationship of individuals reciprocally transmitting a certain pattern of attitudes and behavior. There are two phases to this process. Sumner[5] refers to these as "concept" and "structure": "An institution consists of a concept (idea, notion, doctrine, interest) and a structure." The structure is the obvious and perceptual part of the institution, its physical extensions in the form of buildings and tangible tools. Too often the structure is interpreted as the whole of the institution,[6] when essentially it is secondary to the basic concept, a means for the transmission of the concept. Certainly, the public library as a social institution has been thought of as buildings, techniques such as cataloging and circulation systems, and a personnel to administer these. Such objective and material forms of organization, however, do not comprise the totality or even the essence of the library as a social force; manners, for example, or the ethical institution of morality, require hardly any physical extensions of this type. The social nature of the public library is composed also of the factors of relationship. This nature can best be indicated by outlining these factors, by breaking down the foregoing definition into its component parts.

An idea exists at the basis of every institution. "An institution is always at bottom an idea."[7] This underlying concept is closely related to the purpose of the institution, the vital human need which it meets; it is a conscious formulation of the purpose. The character of the idea is always the ordered relationship of the individual with some aspect of group life. The essence of the family, for example, is a principle of ordering sexual relations and the relation of children to parents; property as an institution is a theory regarding ownership. The general group need at the basis of the public library is the need for the transmission of the cultural heritage from generation to generation, and the specific need is the transmission of that part of the heritage which exists in books and printed materials. In a sense, this specific need is a relatively recent one, as printing is a recent development (although, in another sense, the series of inscribed bricks of ancient Assyria were also a library). This group need is not dissimilar from that which has produced educational systems, for they, too, are maintained for the purpose of transmitting the group culture, and they employ books as a means to this end. Certain distinctions do, however, characterize the two interdependent institutions, as we shall later note. The social need which has engendered the library gives rise to the definition: the library is an institution for the transmission of group culture and knowledge as recorded in printed materials. This idea forms the core of its being.

Another factor which comprises an institution is the socio-psychologic qualities of the individual and their objectification in culture traits. They are something nonmaterial, but yet existent; they are that which is united in the social relationships which make up society in general and the institution in particular. In reality, this is a complex group of factors, variously named, one shading off into another. Without attempting too close a division of these factors, this discussion will treat them in two groups, the first that of attitudes and habits, the second that of a pattern of folkways, mores, and customs. Actually these two artificially divided groups are facets of the same thing—one the property of the individual, the other of that abstract human conception called "society."

Attitudes in the individual are mind-sets, ways of being set for or against things. Mind-sets against books are not impossible or uncommon; an individual with this attitude can be said not to possess the institution of the library (for where is an institution, except in the individual?). Attitudes are directed by the group into one channel, and away from another. Society guides the blind drives of the person toward definite goals which are dictated by the values which the group respects. Attitudes are existent in the group before

coming to the individual, and they come to him by a process
of social definition. Habits may be thought of as the physical
expressions of attitudes. Numerous attitudes of the individual
comprise part of the institution of the public library. The
attitude of a respect for books, and the habit of their use, we
have already noted. Part of the institution of the library is
what might be called a "socialistic" attitude; that is, acceptance of taxation of the group for the provision of facilities by
the state. We think of Franklin's Philadelphia Library Company, with its membership fees and yearly dues, as imperfect
for a public library, and so it was by our present standards.
Yet, had it been possible to present in 1731 a plan of our
present library system, it would not have been used; an attitude which comprises it had not developed in that day.
Quincy's essay[8] justifying educational books but denying a
place for fiction in the town library shows the absence of a
current attitude which places a group value on recreational
activities. The complex of attitudes which are embodied in
the public library need not be enumerated in detail. Suffice it
that they be recognized as part of the institution, certainly as
fundamental as buildings or catalogs.

The group possessions of folkways, mores, customs, and
traditions are the forces which accomplish the process of
social definition, the fixing of attitudes, in the individual.
Certain of these, the folkways and the customs, are irrational
in character; their basis is essentially emotional. Some institutions have more of custom than others. Monogamy and etiquette are examples of behavior patterns depending almost
entirely on their custom content. The library has relatively
little. In consequence it has a minimum of emotional support
to perpetuate it, although community reaction when libraries
have been closed in recent years indicates that this element is
developing rapidly. Lacking a high proportion of custom, and
its concomitant of rigid formalism, the library is in an advantageous position for adjusting itself to rapid social change.
Gaining custom, it may pass from the group of what Ballard[9]
has termed "sanctioned" institutions—those voluntarily supported and used—to the group of "basic" institutions, to

which the group demands conformity. The significance of these factors of folkways, mores, and customs in the structure of the library is, first, that it has an origin in the past of the group, and, second, that it is a changing, relative growth, not the result of an effort that man has been making since history began, but the product of a set of conditions peculiar to recent times.

A third group of factors comprising the library as a social institution is the previously mentioned physical extensions. A building in which the relationship that is the library can objectify itself, a technique of cataloging and classification, charging systems, readers' bureaus and publicity methods, and a personnel—all these are part of the institution. In the code of the public library—that is, its legislative alliance with government and its legal contract with the patron—we possess an objective formulation of the basic relations which constitute the social institution. No attempt should be made to minimize the significance of these physical extensions. In fact, Bernard[10] has concluded that "the social institution will be effective in proportion as it develops both a good administrative organization and an efficient physico-social apparatus for carrying its controls into effect." The point to be stressed is only that its material organization is not the whole of the library. At least equally important are the patterns of individual attitudes and the group ways, and the ideation which runs through the institution, unifying it, relating a loosely assembled mass of relationships and giving them meaning.

SOCIAL FUNCTIONS OF THE PUBLIC LIBRARY

The function of a social institution is the operation in fulfilment of its purpose. Economic institutions function in the attainment of the production and distribution of needed goods; religious institutions function to maintain an ordered relationship between the individual and the unknown world round about. A unique feature of this institutional organization is the use of co-operative effort, the unified action of many persons. The private libraries of the Colonial period, lacking co-operative effort, failed to fulfil the wider group need for reading matter.

Institutions provide lanes of conduct for the individual. As pillars in the social structure ("Social life depends on institutions as a sort of skeleton or frame-work"[11]), they define the particular behavior which the individual must follow out of all the possibilities open to him. This behavior is directed by social institutions toward social solidarity and well-being. In other words, they are means of social control. From the many tendencies of human conduct, some beneficial to the group and others harmful, institutions select the beneficial reactions and define them in such a manner as to make them the spontaneous reactions. This is done sometimes by a process closely akin to psychologic conditioning, but more often by a process of definition in which the individual comes to recognize rationally the value of a particular response. However, institutions exist not only to control and repress the person but even more basically to provide him with freedom and opportunity for self-expression and self-fulfilment. Societal processes must produce not mechanical units in a social machine but human personalities in a social organization. Only when an institution becomes so over-developed as to lose sight of the individual and becomes an end in itself— only then does it fail in this last function.

Both of these aims of social institutions are clearly evidenced in the public library. As a control agency it conserves the cultural heritage and transmits it. These in reality are two distinct functions, for chronologically the library has gone through first a stage of conservation, and more recently a stage in which transmission is added.[12] Currently a third stage emerges, that of evaluating the printed productions of the group and selecting a part of these for conservation and transmission. This last is a qualitative stage. Conveyance and distribution of one portion of the group culture leads directly to social solidarity and social homogeneity. The racial experience, recorded in books, directs the attitudes and behavior of one and all into sanctioned and prescribed forms. Standards of value are inculcated, socially desirable habits are defined, behavior patterns are fixed—in short, the individual is socialized.

Clearly evident also, and perhaps more characteristic of it, is the individualizing function of the library. Every human being, though hardly distinguished from his fellow-men in body or emotions or habits, is unique in mental and intellectual qualities. Rationality is the arena of singularity and specialization. Like man's other attributes, it is the product of his culture complex, but unlike them it possesses some degree of free range when mature and it can turn back to critically evaluate the environment in which it developed. This quality it is that makes man more than a slave of his social heritage, for it enables him to produce social inventions and social leadership—the means by which he can alter this heritage. In various ways the public library promotes intellectual life. It distributes information and by its organization integrates that knowledge. The individual is thus enabled to begin his quest where the previous generation left off, equipped with an understanding of the culture which he inherits. It provides intellectual tools; the library might be termed a laboratory for the mind. "Reading," says Ross,[13] is rapidly taking the place of oral discourse as a source of ideas." And aesthetic life, equally, is promoted and refined by easy access to books. Not so closely related to reciprocal social action, but nonetheless desirable, is the intellectual recreation made possible by the library. Certain institutions in our caste-less and consequently mobile society enable the individual to alter his position in the social structure, both economically and culturally. The library, along with the school and, in some areas, the army, may be thought of as one of the "social elevators."

We have seen that the library promotes both socialization and individualization. On the one hand, it transmits the social heritage and inculcates the values and experiences of the past into the group, with a unifying effect; on the other, it enables the individual to appraise present trends and future values, enhances the quality of his personal life, and provides a means for climbing the social ladder. It is therefore an

integral factor in both the anabolic and the katabolic processes which comprise the metabolism of social life.

SOCIAL ORIGINS OF THE PUBLIC LIBRARY

Inquiry and conjecture concerning the forces in the social
scene that fostered the public library less than a century ago
are not lacking today. The former fog and fiction is being
dispelled by healthful self-inquiry. "Librarianship . . . . can be
fully appreciated only through an understanding of its historic origins."[14] Understanding the library can only mean
comprehending the purpose for which it evolved, the social
need which created it, and thence evaluating the extent to
which the contemporary institution continues to serve that
need and the new problems which it faces. Such inquiry
should be fruitful; detailed analysis should be possible, precisely because a relatively short time has elapsed between the
events themselves and our realization of their historic significance. Records still exist of the events, but we are sufficiently
removed to treat them objectively. And we can therefore
soon expect something more than hopeful deduction and
logical construction in the formulation of the problem.

Characteristically, however, the opinions thus far advanced have been marked by a tendency to oversimplify the
issue, to abstract a few related threads and weave the whole
pattern from them. The fallacy of one-sided causation has
ever been the first result of the coming of social consciousness to any social discipline. One study,[15] for example, ad-
vances the theory that the American public library was the
result of minority-group efforts of a philanthropic, even
paternalistic, nature. Not activity from below, from the people themselves and from the flow of social processes, but
beneficial impetus from above was the cause of the appearance of the library. The Carnegie endowments are used to
clinch the argument, but it is well to remember that these did
not enter the field to any extent until after 1900; previous to
1898 Carnegie grants numbered only fourteen, as compared
with a total of over four hundred in 1917.[16] Now, no one can
deny that the efforts of altruistic individuals and groups

played a role in nineteenth-century library development. But it must be equally obvious that such appropriations, while helping to serve a social need, did not and could not create that need. Related to our earlier analysis of the nature of a social institution, philanthropic grants can contribute only to the more obvious forms of an institution—its physical extensions—and not to its essence in ideas and attitudes (although library buildings, once constructed, do become part of the dynamic institution of the library and aid in serving certain ends and fostering certain values and attitudes). Furthermore, explanation of the evolution of the public library in terms of altruistic dispensations entirely disregards a unique quality of the early library—its use of co-operative activity in a time of rampant individualism.

Another facile "explanation" of the origin of the public library is as an extension of the educational aystem, and copious quotations of the early founders can be cited to support the contention. There is nothing incorrect in the statement that the emerging library was part of the growing educational scheme (although it is worthy of note that from the beginning the library advocated individualization as well as socialization, while the school did not attain this second ideal until the turn of the century). The difficulty with the statement, however, is that it describes rather than explains the situation. It merely transfers our question from "What were the social forces which produced the public library?" to "What were the social forces which produced the school and the public library?" and only makes the problem more difficult because less selective. Nor can the statement that "the rapid multiplication of libraries between 1850 and 1900 was synchronous with the labor movement"[17] be given general credence in view of the rise and fall of the Knights of Labor, the fact that the American Federation of Labor definitely abandoned social reform as one of its aims, and the failure of a labor-class feeling to develop until after 1900. The shorter working hours that A.F. of L. activities promoted was a contributory factor, but hardly the only one, as the whole of Mr. Borden's article itself indicates. Apparently no snap, simple cause exists to solve in a single formula the social origins of the American public library.

Small and Sumner both localize the source of institutions in the "interests" of mankind.[18] The religious interest developed the church, political interests the institutions of government and law. We may translate these interests into the more concrete concepts of individual wants and social needs. "There never was a human institution that was not called forth in response to a social demand, which from the scientific standpoint means a social necessity."[19] The social need which produced the public library is apparent. A vast body of group culture had accumulated, owing both to new historical interests and to the technological revolution. No longer were the family and the school capable of passing on this heritage. The problem of molding a unified society was particularly acute in late nineteenth-century America, for large groups of immigrants were entering the country.

It is important to note that this need had not suddenly appeared full-fledged about the year 1850. Certainly it had been felt as early as 1731 in the organization of what was later named the Library Company of Philadelphia. The numerous later social libraries of both the proprietary and the subscription types attested to the felt need, as did the faltering school-district libraries. Particularly significant were the mercantile and mechanics' libraries of the early nineteenth century. The membership of these organizations was composed of young workers, artisans, and clerks. Fees were sometimes as low as a dollar per year, and few restrictions were placed on membership. Of added weight is the fact that official approval and protection was extended by state governments to these organizations,[20] occasionally in the form of tax exemption. No doubt the need was there. It was merely that a pattern of conditioning factors—population density, accumulation of surplus wealth, the rise of the common man, the maturation of the democratic ideal—had not yet set the scene for that which we term the public library, an institution organized by law, supported by taxes, and accessible free of charge to all the citizens.

Highly important among these conditioning factors is the democratization of knowledge that had attended the rise of the common man. Jacksonian democracy had been materialistic and uncritical in nature. "The generation of the thirties and forties did not evaluate, it destroyed taste . . . . it saw the acme of a particular development of individualism."[21] But the eventual contact of this western tendency with the aristocratic culture of New England, the New England of the flowering in such literary figures as Everett, Bancroft, Prescott, and Ticknor, as Emerson, Hawthorne, Whittier, and Lowell,[22] converted the "manifest destiny" principle into less material channels. The artistic fruits of mankind, it was held, could be democratized without being vulgarized. It is not surprising, therefore, that the first rise of libraries centered in New England; in 1875, 53 per cent of the "public" libraries were in this geographic division, and 58 per cent of the total library volumes.[23] A fact of possibly equal significance is that the North Atlantic states at mid-century had advanced farthest with the process of industrialization. The former home industry, which had constituted the whole life of the artisan, his job and his leisure alike, gave way to the factory system. Its concentration on the repetition of limited phases of the manufacturing process left the worker with a new leisure. A stirring of intellectual interests, profound in its far-reaching effects, rose to fill the void. A certain minimum of surplus and per capita wealth (this was $780 in 1870, as compared with $308 in 1850)[24] was prerequisite to the development of public libraries. Expanding industry and the exploitation of newly discovered natural resources—gold and silver, iron and coal—furnished the required wealth. A certain urbanization of population was necessary (in 1840, 8.5 per cent of the total population lived in cities of eight thousand inhabitants or over; in 1860 16.1 per cent; and the figure had again doubled by 1900 to 32.9 per cent).[25]

In short, the social scene had been set in changed conditions and the new attitudes of democracy and co-operation. The mercantile and mechanics' libraries had attested the possibilities of public libraries. Similarly the need and the basic idea had long been pressing for fulfilment. And then the direct factors of an expanding educational system with the need for extension in the adult field, the demands of labor and other organized groups, the financial aid of philanthropic individuals, and the influence of a far-flung Lyceum movement had crystallized the process. The social product was the public library. The elimination of any one of these factors would have changed the picture, but no one of them is wholly responsible for it.

SOCIAL CHANGE AND THE PUBLIC LIBRARY

Related to the origin of the public library, in fact continuous with its emergence—for the appearance and development of an institution is not an isolated but rather a continuous process— is the question of the public library and social change. An institution is never independent of the scene in which it has its being; it does not wander from its essentially social origins to pursue a disconnected existence.

The public library has been the expression of its age. We have already noted that the school and the library were among the first examples in American life of conscious co-operative effort applied to the development of individual potentialities. Fifty years before other activities, they proclaimed a balanced conception of individualism and democracy, a conception which recognized that the well-being of the individual is intimately bound up with the condition of society as a whole. Today the same idea is being applied to such separated fields as artistic production and social security. The changing intellectual life has left its impress on the library. From an institution of a primarily educative nature, it has swung to one of a wide recreational character, even as the mass of people have made themselves more articulate. Today the public library expresses the temper of the numerical majority of the people more than formerly, and this is intimately linked with the dwarfing of the earlier standard-setting *petit bourgeoisie* before growing numbers of workers united as a distinct laboring class.

Many and varied are the forces which have conditioned

and defined library development. The frontier left its impress in the form of local control, while its passing was expressed by the formation in 1876 of the American Library Association, a subsequent force of deep significance. Urbanization has been intimately related with the public-library movement; on the face of the evidence a high correlation is probable between the growth of libraries and the degree of concentration of population, both in the urbanized North and in the rural South. The new leisure created by an average decline of twenty hours[26] in the working week has a direct influence on a recreational institution. Many social changes have had an effect that is difficult to measure: the extended suffrage, for example, or the changed status of women, the sustainers of the country's feeble cultural life. Important also is the intensified interest of the people in art and science and social problems, both through extended education reaching up, and popularized forms of art, science, and sociology reaching down. Currently the same nationalizing process that increasingly organizes business and labor on a nation-wide basis under government jurisdiction invades library activities, and a federal library bureau is about to be created. Nor has the library escaped the monotonizing effects of a machine civilization; more people read books, but they tend more and more to read the same titles. Current trends such as the increasing concentration of economic power without a corresponding acceptance of social responsibility, and the implied threat to American democracy from the clash of world political ideas, play a part in the scene today that librarians cannot afford to ignore.

Few if any of the currents of the swift-flowing years have cut a path around the public library.

In the face of rapid social change, which so modifies social needs as often to remove the basis for which a particular collective action pattern was evolved, institutions—if we may speak so abstractly—possess a kind of defense. This is formalism: the institution ossifies, builds about itself a shell in the form of individual sentiments and habits. An example of this is a form of etiquette which persists long after the need which created it has disappeared, although the example may be an unfortunate one in that it does not indicate the danger inherent in formalism. The tendency of an institution to perpetuate itself, to become an end in itself rather than a means for life fulfilment, can be understood in terms of its nature. Institutions emphasize authority and precedent. They are control agencies and autonomous—that is not looking beyond themselves for reasons for their own existence—and they are products of the past and therefore "backward-looking." The tendency for institutions to become "bearers of social fossils—crystallized dispositions of archaic attitudes, beliefs, codes and habits"[27] is, in a sense, the purchase of security at the price of progress. The public library is not yet formalized. As a sanctioned rather than a basic institution it faces the continual task of serving the needs of the time. Neither structural rigidities nor excessive emotional prejudices have adhered to it. It therefore has, at the moment, no need to fear the social upheaval that eventually breaks the shell of institutional formalism, and it possesses a flexibility that should enable it to adjust itself to changing demands.

SOCIAL VALUES AND THE PUBLIC LIBRARY

The threat to the library, however, comes not so much from inner tendencies toward formalism as from a shifting social scene that may possibly undermine the need for which the public library exists. Competition is rife in the field of recreation. The expanding radio and motion-picture industries cut increasingly into library activities. The eventual significance of huge numbers of automobiles and trailers, the social structure of a "country on wheels," can hardly be predicted. The declining use of libraries in prosperity years may well be an index to the future. J. H. Shera[28] suggests a "central planning agency, composed of the best minds in the profession, and existing not in a merely advisory capacity, but with broad and very definite powers of control" as a solution to the wastefulness of institutional competition. The importance, also, of mounting standardization of not only technological culture traits but also of ideas and books is possibly

considerable; a society of Middletowns, with narrow standardization of thought and activity, may require a library
somewhat at variance with present hopes. Educationally, too,
the public library can be interpreted as faltering because
patrons of this group, a support comparatively impervious to
material social change, have evidenced a tendency to use libraries of a specialized type. This whole point, however, can
readily be stressed too strongly. No unsurmountable reasons
exist to prevent adjustment to these changed circumstances.
Yet it is well, after accepting the library as a social institution, to remember that institutions are relative to group needs
and, therefore, not necessarily permanent. It is well to emphasize the need for increased financial support, extended
professionalization, and a constructive program of adult education closely co-ordinated with other agencies in the field.

The preceding analysis of the immediate relation of the
public library and social change may have left an impression
of the library as a mere whim of the social environment, help-
less and lacking in individuality. Such is hardly the case; institutions are not solely social products but an integral part of
social processes. Institutions preserve and guarantee great
social values and also create values. They become part of the
environment. The public library preserves and promotes
values—scientific, artistic, cultural, even religious and ethical.
In our discussion of the functions of the public library we
saw that it both socializes the individual through its preservation of the social heritage and individualizes him through its
promotion of personal development. This second achievement is the foundation of all institutions, for, in any balanced
conception, the final and absolute end of society is the production of fully developed individuals, realizing human
potentialities in a socially acceptable manner. Full personal
life is the aim, and all other values may be thought of as
derivative. The library, with its freedom from restrictive behavior patterns and autonomous formalism, and in its books
reflecting the whole play of living, is favorably equipped to
assist the realization of personality and the encouragement of
self-expression. The organization of the public library

provides a means to the interpretation of the cultural heritage in relation to a new environment, and it is for this reason that cultural lag is particularly dangerous in this institution. The probable truth of the statement that "institutions are almost certainly representative of the best experiences of the past, but seldom, if ever, of the best experiences and experiments of the present"[29] should give librarians, as the guardians of an institution, pause to be ever self-critical. Furthermore, the necessity that the library faces of operating through impersonalized secondary-group contacts should indicate its path for the future—contacts of a growing personal nature between library staff and the public. Continued urbanization, concentrating the library into larger units, renders the problem more difficult and its solution more mandatory.

Revision of institutions on the findings of scientific investigation is not far distant. Critical and enlightened analysis of the library will reveal those points at which it is inadequate. Thereupon individual leaders must rise above the present and lift the library after them to a higher plane of effectiveness. This new method of revising social institutions possesses remarkable possibilities, because such knowledge may enable us to perpetuate a continuous adjustment of library activities, keeping them ever abreast of the times. That such adjustment of the library to social change and to social value is its fundamental problem is indicated by its inherent nature as a social institution.

[1] *The protection of majorities* (Boston: Roberts Bros., 1876), p. 105.

[2] U.S. Bureau of Education, *Public libraries in the United States* (Washington, 1876), Part I, p. 390.

[3] F. H. Allport, "The nature of institutions," *Social forces*, VI (December, 1927), 168.

[4] C. H. Judd, *The psychology of social institutions* (New York: Macmillan, 1926), p. 127.

[5] W. G. Sumner, *Folkways* (Boston: Ginn, 1907), p. 53.

[6] L. L. Bernard, *Introduction to social psychology* (New York: Holt, 1926), p. 564.

[7] G. D. H. Cole, *Social theory* (New York: Stokes, 1920), p. 43.

[8] *Op. cit.*, pp. 96-108.

[9] L. V. Ballard, *Social institutions* (New York: Appleton-Century, 1936), p. 12.

[10] *Op. cit.*, p. 578.

[11] J. O. Hertzler, *Social institutions* (New York: McGraw-Hill, 1929), p. 25.

[12] Douglas Waples, "Social implications of the public library," *Encyclopaedia of the social sciences*, XII, 622.

[13] E. A. Ross, *Outlines of sociology* (New York: Century, 1923), p. 218.

[14] Pierce Butler, *An introduction to library science* (Chicago: University of Chicago Press, 1933), p. 81.

[15] J. H. Wellard, *Book selection* (London: Grafton, 1937).

[16] W. S. Learned, *The American public library and the diffusion of knowledge* (New York: Harcourt, Brace, 1924), p. 71.

[17] A. K. Borden, "The sociological beginnings of the library movement," *Library quarterly*, I (July, 1931), 282.

[18] A. W. Small, *General sociology* (Chicago: University of Chicago Press, 1905), pp. 425-36; W. G. Sumner and A. G. Keller, *The science of society* (New Haven: Yale University Press, 1927), I, 85.

[19] L. F. Ward, *Pure sociology* (2d ed.; New York: Macmillan, 1925), p. 268.

[20] C. B. Joeckel, *The government of the American public library* (Chicago: University of Chicago Press, 1935), p. 5.

[21] C. R. Fish, *The rise of the common man* (New York: Macmillan, 1927), p. 337.

[22] V. W. Brooks, *The flowering of New England* (New York: Dutton, 1936).

[23] U.S. Bureau of Education, *Public, society, and school libraries in the United States* (Washington, 1897), p. 351.

[24] U.S. Bureau of Foreign and Domestic Commerce (Department of Commerce), *Statistical abstract of the United States* (Washington, 1935), p. 258.

[25] *Ibid.*, p. 6.

[26] President's Research Committee on Social Trends, *Recent social trends in the United States* (New York, 1933), II, 828.

[27] Hertzler, *op. cit.*, p. 80.

[28] "Recent social trends and future library policy," *Library quarterly*, III (October, 1933), 351.

[29] C. C. Taylor, *Rural sociology* (New York: Harper, 1926) p. 375.

A NOTE ON THE THEORY OF BOOK SELECTION

Herbert Goldhor

I

An increasing amount of attention, reflected in the growth of
the literature, is being devoted to the theory of book selection in libraries. Many of the pertinent investigations were
not undertaken with the sole or principal aim of contributing
to the formulation of such a theory, but they have so served.
The librarian who has kept abreast of professional studies and
has pondered on their implications in this connection will be
aware of the broad outlines of the theory that is being
evolved. This paper represents not an attempt at the presentation of the whole theory but only a tentative elaboration of
certain important points in it which the author feels have not
been clearly explained and of whose significance there has
been too little appreciation hitherto.[1]

If there is one idea more basic to the theory of book
selection than any other, it is this: Librarians have long selected books according to literary criteria, while the reading
situations with which they are concerned are to be understood only in sociological and psychological terms. The main
question that the book selector must consider is: "What happens to people when they read?" From this question of the
effects of reading, the whole theory flows.

Reprinted from *Library Quarterly* 12 (April, 1942):151-174, by permission of the author and the University of Chicago Press.

A good way to begin the consideration of what happens to people when they read is to look at the unit combination with which we are concerned—the individual and the publication he is reading. In every situation in which an individual reads print three factors are always present: (1) the reader with certain personal characteristics;[2] (2) the publication, with a certain content and style; and (3) the goal (or goals) sought by the act of reading, which reflects the reader's personal wants as stimulated and modified by his present social environment.[3]

These three more immediate factors occupy the foreground. In the background, more remote and indirect in their influence, are two other factors that must be considered in explaining the communication of ideas by print. These are (1) the author—his purposes, characteristics, and the social forces at work upon him—and (2) the previous social conditions and environmental influences that explain why the reader seeks the effects that he does seek.[4] Broadly speaking, the analysis of the author can be subsumed under the study of the publication and the analysis of the reader's background under the study of the reader. Technically, these second-rank factors should be treated separately.

The extent to which the reader obtains the desired effect describes the efficacy with which a given type of publication produces that effect on such an individual. The reader's purpose is often not the same as the effect produced upon him by his reading; the more nearly identical are purpose and effect, the more successfully was this publication selected for this reader, assuming that purposive selection and not random choice was involved.

To borrow the figure of the "economic man" from classical economic theory, each "economic reader," ideally, is conscious of his own traits, identifies his desires, and proceeds to that print-distributing agency which is best suited to his purpose, wherefrom he selects, or is helped to select, the most appropriate publication.[5] Actually, of course, the process is far less painfully conscious and less rational, but this figure of the "economic reader" brings out the final factor needed to explain the individual reading situation—the distributing mechanism whereby print and readers are brought together.[6]

Every time a publication is read, some means of distribution is involved. The distributing agency may be identical with the author, as when a commercial firm writes, prints, and mails out a piece of advertising copy; or with the reader, as when he selects his reading from his personal library. Sometimes the distribution is entirely informal, as when publications are borrowed from friends, read in doctors' offices, or received unsolicited by mail or by hand. But generally the distributing unit is a separate agency formally organized for the purpose, for example, bookstores, rental libraries, public libraries, or newsstands. It is this last broad group that is meant when any reference is made hereafter to print-distributing agencies.

In considering the functions of the organized agency, there are certain differences that can be distinguished between selection to fit the individual reader's needs and the chronologically earlier and necessarily previous process of "institutional" selection involving the policies and procedures by which agencies, formally organized for the distribution of print, decide on the types and kinds of publications they shall stock and make available to their patrons.[7]

This institutional book selection, as distinguished from the process whereby the individual reader chooses from a given collection, is the general topic for consideration here. The justification for the separation of institutional book selection from book selection for the individual reader and the necessity for analyzing the former apart from the latter spring from the fact that the two processes, though related and similar in many respects, turn on essentially different bases.

The process of institutional book selection operates with full attention to the individual reading situations which are expected to result from the functioning of the institution. The agency seeks to avoid selecting publications that will not be used by the people it hopes to reach. It either plans to sell the materials it stocks or hopes to rent them out or to circulate them gratis or to allow them to be used only on the premises. Whenever a distributing agency selects publications for its shelves, it does so for a purpose; and that purpose can be thought of in terms of the individual reading situations which the agency aims to encourage and help consummate.

Agencies differ widely in the degree to which they recognize the factors involved in book selection for the individual. Yet the more clearly the agency understands the nature of the reading situations it aims to satisfy, the more successful will it be in selecting books for its own purchase and in achieving its basic goal—whether that goal is to make a profit, as in the case of a bookstore, or to build up the best possible collection in a subject field, as in the case of a university departmental library.

But in the process of institutional selection itself the three main factors found in the individual reading situation—the reader, the publication, and the effect desired—are not all duplicated. It is chiefly with regard to the third factor—the purposes of reading, or the effects which it is desired to produce by reading—that there spring the differences between the selection of print by institutions and the process of book selection for the individual.

One reader can express an infinite diversity of purposes in reading at different times and in different places, subject only to the limits imposed, first, by his own background—his education, experience, and maturity—and, second, by the range of publications of which he is aware or to which he has access. Because of the wide diversity of purposes expressed by individual readers, print-distributing agencies have generally found it necessary to limit the area of readers' wants to which they will address themselves.[8]

This delimitation follows two lines. First of all, each agency will devote its efforts to meeting those requests of readers which are in closest harmony with its main objectives. Thus a rental library strives to make as large a profit as possible; with this goal in mind, the proprietor is able to decide whether to serve those individuals who seek the knowledge to be had from a study of higher mathematics, in place of or in addition to those who seek relaxation in the reading of detective stories. The concreteness of this agency's goal offers a sharp criterion by which to identify the readers' desires it shall attempt to meet.[9]

A second basis for exclusion is found in the desire to avoid competition with other agencies in the same geographical area. Once an agency has decided what type of readers' wants are most directly associated with its own goals, it soon finds that an important factor affecting the efficiency of its operation—in terms of those goals—is the presence of other agencies in the same area and with substantailly the same objectives.[10]

In the case of profit-making agencies, this means that there is economic competition between bookstores, for instance, whereby each strives to build up its own body of steady patrons, either by doing a better job of fitting print to readers or by narrowing the field of readers' needs with which it deals and thus specializing itself out of competition, e.g., the "rare-book" store. In the case of print-distributing agencies that are noncommercial, this delimitation of the field of readers' needs recognizes the wastefulness of duplication; thus the main research libraries in a city may agree on a program of co-operative buying and the assignment of special fields of subject knowledge for emphasis by each (cf. the agreement of this kind in the city of Chicago between the John Crerar, Chicago Public, and Newberry libraries).[11] Such agreements represent a tendency toward specialization in defining the particular purposes of readers on which each agency will concentrate.

It should be noted that sometimes the two bases of delimitation may take effect in the reverse order. This occurs, for instance, when there is a bookstore in a town but no public library. The bookstore can be expected to assume broad objectives in terms of readers' requests, even though it may mean that some of the services offered produce no direct profit. With the establishment of a public library in the community, the bookstore will abandon those services that the

library can perform more efficiently and will reformulate its
criteria for stocking publications on the narrower base of
readers' needs that it now strives to meet under its reduced
program.

In short, the objectives of a print-distributing agency
serve to indicate (*a*) the wants of readers it wishes to serve
and (*b*) those wants which it has no interest in meeting. The
institution which will now be considered in this regard is the
public library, though there is no reason why analyses, similar
to that which follows, cannot be made for any agency formally organized for the distribution of print.

II

What we are now concerned with, then, is a statement of
the factors that should be considered in the selection of print
for public libraries—an example of the general area of institutional book selection. If one looks at contemporary practice
in this matter of public library book selection, he cannot but
be impressed by the number of assumptions on which current procedure rests and the extent to which they are unrec-
ognized by the practitioners.

One of the major evils which flows from this situation—
because of the failure to recognize the relationship of the
book-selection process to the individual reading situations
that the library wants to encourage—is the concept that the
library's collection should be "well-rounded."[12] The term is
vague and open to numerous interpretations, but presumably
what most librarians mean when they seek to make their collections "well-rounded" is that, first of all, there be some
material on every branch of knowledge and creative composi-
tion[13] and that, second, purchases he apportioned among all
the possible fields according to a rough, subjectively esti-
mated composite of the amount of literature published in
each field,[14] the distribution of previous circulation between
the various classes of the Dewey system,[15] and what the librarian's experience indicates to him, in a general way, the
registered reading public is likely to request.[16]

Not only is the goal of a "well-rounded" collection of

questionable practicability, if indeed it is desirable at all, but an entirely different approach to the whole problem of book selection for the library is called for when the implicit assumptions underlying the practice of book selection are made explicit and when the essential factors basic to book-selection policy are pointed out and recognized. The approach so suggested will start with the library's patrons, actual and potential, whereas the older concept starts with the book collection. It will limit itself to those wants of readers which the library wishes deliberately to develop and encourage and, of this group, to those which it is best able to meet; whereas the older concept strives to take account of as many interests as possible. It will emphasize the individual reading situation, striving to bring the right book into contact with the right person at the right time whereas the older concept emphasizes the building of the book collection as such, in which all and sundry may stumble or pick their way through the great (and not so great) books of the world.

To summarize what has been said so far, it was pointed out that the three most important elements in the individual reading situation are the predispositions of readers, the characteristics of publications, and the effects sought in reading. The process of institutional book selection must of necessity be fashioned to accord with these ultimate factors; and the greater the degree to which this fact is recognized, the greater the extent to which institutional book selection is a rationalized, conscious, and effective process. In the light of this, the three main elements for consideration by a public library in determining its book-selection policies are: (1) the predispositions of its public, (2) the characteristics of available publications, and (3) the objectives of the institution. Of these, the third will be discussed first.

It would be difficult to overemphasize the importance of the institution's objectives in this connection. To put the matter in the context supplied above, it should be remembered that, though the reading wants of even one individual are theoretically infinite in scope and diversity, each print-distributing agency must delimit the sphere of readers' requests to which it will address itself. The necessity for this delimitation arises from the demand for increased efficiency in administration and service, which can best be achieved by specialization of function. The delimitation itself is set by the terms of the institution's objectives and occurs along two lines: first, those desires of readers will be served which most closely conform to the main objectives of the institution in question and, second, attention will be focused on those wants in this group which can be better served by the institution than by similar agencies holding more or less the same general objectives.[17]

The inability of librarians to state the wants of readers for which they purchase books strongly underlines the weaknesses that result from the lack of clearly defined institutional objectives (compare the definiteness with which a special library can state the factors which decide its purchases). An appreciation of the bases on which institutional book selection proceeds will throw light on the appropriateness of the various objectives that a public library can consider for itself; thus the flow of influence is not all one way.

The sources of contemporary public library objectives can be found in such factors as the social origins of the institution, the convictions of the chief librarian and the trustees, the general social milieu, etc.[18] The currently accepted objectives can be summed up, with a fair degree of adequacy for our purposes, as information, recreation, and education. Information and recreation themselves warrant critical investigation, but they have certain standard denotations; while education is such a diffuse term and, in view of the current emphasis on adult education, is of such importance that our attention here can best be concentrated on it.

The cardinal weakness with "education" as an objective, so far as guidance in book selection is concerned, is that it offers little help to the library's book selectors in pointing to the specific wants of individual readers which the library can attempt to meet.[19] This objective may serve satisfactorily if one accepts the concept of the "well-rounded" book collection; it is decidedly deficient when the library strives to fit specific books to individual readers with particular needs.

An objective, of course, can be arbitrarily sharpened; theoretically the librarian and the trustees are at liberty to set up any objective they see fit. They could also define it so rigidly as to make it a technically efficient guide to book selection. As opposed to such arbitrary action, however, it is suggested that a body of factual information, useful for indicating possible and practicable objectives, should be secured by a study of the actual use which patrons make of the library's book collection.

On the basis of existing evidence[20]—admittedly incomplete—one might hypothesize that three major uses which people make of the public library account for the overwhelming bulk of satisfactions so derived. These three uses are for instrumental purposes, for respite, and for reinforcement.[21]

The instrumental use of the library corresponds in large part to the current objective of providing an information service but has a broader scope. Whenever an individual reads print in order to secure "fuller knowledge of a practical problem and greater competence to deal with it,"[22] his reading serves him directly as a means of accomplishing a certain result. Examples of instrumental use would include the determination of the market price of a particular stock, the use of a cake recipe, the checking of a chemical formula against laws and principles laid down in a textbook, the study of the career opportunities in nursing, etc.

Similarly, the use of public library books for respite roughly approximates the objective "recreation," though again it is something more than that.[23] Reading for respite would cover such uses of print as reading for vicarious adventure or for stimulus to the imagination or for relief from tension. Examples of reading for respite are provided by the scholars who pursue highly intellectual hobbies as a change from their usual work, the vast bulk of detective and western story fans, and the convalescents who read voraciously for no other reason than to fill up their time.

Reading for reinforcement is not easily explained without a consideration of the place of reading as a medium of communication. According to one theory of psychology, at least, humans have various basic drives, eg., sex, hunger, and the avoidance of pain, and corresponding basic needs which they attempt to satisfy as well as they can. In a complex society like our own such satisfactions cannot be secured without help from others, a situation that demands an organized system of communications between individuals. In the course of time various mediums of communication have been developed—conversation, print, the radio, and the motion picture. Of these, conversation is the most used.[24]

Since reading is only an alternative method of securing satisfactions,[25] it is obvious that it will not be used except when it is found to be superior for this purpose to other mediums of communication. From this point of view, to urge reading for its own sake is no different than to recommend conversation as such.[26] But reading does possess, in addition, certain unique values. Because of the peculiar characteristics of print (e.g., it can be more accurately aimed at the predispositions of minority groups than are the movies; it can be more selective in its appeal than is the radio; and it can disseminate widely the work of the most effective writers, while conversation at best is limited to a relatively small group), it is superior to variant forms of communication in offering people the opportunity to be told, for instance, that they represent values or possess traits more desirable than those attaching to other groups in the population or in offering people the opportunity to identify themselves in their imagination with individuals having such superior standing.[27]

A stenographer may thus turn to stories of romance to find vicariously the emotional satisfactions she craves and is unable to secure in the real world about her. For this purpose, in some respects, books are superior to conversation, for few of her acquaintances are likely to be able or willing to build a word picture suited to her needs; to the radio, for she need observe no set schedule; and to the motion picture, for she can re-read any passage at will. It is possible that this same generalization holds true, in an entirely different area, for political radicals and conservatives; though public libraries supply the literature of both sides, few individuals take

advantage of the availability of the opposing literature to
read it and be converted. In other words, the radicals read the
radical literature, and the conservatives the conservative
literature, because each group thus secures the soothing experience of finding that the author's attitudes agree with
their own predispositions.[28]

When print is so used, the effect is a reinforcement of
the reader's self-esteem, a strengthening of his self-confidence,
and a lulling of incipient doubts as to the correctness of his
position. Such a use of print is directly antithetical to that
which education demands.

A comprehensive statement of the nature of education
is quite beyond this author's purpose and would lead far
from the subject of this paper. But there is one important
characteristic of education that is relevant. Successful education may be said to involve a relationship between the teacher
and the student of such a kind that the mind of the latter is
led in a certain direction; in this sense, education can be
thought of as a series of planned experiences such that the reaction patterns of the student are altered in a way that the
instructor wishes, by his exposure to certain experiences and
not to others.[29] It is this characteristic of education that
requires of every curriculum a clear statement of the goals to
be sought.

It may be objected that to require this element in every
educational situation makes for too narrow a definition. If
the term is to mean anything, however, it must be defined
rigorously to distinguish it from such allied terms as learning
and knowledge and training[30] and to differentiate it from the
concept of education that would identify it with all of life.[31]
This factor of change on the part of the pupil, directed and
purposive change and other than that due solely to growth, is
possibly the *sine qua non* of true education. This makes education a painful process, for it involves the acquisition of
strange new patterns of thought, if not also the destruction of
existing and therefore pleasantly familiar patterns.

Education as thus defined is not a common occurrence;
it is found most often in the family relations of a child to his

parents, where the well-nigh perfect combination of circumstances occurs. The parents know clearly the goal they wish
to achieve (e.g., the inculcation of proper eating habits), they
have control over the child's behavior, and they have numerous occasions to instil the lesson and equally numerous occasions to test the pupil's mastery of it.

Outside the family, education occurs most often in the
school,[32] though not all that takes place in the school is education in this sense. It rarely occurs elsewhere in any systematic fashion. Thus it is that the teacher and the school have
always been of great social importance. The story of Socrates
illustrates the influence that can be wielded by an effective
teacher, and the dictators of our day have learned the lesson
well. In a democratic society the teachers have a certain
amount of freedom to decide the direction in which they will
lead their students.

The public library, however, is in a poor position to
accomplish any great amount of education in this sense.[33] It
has no power to compel people to read; it cannot force the
patrons it does secure to read the materials that it feels are
"best" for them; it has no staff of pedagogues and no opportunity to supervise the reading of its patrons, since the use of
library books is typically a solitary, voluntary process that
takes place outside the library; and it can administer no testing program to determine how well it has succeeded in "educating" a reader to a certain point of view.

Not only does the library lack the powers and facilities
to conduct education but librarians strenuously disavow the
possession of any fixed goals toward which they would lead
their patrons.[34] They maintain that whatever changes occur
in readers are for the readers themselves to decide. It is as
though they posted a sign: "THIS LIBRARY ASSUMES NO
RESPONSIBILITY FOR WHAT HAPPENS TO YOU AS A RESULT
OF READING THESE BOOKS." Librarians seek thus to delegate
to readers the responsibility that teachers assume in relation
to students. And yet, as a matter of fact, the library is not
completely neutral, because it too exposes people to selected
experiences by making available on its shelves the works of

certain authors and not of others. But the difference is that the library's materials are not purposely selected with an eye to the individual reading situations that will result or in line with clearly defined and practicable goals; on the contrary, as under the concept of the "well-rounded" collection, the library in effect educates in all directions.[35]

There has been a great deal said about adult education and readers' advisory work, but it must be admitted that the number of people so reached constitutes but a fraction of those who come to the library for other purposes.[36] And of those who do use the adult education facilities of our libraries, few indeed seek education that involves directed change. Materials on welding, the history of Greek architecture, how to write business letters—these are worthy interests beyond question, but they are not education in the sense of purposively guided change.

The probability is that the bulk of our public library patrons seek clarification and reinforcement in their thinking rather than the unsettling experience of education. While the school has an obligation laid on it by society to direct the education of youth so as to mold their thinking in line with the mores of the race and to develop in them the mental equipment they will need to carry on civilization,[37] the library is under no such obligation. Analysis of the conditions under which it operates shows that the public library is unsuited to accomplish any great amount of real education; analysis of the actual functioning of the public library reveals that an important use to which people are putting its resources is that of reading for reinforcement.

Where education results in breaking down existing patterns of thought and to that extent unsettling the individual, reading for reinforcement involves a cementing of those patterns and the reassurance to the individual of the worthwhileness of his place in society. Consider what would happen if all that we read did violence to our established attitudes, or if every conversation we had involved the presentation of a point of view sharply challenging our own. Children live in a world of immediate gratifications; with maturity and education, the length of time during which no reinforcement need be secured can be extended and a more remote substituted for a more immediate return. But the need for such reinforcement is still present; and surely if society is willing to support schools to change the direction of thinking, it will find it advisable to support libraries for their influence, among other things, in reinforcing the personalities and thought-processes so established.

This is not a plea for "reinforcement" as against any other goal of library activity. But it is an attempt to point out the probable dominance of that effect of reading, here called "reinforcement," in the area which is presumably covered for the most part by the currently accepted library objective of "education." If the hypothesis is verified—that reinforcement is the dominant effect of reading sought by public library patrons—then it will be necessary for librarians to orient whatever objective they choose to set up in this area from that fact. Such an objective may find its place at any point in the range from the intensification of reinforcement to the opposite extreme of education as defined above.

"Education" is a noble and high-sounding term. "In America education is and has always been the magic word."[38] And education is a vital necessity in society. If we wish to establish it as an objective of our libraries, we should do so only with a full realization of the present situation and of the difficulties in our road. It is possible, perhaps, for the public library to become in face as well as in name an educational institution, but we need to implement that objective far better than we have done in the past, for our performance to approach our goal.

In public library administration objectives lead to policies, policies to programs, and programs result in uses of print by individual readers. The natural tendency is to formulate objectives, policies, and programs with increasing deference to uses. If we seriously go to work to establish education as an objective of the public library, we face the task of replacing certain uses of print with certain other uses and of forcing the day-to-day uses of library materials to accord with the programs and policies that spring from our objective.

III

In any case, whatever objectives a librarian sets for his institution, this analysis of their role in the process of book selection would be equally valid. The degree to which the book-selection process can contribute to the achievement of the goals set up will depend on the clarity, fulness, and explicitness with which they are stated and the extent to which they are feasible and in accord with the facts as to the library's position in the life of the community. The function of the library's objectives in the process of book selection, on the other hand, is that of delimiting the field of readers' wants to which the institution will address itself.

Given a complete statement of the institution's objectives, the operation of the process of book selection depends upon knowledge of the two other factors involved—the reader and the publication. The library must have data on the psychological and sociological traits of the people it attempts to serve, that is, its patrons both actual and potential.[39] This is to be secured through periodic community analyses and reading studies.[40]

This whole approach of the psychosociological study of the people of a community is in flat opposition to the assumption, underlying present public library book-selection practice, that the library's collection should be built to meet and answer present interests of readers.[41] This latter policy is faulty in that it limits itself for the most part only to those readers registered with the library and ignores the readers in the community who are not so registered, not to speak of those who are nonreaders at present.[42] But, more important, it is faulty in assuming that what people read is determined by what they are interested in. It seems clear that in reality the determining factors are accessibility and readability, with subject interest a poor third.[43]

The identification of the subjects on which most reading is being done or on which most people say they would like to read should be a minor aspect of a library's study of its community and of the reading done therein; more important are data on the other print-distributing agencies in the area and on the predispositions and socioeconomic status (e.g., sex, age, education, occupation) of the population.[44] Such data will indicate of themselves the subjects to which the threshold of receptivity is low; but, more to the point, they will indicate what types and kinds of print are needed within any one subject field to produce certain specified effects on these readers. And that, after all, is the heart of the problem.

As for the factor of the publications that are available, there is need for a continuing process of analysis of the content of new books. This content analysis need not be so refined and complete as would be necessary in the case of a research study that used this technique, but neither should it be as haphazard, unformed, and unconscious a process as present book-selection practice involves. It is possible, given the stated objectives of the library and knowing the important facts about the patrons, to set up a number of categories by which to analyze the content, style, authorship, etc., of a piece of print.[45] These categories must be worked over until meaningful relations are found between them and the traits of the library's patrons. They will then serve to guide the librarian in purchasing those items which, in view of the characteristics of his patrons, will best help him satisfy those needs and secure those effects which conform to the library's objectives. All three bases of institutional book selection are in need of serious investigation by students of librarianship, but the one that needs most attention first is this matter of content analysis.[46]

The development of each of the three basic factors— library objectives, community analyses and reading studies, and content analysis—is to be made in terms that are significant for the others. The content analysis should be based on the known characteristics of the readers and nonreaders.[47] The community survey should seek data relevant to the institution's objectives. And those objectives should have their basis in existing relationships between readers and public library materials.

Once the development of these three factors has been well started by the institution, it will mean that the analysis of new publications goes on currently, regular studies are made on the reading and readers (and nonreaders) in the community, and the library's objectives are being constantly refined, clarified, and retranslated into operational terms. When these things are being done as a matter of current practice and are properly integrated (e.g., by a formal statement of the library's book-selection policy and procedure), the institutional process of book selection so carried on should better serve to carry out the library's objectives in the community than would any other policy of book selection.[48]

If one looks at this institutional process of book selection from the functional point of view, it might be described in some such terms as these.[49] The announcements and reviews of new publications are scanned by the book-selecting staff, and those titles are ordered which appear to offer a possible contribution in furthering any one of the library's objectives among any substantial group of patrons possessing certain psychosociological characteristics in common. Thus the public library in a small town would probably ignore the publications of the Brookings Institution but might buy the popular digests of them in the form of *Public affairs pamphlets.*

Once the material was received, it would be examined by one or more staff members and a record of the analysis made. Unless this analysis, when viewed against the known characteristics of the community, indicated that the publication would serve to meet a want of any group of these people (as defined by their distinguishing traits)[50] which conforms to one of the institution's stated objectives, the item should not be purchased. Any objective will have to be shifted in its main emphasis from time to time, new data on the people of the community will be absorbed, and the categories for the analysis of publications sharpened and adapted to these changes; but the process as such will be the same.

Probably no library will be able to buy all the books that it finds can pass this test, but to determine which of these books to select is merely a matter of identifying those items that most nearly hit the center of the target—to produce a desired effect on a given type of reader. Other considerations that would be involved in applying the library's objectives are fairly obvious. For example, does a book that is being considered for purchase duplicate material already in the library? Is it readily obtainable elsewhere in the community? For how large a group of patrons is it likely to be useful?

It might be objected that this institutional process of book selection is entirely too complicated and difficult to make it worth while for most public libraries to adopt. To this, three things can be said. First, this very process as described above is going on in every public library in America today—but without the implications of the assumptions on which it rests being recognized as such. Every librarian who selects books has vaguely in mind the general purpose of the institution, the general characteristics of the readers served (usually ignoring the non-readers), and the general nature of the publication under consideration. If this were not so, it would be difficult to explain why the Denver Public Library has not built up its holdings on marine architecture, why the Newark Public Library Business Branch does not have a fiction collection, and why the New York Public Library does not stock the pulp literature than can be secured on the newsstand outside its doors.

Since the process is going on under the surface, to call for an awareness of the situation, a self-consciousness as to what is being done, is to seek to make the criteria involved more objective, more precise, and more definite and to substitute valid generalizations for vague generalities. This is the first step in science—to uncover assumptions and to make clear what it is that you are trying to do and how you propose to go about it.

Second, the full development of the book-selection process described here is important not alone for the selection of materials for the library's shelves; it is also a fundamental of adequate reader's guidance, i.e., the selection of books for a particular reader from what is available in the institution. It was pointed out before that the whole process of institutional book selection must be focused on the individual reading situations that the library seeks to encourage. The interrelationship between the two ends of the activity appears even more close when one examines its actual operation. Much of the data on reading and readers will be secured through the readers' advisers, and to them the content analysis of the publications selected will be as the breath of life.[51] And this is as it should be, for if the results sought by institutional book selection are in terms of individual reading situations, then the role of the readers' adviser in directly influencing the latter process turns on the data used and decisions made in connection with the former.

And, finally, to justify the present state of book-selection practice in our public libraries is to ignore the dangers that lie in a policy of drift by a social institution that takes no steps to align its activities with the dominant trends of its age. This institutional process of book selection not only demands a concrete statement by the librarian as to the objectives he seeks to achieve (in itself a desirable by-product) but also contributes to the formation of that statement by the light it throws on the reading situation that the library faces in its community.

But, most important of all, this institutional aspect of book selection is designed to make effective the objectives set up for a library in the only sense that a public library can be effective, and that is in terms of the reading satisfactions that it is able to effect in its community. These are the potential contributions that an able and effective process of institutional book selection can offer. □

[1] Those who are familiar with the work of Dr. Douglas Waples will recognize the great influence it has had on the preparation of this note. The best sources that can be cited for background to the present paper are James H. Wellard, *Book selection: its principles and practice* (London: Grafton, 1937), esp. pp. 102-13; and Douglas Waples, Bernard Berelson, and Franklyn R. Bradshaw, *What reading does to people* (Chicago: University of Chicago Press, 1940), esp. chap. iii, "Distribution of publications," pp. 44-61.

[2] For evidence on the association of readers' traits with the quality and quantity of reading see Robert A. Miller, "The relation of reading characteristics to social indexes," *American journal of Sociology*, XLI (1936), 738-56.

[3] To be precise, a reader's goal is one of his personal characteristics; but the individual's purpose in reading is such an important factor and is so clearly dissimilar from the other personal traits of the reader (e.g., age, sex, education, and occupation) that clarity in analysis is facilitated by setting up a separate category for it.

[4] Such influences can cover a wide range, e.g., seeing a movie based on a book, the closing of the plant in which the reader works, the entry of the nation into war, etc. In selecting books for the library, only those factors can be considered that affect groups of people; the readers' adviser, however, in selecting books for a particular reader, will need to know about the relevant personal factors influencing that individual. See below, no. 50.

[5] The most purposeful readers in this connection are scholars. For a study of the extent to which they will go in the search for their material see Douglas Waples, "Belgian scholars and their libraries," *Library quarterly*, X (1940), 231-63.

[6] For a full development of this brief and highly simplified statement of the factors involved in the individual reading situation see Waples, Berelson, and Bradshaw, *op. cit.*, and for a critique of the assumptions on which their analysis is based see Hans Muller, "Two major approaches to the social psychology of reading," *Library quarterly*, XII (1942), 1-28.

[7] An even earlier stage of selection is found in the process by which publishers determine, from among the manuscripts submitted to them, those which they shall publish. The present-day attempts to rationalize that process indicate the need for the same kind of criteria that this paper undertakes to explore for the middle stage, that of institutional selection.

[8] The best evidence that different kinds of people secure different kinds of publications from different sources is to be found in Ralph E. Ellsworth, "The distribution of books and magazines in selected communities" (unpublished Ph.D. dissertation, Graduate Library School, University of Chicago, 1937); and in Douglas Waples, *People and print: social aspects of reading in the depression* (Chicago: University of Chicago Press, 1937).

[9] Similarly the reading wants to which school and college libraries will attend are likely to be clearly defined because of the dominance of the institution's teaching objectives (see Edward A. Wight and Leon Carnovsky, "The library," *Reading in general education: an exploratory study*, ed. William S. Gray [Washington, D.C.: American Council on Education, 1940], pp. 425-27).

[10] From the point of view of the individual agency, an important characteristic of this second basis is that, for the most part, it lies outside its control—as compared with the first basis, the determination of its own objectives. See below, p. 159.

[11] Carleton B. Joeckel and Leon Carnovsky, *A metropolitan library in action: a survey of the Chicago Public Library* (Chicago: University of Chicago Press, 1940), pp. 391-93.

[12] "Every library collection should be built up . . . . so that certain classes will not be overemphasized and others neglected. The needs of the library exist and should be met, as well as the needs of its readers" (Helen E. Haines, *Living with books: the art of book selection* [New York: Columbia University Press, 1935], p. 16).

[13] Lionel R. McColvin states that "the public library is a universal provider, that it must embrace, as far as possible, all knowledge and activity" (*The theory of book selection for public libraries* [London: Grafton, 1925], p. 18). "It is normally desirable to provide an initial stock of wide general appeal and to expand it as future demand indicates." (W. A. Munford, *Three thousand books for a public library: some significant and representative works for a basic stock* [London: Grafton, 1939], p. 6).

[14] Haines offers as a "principle" of book selection the injunction: "Keep abreast of the changing currents of thought and opinion, and give adequate representation to the scientific, social and intellectual forces that are shaping the modern world" (*op. cit.*, p. 34).

[15] See Francis K. W. Drury, *Book selection* (Chicago: American Library Association, 1930), pp. 12-13.

[16] McColvin, *op. cit.*, p. 62. For evidence of the unreliability of this last factor Douglas Waples and Ralph W. Tyler, *What people want to read about* (Chicago: American Library Association and University of Chicago Press, 1931), esp. pp. 42-47.

[17] In connection with this point see, on the one hand, the proposal for regional cooperation between libraries in the delimitation of objectives, in Wellard, *op. cit.*, pp. 176-88; and, on the other hand, the recommendation that the public library no longer buy fiction of the type duplicated by the typical radio serial drama, in Frances Henne, "Library-radio relationships," *Library quarterly*, XI (1941), 476-94.

[18] Wellard, *op. cit.*, pp. 3-68; Carleton B. Joeckel, *The government of the American public library* (Chicago: University of Chicago Press, 1935), pp. 1-19; Arnold K. Borden, "The sociological beginnings of the library movement," *Library quarterly*, I (1931), 278-82; Lowell Martin, "The American public library as a social institution," *Library quarterly*, VII (1937), 546-63; and Clarence E. Sherman, "The definition of library objectives," in *Current issues in library administration*, ed. Carleton B. Joeckel (Chicago: University of Chicago Press, 1939), pp. 22-46.

[19] "The province and purpose of the public library is to provide for every person the education obtainable through reading" (Haines, *op. cit.*, p. 16).

[20] William C. Haygood, *Who uses the public library* (Chicago: University of Chicago Press, 1938), pp. 29-36; and Helen L. Butler, "An inquiry into the statements of motives by readers," *Library quarterly*, X (1940), 1-49.

[21] It is easy to appear precise in dealing with this question, and the reader should not be deceived. All that one can say with surety is that certain broad effects can be isolated. In Waples, Berelson, and Bradshaw (*op. cit.*, chap. vi, "The effects of reading," pp. 101-33), five major effects are distinguished—instrumental, increased self-esteem, reinforcement (and its opposite, conversion), aesthetic enjoyment, and respite. The present writer construes the effect of reinforcement in a somewhat different light so as to include the second effect above, increased self-esteem; and aesthetic enjoyment is discounted as quantitatively unimportant in the use of public library materials.

[22] *Ibid.*, p. 13

[23] From one point of view, all reading whatsoever can be thought of as providing respite in the sense that the activity required in reading constitutes a relief from boredom or a variation from previous activity and will not be continued beyond the point at which such return fails to overbalance the deterrents involved in the expenditure of energy in the physiological process of reading. In this paper, however, respite is being used in a narrower sense as explained in the text.

[24] See William Albig, *Public opinion* (New York: McGraw-Hill, 1939), esp. chap. iii, "Communication," pp. 26-52.

[25] For an analytical comparison of reading with other mediums of communication with regard to its usefulness in the learning process see Edgar Dale, "Relation of reading to other forms of learning," in *Reading in general education*, ed. Gray, pp. 45-76.

[26] "Like other forms of experience, however, reading may produce undesirable as well as desirable reactions, and negative as well as positive personalities" (William S. Gray, "Reading and factors influencing reading efficiency," in *Reading in general education*, ed. Gray, p. 31).

[27] Waples, Berelson, and Bradshaw, *op. cit.*, pp. 91-94.

[28] The reasonableness of this hypothesis is supported in part by the existing evidence that people like to read about subjects that concern themselves, and such interests vary directly with certain objective social characteristics of the readers (see Waples and Tyler, *op. cit.*, esp. pp. xxiii-xxiv and 15-30). Furthermore, Waples and Berelson found that the most important influence that determined agreement or disagreement with political campaign arguments encountered in print was the predispositions of the individual voters (see Douglas Waples and Bernard Berelson, "Public communications and public opinion," in their "Public communications and public opinions" [Chicago: Graduate Library School, University of Chicago, 1941], pp. 1-76 [mimeographed]).

[29] A classical statement of the concept of education, from this point of view, is to be found in John Adams, *The evolution of educational theory* (London: Macmillan, 1912), esp. chap. i, "The nature and scope of educational theory," pp. 1-40.

[30] See Abraham Flexner, " 'The gates of excellence': a plea for distinction between education and training," *Journal of adult education,* IV (1932), 5-7.

[31] See Ruth Kotinsky, *Adult education and the social scene* (New York: Appleton-Century, 1933), especially the Foreword by William H. Kilpatrick, pp. v-vi, and chap. ii, "Schooling as life, and life as education," pp. 30-69.

[32] For a statement on the use, in the school, of specific titles to produce changes in students' thinking see Leroy H. Buckingham, "The development of social attitudes through literature," *School and society,* LII (1940), 446-54.

[33] It is possible that what librarians mean when they speak of education as an objective of the library is really covered for the most part by the purely instrumental use of books (see Wellard, *op. cit.,* pp. 76-79).

[34] Conspicuous for their deviation from this accepted pattern are the suggestions found in Leon Carnovsky, "Community analysis and the practice of book selection," in *The practice of book selection,* ed. Louis R. Wilson (Chicago: University of Chicago Press, 1940), pp. 20-39; and Bernard Berelson, "The myth of library impartiality," *Wilson bulletin,* XIII (1938), 87-90.

[35] Cf. Grace Kelley, "The democratic function of public libraries," *Library quarterly,* IV (1934), 1-15.

[36] Joeckel and Carnovsky, *op. cit.,* pp. 346-50.

[37] National Education Association, *The unique function of education in American democracy* (Washington, D.C.: Educational Policies Commission, 1937).

[38] Alvin Johnson, *The public library—a people's university* (New York: American Association for Adult Education, 1938), p. 46.

[39] Waples, Berelson, and Bradshaw, *op. cit.,* chap. v, "The readers' predispositions," pp. 82-100. For evidence on which are the most important reader characteristics see Waples and Tyler, *op. cit.,* pp. 122-47. A characteristic of the reader which is of prime importance to the library is the level of his reading ability; for a good introduction to the physiology of reading see Guy T. Buswell, *How adults read* ("Supplementary educational monographs," No. 45 [Chicago: University of Chicago Press, 1937]).

[40] No adequately comprehensive and systematic community analysis has yet been made for library purposes. Fruitful suggestions in that direction will be found in general works on the social survey (see also Wellard, *op. cit.,* pp. 92-101 and 120-62; Haygood, *op. cit.;* Helen A. Ridgway, "Community studies in reading. III. Reading habits of adult non-users of the public library," *Library quarterly,* VI [1936], 1-33;

and Lowell Martin, "Public library provision of books about social problems," *Library quarterly*, IX [1939] , 249-72). Joeckel and Carnovsky suggest the use of an ingenious registration system that would make a large amount of data available at once on library patrons (*op. cit.*, pp. 387-88). A modification of this system is being tried out now in a branch of the Chicago Public Library (see Lowell Martin, "Outline of experimentation in the South Chicago Branch Library" [Chicago: Chicago Public Library, 1940] , pp. 10-15 [mimeographed]).

41 In the Graduate Library School Institute of 1939 Carnovsky objected to this same aspect of present book-selection practice and suggested that it be replaced by selection that would bring to library shelves only publications that supplied the truth. To put this in the terms used here, he was in effect setting up an objective for the library; such an objective could be served by the process of book selection described above, though—like the objective of "education"—it might be implemented less easily than other possible objectives (Carnovsky, *op. cit.*, pp. 27-34; see also his "The evaluation of public library facilities," in *Library trends*, ed. Louis R. Wilson [Chicago: University of Chicago Press, 1937] , pp. 301-9).

42 Ridgway, *op. cit.*

43 Leon Carnovsky, "Measurements in library service," in *Current issues in library administration*, ed. Joeckel, p. 244; Leon Carnovsky, "A study of the relationship between reading interest and actual reading," *Library quarterly*, IV (1934), 76-110; Harold A. Anderson, "Reading interests and tastes," in *Reading in general education*, ed. Gray, esp. pp. 242-49; Douglas Waples, "Community studies in reading. I. Reading in the lower east side," *Library quarterly*, III (1933), 18-19, and "The relation of subject interests to actual reading," *ibid.*, II (1932), 42-70; and Ethel L. Cornell, "The voluntary reading of high school pupils," *A.L.A. bulletin*, XXXV (1941), 295-300.

44 That the social characteristics of population groups are closely associated with and probably the determinants of social behavior is becoming increasingly clear. For evidence on the association of these characteristics with reading behavior see Miller, *op. cit.* He suggests indeed that reading itself may serve as a reliable social characteristic. The 1940 study of Sandusky, Ohio, conducted by the Office of Radio Research of Columbia University, has produced evidence on the association of such traits as economic status, age, religion, and rural-urban residence with voting behavior in that community (see Paul F. Lazarsfeld [ed.] , "How the voter makes up his mind" [to be published by the University of Chicago Press]).

45 By 1940 Columbia University's Readability Laboratory had laid plans for and started work on a basic analytical bibliography (to be supplemented by a current service for new books), in an attempt to describe specific titles in terms that relate to various, closely defined groups of readers. The major emphasis in the analysis is apparently to

be on readability, i.e., stylistic analysis. This is the first large-scale project to consider the evaluation of specific books by nonliterary standards. See the "Memorandum on estimating readability, prepared by the Readability Laboratory of Teachers College, Columbia University, for examination by members of the A.L.A. Subcommittee on Readable Books," unpublished exhibit from the minutes of the November 29, 1940, meeting of the Subcommittee.

[46] There are three major classes of references here, characterized by decreasing directness of application.

I.   For an explanation of the theory of content analysis see Waples, Berelson, and Bradshaw, *op. cit.*, chap. iv, "The content of publications," pp. 62-81, and Appen. B, "Notes on content analysis," pp. 145-57; Waples, *People and print*, pp. 30-36; and Waples and Berelson, "What the voters were told," in their "Public communications and public opinions," pp. 1-77.

II.   Most attention so far has been given to content analysis in relation to the level of reading difficulty represented by the publication (see William S. Gray and Bernice E. Leary, *What makes a book readable* [Chicago: University of Chicago Press, 1935]). A corrective to the point of view there expressed is to be found in Mabel E. Jackman, "The relation between maturity of content and simplicity of style in selected books of fiction," *Library quarterly*, XI (1941), 302-27.

III.   Students who investigate the problem of content analysis from the point of view of library book selection will find valuable suggestions, especially as to techniques, in the work of educators in evaluating textbooks for use in the schools.

[47] "The concept of readability can be sensibly discussed only in terms of the particular reader. Nothing is ever readable in general. The intelligibility of anything in print depends upon the person who is trying to read it; upon his reading skill, his knowledge of the subject, and his interest in it at the moment" (from th digest of Lyman Bryson's remarks at the 1940 convention of the American Association for Adult Education, *Journal of adult education*, XII [1940], 529).

[48] Possibilities for further investigation lie in a comparison of the process of institutional book selection with that of curriculum construction. Because of the extent to which the school men have carried their analysis of curriculum construction, there is an abundant literature, from which librarians can learn much (see W. W. Charters, *Curriculum construction* [New York: Macmillan, 1924]; Henry Harap, *The technique of curriculum making* [New York: Macmillan, 1928]; and H. E. Caswell and D. S. Campbell, *Curriculum development* [New York: American Book Co., 1935]).

[49] It should be emphasized that the theory of institutional book selection is not yet so well established that one can readily draw up practical procedures to put the theory into operation. The devising of such procedures is a second and later step than the development and

statement of the theory itself. It is with this latter aspect that this note is primarily concerned. Furthermore, such procedures must be fashioned so as to accord with the particular circumstances of the individual library and can be left to the ingenuity of practicing librarians once the theory itself has been demonstrated to be sound. What is offered here, in regard to practical procedures, is only for purposes of illustration.

[50] Note that groups, not individuals, are to be considered. This is so because groups represent relatively permanent categories among whch individual readers can and do shift; but while an individual is one of a group, he tends to read much the same material and for the same reasons as do his fellows in the group. Thus it is that, though individuals and not groups do the reading, institutional book selection is for the group and not for the individual (see Waples and Tyler, *op. cit.*, pp. xix-xx, 122-47, and 172-86).

[51] See Jennie M. Flexner, "New experiences with books," *Journal of adult education*, VII (1935), 413-14.

THE BELLIGERENT PROFESSION

Frances Clarke Sayers

If to the man in the street the profession of the librarian
seems either a scholarly pursuit, an esoteric matter of bibliographies and intricate cataloguing performed in professorial
quiet, or, in the case of the ordinary public library, a matter
of keeping records by shuffling cards about and smiling
amiably or not smiling at all—if, I say, these are the only ideas
the public holds of a magnificent profession, it is probably
the fault of the librarians themselves who have not bothered
to state, or indeed have not formulated in their own minds,
the purposes of their profession.

Two branches of librarianship are perhaps clearer in
their concepts than any others: the university librarian, who
forthrightly serves the cause of scholarship, and the librarian
for children, who realizes that the first picture book opened
up by the three-year-old is the "beginning of wisdom" and
will at last result in the flowering of the adult, the judicious,
the discriminating or scholarly, mind. For this reason, then, it
is not entirely inappropriate that a children's librarian should
write a piece in the name of one of the foremost librarians of
a great university library—William Warner Bishop.

Reprinted from Michigan *Alumnus* for March, 1950, by permission of
the University of Michigan Alumni Association and from *Summoned by
Books:* Essays and Speeches by Frances Clarke Sayers, compiled by
Marjeanne Jensen Blinn (New York: Viking Press, 1965), pp. 27-37, by
permission of the author, the compiler, and the Viking Press.

As I have read Dr. Bishop's interpretation of librarianship, I have been captivated by the breadth of his vision and the measured strength of his prose. I was fascinated by the variety of his interests. He is historian, archaeologist, architect, and educator, as well as a librarian who has been an expert administrator and cataloguer. He is a man for whom scholarship is an exhilaration, and the reading of books a joyous obligation rather than an intellectual discipline. For him the profession has been a magnificent task. He lived it belligerently. The quality of belligerency was never more greatly needed in the profession than it is at this moment. We have been called many things in our time—gentle and genteel; modest and mousy; learned and lame; dedicated and dowdy; unprepossessing and underpaid. I hope for the day when we shall be called the belligerent profession; a profession that is informed, illuminated, radiated by a fierce and beautiful love of books— a love so overwhelming that it engulfs community after community and makes the culture of our time distinctive, individual, creative, and truly of the spirit.

I would have us belligerent first within the ranks of our own profession. We have never, in my opinion, stood our ground firmly enough and declared what our peculiar, unique function was to be, and then held to it and accomplished it. The men and women who founded the profession knew what it was they were to do. William W. Bishop's concept of librarianship is as clear as glass, and all the methods he writes of are bound to the main and primary concept with strong cords of direct relationship. Read Dr. Bishop on the history of the card catalogue; on the use of reference guides; on the indexes and tables of contents. It is exciting reading because never for one moment is the purpose of all this forgotten—namely, the reading of books, what he calls "the mastery of books." Everything these men and women did—O blessed pioneers— led to the reading of books. If you doubt it, go back into the early proceedings of the American Library Association and read the speeches, the addresses. All the techniques there discussed—their descriptions of processes, the invoices, ordering procedures—have a glow about them because they were a

means to a glorious and clearly perceived and deeply experienced purpose.

This initial impulse, this enduring faith in reading books
to know them and to make them useful, has somehow been
lost—not, I feel, because we are of lesser stature than our
predecessors, but because, perhaps, there have been such pressures, such multitudinous forces at work upon the culture of
our generation—economic, political, mechanical, and inven-
tive—and the joyous obligation to read and to induce others
to read seemed too simple a function in a world where everything and everybody were being mechanized, organized,
industrialized, streamlined, geared for action in two wars,
emotionally adjusted for a depression, progressively educated,
and made socially conscious. Aldous Huxley writes in his
Texts and Pretexts:

> Science advances from discovery to discovery, politi-
> cal and economic changes follow one another with a
> bewildering rapidity. The educated have to "keep up."
> They are so busy keeping up that they seldom have time
> to read any author who thinks and feels and writes with
> style. In a rapidly changing age, there is real danger that
> being well informed may prove incompatible with being
> cultivated. To be well informed, one must read quickly
> a great number of merely instructive books. To be culti-
> vated, one must read slowly and with a lingering appre-
> ciation the comparatively few books that have been
> written by men who lived, thought and felt with style.

It was no doubt this dilemma which forced us to abandon our initial function as a "cultural" profession and to let
ourselves become attached to the educational movement of
the 1920s and the '30s.

Our profession did not have strength of character to
stand firm and interpret this swift pattern of change in its
own media of books, individual reading and individual opinion. We too felt we must assume a science if we had it not.
We indulged in a sickness of our time—namely, "the unctuous
explanation of the obvious." We felt the need to participate

in the discipleship of the special jargon and the befuddled but "highfalutin" terminology. We developed library science and produced our own textbooks. We aped the schools of education—whose function is not our function.

Jacques Barzun, in his *Teacher in America,* paints a grim picture of a philosopher's impression of library science. It is not true, of course, but there is enough truth in it to make it sting. He begins well enough, but further reading proves he has his tongue in his cheek.

> Librarians doubtless develop through their training a passionate love of books. But need it be so possessive? Why must many of the rules that they make suggest the bad governance which galls without repressing? Should a common enough attitude—the pursed lips, the tone of suspicion, the pouncing manner—become professional traits? Most important, is it so arduous a task to learn the Dewey classification system and the use of bibliographies that there is no time left for librarians to learn about the insides of the treasures they hoard?

The use of books by fighting men brought about a renaissance of reading. There was an immediacy about reading in the South Pacific, on shipboard, and during the long periods of waiting, that should have renewed our faith in ourselves. But no, here we are once again about to take off on bright wings of a fresh vocabulary—this time the vocabulary of sociology and psychology. The profession is in the throes of being surveyed and analyzed by the Social Science Research Council,* under Dr. Robert D. Leigh, who disclaims "any foregone conclusions" in the *ALA Bulletin* for March 1948. Nevertheless, my spies tell me that whenever he encounters a children's librarian, he states a very definite opinion that all work with children should be assigned to the public schools because it will save money for the taxpayer, and this at a time when the schools have reached a low ebb in

---

*The reports of the survey were published in *The Public Library in the United States* by Columbia University Press, 1950.

staff and equipment. But is it not significant that as a profession we are always willing, ready, and waiting to be dissected by whatever group has adopted us, and too ready to take their advice, not judiciously, but to swallow it whole—hook, line, and sinker?

I distrust the questionnaire method, having submitted to a session of several hours' duration on the questionnaire for Dr. Leigh's survey, when I might better have been reading Herbert Read's *The Innocent Eye,* which I have just discovered. "What was your greatest gain from library school?" runs the questionnaire. And then, since "they" know all the answers, replies are listed for the victims to check. Now I was in library school at Pittsburgh in a golden era of the school. Among my instructors were Margaret Mann, Sarah C. N. Bogle, Ernestine Rose, Elva Sophronia Smith; and my greatest gain from library school was a knowledge of stamina, scholarship, and vision of these personalities.

There is no place in the sociologist's world for the force of personality. "Why did you accept your first position?" and as though you were incapable of knowing, again the list of possible replies is furnished. And again, the power of personality is ignored. I accepted my first position because I was stirred by the personality of the librarian under whom I was to work—Anne Carroll Moore. And who among the checkers will be able to interpret my answer on pairs of choices, checked rapidly as instructed, which reveals me as longing to be a contractor? I know that my check reflects my acquaintanceship with a contractor whose chief interest is books and whose spirited friendship I have long enjoyed, but the machine that tabulates replies will never understand this interesting fact.

In this instance the final judgment on us, I presume, will be handed down by the Council's advisory committee, which consists of a political scientist, an economists, a sociologist, a psychologist, a historian, and two librarians. Each will look at us, I suppose, from the intense and narrowed vision of his own specialization, the two librarians somewhat timidly, being host to the infection. And what profession cuts across all these fields, these specializations, and turns over from the plowed ground the taproots of all of them? It is the librarian's profession. It is this profession that upholds, as does no other, the right of any man, whether or not he is trained, educated, classified, and certified, to explore all these fields on his own. It is the profession that should have in greatest measure the gift, the skill, the imagination, the art, to invite and entice readers in all these directions. For reading is an art as much as it is anything. And yet no artists, no writers, no poets, no dramatists, no practitioners of letters, are invited to appraise us—no gifted readers!

In the new courses of study which are now to be introduced into library schools, we are to stress *the psychology and sociology of reading! The study of the motivations, needs, and purposes of readers!* I cannot predict what this will mean for the adult readers. It conjures up in my irrelevant mind a grim picture of some gentle old lady who has been reading for years along her own lines of interest suddenly encountering a bright young thing just out of library school who insists upon psychoanalyzing her before she is allowed to read *Hugh Wynne, Free Quaker*. But in my own field, I can tell you what happens to books when they are put to these uses. They are examined for "developmental values," or read because they teach the concept of "relative size," or because of "good human relations," or "interracial concepts," or "vocabulary content." But when one searches for values and pursues them as if they were plums in a pudding, one destroys the texture and proportion of the pudding itself, and the art of pudding-making and the eating thereof are destroyed.

It is all very well to discuss the use of words beginning with *s* and to define the meter in Shakespeare's sonnet:

> When to the sessions of sweet silent thought
> I summon up remembrance of things past,

but one cannot write a sonnet by this prescription, nor does it explain the poem's effect upon the mind and emotion of the reader.

What happens to the art of reading and of writing in all this sociology of reading? What of sensibility and intuition? As Jacques Barzun says, those things which touch the emotion and the mind cannot be measured by science.

In 1912, in an address delivered at the College of William and Mary, Mr. Bishop said all this in no uncertain terms. He, like Mr. Huxley, affirms his faith in the reader-librarian who reads deeply.

> No one is really trained in the use of books who has not made himself master of a few books. . . . What these books should be is not a matter for dogmatism. One man will feed his soul on Shakespeare, and another on Newton's *Principia.* But certain works should become a part of the very nature of every man of our race, whatever his profession, who dares call himself educated. The English Bible is still the greatest work in the English tongue. The youth who reaches maturity without a thorough knowledge of its wonderful prose and poetry, and its message of personal religion and of duty toward God and man, has missed the greatest intellectual and moral training the language affords. I care not how he interprets it. Let him *know* the Bible from cover to cover, and consider his own relation to it what he will.

> There are other English books, too, which no man can afford not to know, and know intimately. Shakespeare and Milton among the poets; Bacon and Addison and Emerson among essayists; Green, Macaulay, and Parkman among the historians, are but a few of the names which suggest themselves at once. And who dares affirm himself wholly ignorant of Homer and Vergil, of Dante, and of Goethe and Schiller, of Cervantes and of Montaigne? The man who has not as a boy devoted himself to the reading and rereading of at least a few of the world's great books is but poorly prepared to cope with the literary deluge of our day or with the plausible sophistries of the time. He has necessarily a low standard of literary judgment. He has sold his birthright of noble books for a mess of pottage whose chief ingredients are Sunday newspapers and illustrated weeklies.

With this caution, this admonition to think on the high things of the world of letters, I reach my conclusion. He that is faithful to the mastering of a few great books will use easily the tools provided for handling the lesser books. Secure in the possession of some works which the ages have tested, he will welcome the good in the mass of new books, will make the indifferent, or even the bad, serve his need without lowering himself to its level, will show his training in the use of books not alone in the ease with which he masters bookish problems or acquires information, but much more in the character of his thinking and in the standard of his judgments.

"The standard of his judgments." This phrase brings me to the second point at which I should like to see the library profession belligerent—belligerent in its responsibility to the community's standard of judgment and taste. In the *National Plan for Public Library Service* it is stated: "Unfortunately, the sense of purpose . . . [of the public library] is often so vague that neither librarian nor reader can report the function of the public library in concrete terms, and so all-inclusive that energy and attention are diffused." Let us then declare, before everyone, that the purpose of the public library is to foster, promote, and initiate the reading of books which not only serve the community but stretch the minds and imaginations of its constituents to such peaks of their ability as they never dreamed of.

Somewhere, somehow, there has got to be an institution which belligerently attacks the mediocre, the slick, the sentimental, the commercial, that is typical of the mass culture of our day. Not that it came from the masses. It is prescribed for them and is poured upon them by money-ridden, power-ridden, advertising-ridden radio, moving pictures, press, television. In a great measure, as the Harvard reports on the teaching of English so eloquently state, all of these forces are aimed more or less to make us all think, vote, buy, read, listen to, and look at the same thing. I am convinced that the mass mind is capable of much greater distinction in its thought, but how can anyone resist the never-ending pounding on our five senses—eat this, read this, see this, buy so-and-so, and think such-and-such.

Jacques Barzun speaks somewhere of besieging the students with books. Why cannot we besiege our communities with books and the love of reading? I was deeply concerned when I found my own library recommending for moderate purchase *Cry, the Beloved Country,* by Alan Paton, while books of lesser stature for which there was a demand were recommended for extensive purchase. Why cannot we proclaim such a novel as this and spread its name in neon lights across the desks, across the very portals of the library? And talk about it! The book of the week! Or the day. Send people to talk about it in the community who have the power of the Ancient Mariner to hold an audience. Why don't we assail people with books? Why don't we speak their lines over the loudspeaker? We should be noisy about books in a noisy world. For we are like the vintners:

> I wonder often what the vintners buy
> One half so precious as the stuff they sell.

"The stuff they sell." We are employed to give books away!

Only at the hand of some such happy belligerency will the individual escape from death of the spirit in a culture that numbs individuality, chloroforms the imagination, exalts the vulgar, and makes robots of us all. All this—and television too.

In his book *Our Threatened Values,* Victor Gollancz writes:

> Every man is potentially a political, creative, individual creature: his glory is independence and his birthright is spontaneity. I want to see the potentiality realised, the birthright accepted, the glory achieved. I want to see a race of *men,* not of domestic animals however "happy": of self-directing intelligences, not of anthropoid automatons who will do what they are told and think what others prescribe for them. And I say that any ideal pettier than this rests, in the last analysis, on contempt for humanity.

In this cause, then, the cause of humanity itself, let us be about the profession with the belligerency becoming to happy warriors.   □

THE WORLD OF BOOKS

Helen E. Haines

All that Mankind has done, thought, gained, or been: it is
lying as in magic preservation in the pages of Books. . . .
All that a university or final highest school can do for us, is
still but what the first school began doing—teach us to read.
Thomas Carlyle: *The Hero as Man of Letters*

As children learning to read, we step with indifference into
the world of books. How we fare in it afterwards depends on
how soon and in what measure indifference gives place to
inclination and selection. And inclination and selection find
their stimulus chiefly in the influence of what has been read
upon the will to choose what shall be read. "Evolution in
reading" proves its truth in the personal experience of everyone who knows and uses books. Standards are raised, intelligence is enlarged, perceptions are deepened, through the
simple process of reading. Books that meant nothing to a
reader ten years ago, today penetrate his understanding and
stimulate his own deepening realization of human experience;
books that ten years ago were revealing or inspiring, have long
since been outgrown and forgotten. "What may have sounded
like balderdash at twenty, may be the very tissue of truth
when forty winters besiege the brow," says John Mistletoe.

Formal education applies its patterns to the mind; but
only through books does the mind itself enrich, deepen,

Reprinted from Helen E. Haines, *Living With Books: The Art of Book
Selection,* 2nd ed. (New York: Columbia University Press. 1950), pp.
[3]-11, by permission of the publisher.

apply, modify, and develop those patterns in individual life fulfillment. Intelligence must be kept active, playing over the education it is receiving, drawing its own conclusions, making its own observations and its own tests; otherwise we have simply a thin surface coating of applied instruction. Books are the instruments of intelligence. They are also, of course, the instruments of aberration and fallacy; for they are the expression of all the qualities and defects of the human mind. The more we know them, love them, and use them, the more their inexhaustible riches, their ever increasing potencies, are made manifest.

Consider what books may mean in individual development: in the formation of character, in the activation of intelligence, in the enrichment of resources, and in the deepening of sensitivity.

They offer building material for the formation of character through knowledge and thought. Such character making is a continuous unconscious process of self-education in the school of daily life. We may grow in maturity of judgment, in knowledge of the world, in ideals and principles; or we may remain stationary, gleaning nothing from the ripening harvests of experience; or we may narrow and diminish in intelligence, indifferent to changing thought and expanding knowledge, or intolerant and antagonistic toward all that is outside our immediate experience. Growth is a determinate process of change—not in the essence of the individual being; the germ is unchangeable—but in mutation to broader, deeper understanding, to deeper insight and freer range. We may learn much simply from living and working; but the enduring materials of knowledge, prepared for us through centuries of thought and labor, are stored for our use in books.

Through books we gain what John Morley called "the historic sense of progress through the ages," in other words, a background of understanding, a basis of familiarity with the interlocking of events and with the great undercurrents that run, forever changing yet forever the same, through human experience, past and present. There cannot be broad intelligence or sound judgment without this. No one can form valid opinion or pass fair judgment on what is, who has not some ability to compare, to contrast it, with what has been. Man's possessions and equipment today—achievements and realizations that would have been miracles to the men and women who lived only a hundred years ago—are but later waymarks along paths of human effort and research worn slowly through four thousand years. Ambroise Paré plodded toward the shining highway of modern surgery; Copernicus helped break the pathway to Palomar. Every succeeding generation widens and makes more firm the path; but take away the knowledge gained by the labor expended before our own day and what should we have left? Through books we have bridged the centuries and built the world's structure of achievement; through books we receive and enlarge the heritage of the human mind.

This background of understanding in some degree, is indispensable to enjoyment of good reading; and it builds itself from that enjoyment. To care for good reading, to keep on with good reading because you care for it, means that little by little this background takes on substance in the mind, and unconsciously every new subject contemplated, studied, or enjoyed enlarges and enriches it. From every book invisible threads reach out to other books; and as the mind comes to use and control those threads the whole panorama of the world's life, past and present, becomes constantly more varied and interesting, while at the same time the mind's own powers of reflection and judgment are exercised and strengthened. Poetry, drama, novels—books that set the imagination at work—are potent agents in background-building, weaving color and personality into the fabric of history and social progress.

Background reading may be built forward or backward. The present gives stimulus to explore the past; the tides of the past ebb and flow into the present. As the new physics teaches, there is no solid matter—all is change and motion in ourselves and our universe. Through reading we are borne along on this flow and movement of life.

Books give a deeper meaning and interest to living.

There is nothing in daily work, in the most humdrum occupation, that cannot be made more interesting or more useful through books. They are means to proficiency in every calling. They are inexhaustible sources of pleasure. They bring to us the life of the world as it was and as it is now. They supply increased resources. Those able to turn to books for companionship are seldom lonely; nor do they suffer from the need of finding some action, however trivial, to fill an empty hour. They have friends who will come when desired, bringing amusement, counsel, or some absorbing confidence; friends who, unlike the human variety, may be dismissed when their conversation palls, and who may be chosen to suit whatever mood or interest is uppermost.

Books impart deepened sensitiveness to ideals, to beauty, to pleasure, to the best emotions of life. Living is feeling, and the more responsive the spirit becomes, the fuller and richer life it enjoys. There can be no true culture without sensibility. Every thought and every feeling has overtones that can be apprehended only through refinement and extension of the mind's perceptions. To recognize these overtones, to catch their delicate implications and glimpse their variant elusive radiations, is one of the keenest and most enduring pleasures of life. This is the "meaning of culture," as John Cowper Powys says:

A mind that is totally uncultured gets its own special thrills, no doubt, from a raw, direct contact with unmitigated experience; but a cultured mind approaches everything through an imagination already charged with the passionate responses of the great artists: so that what it sees is a fragment of Nature, double-dyed, so to speak—a reach, a stretch of time's whirling tide, that carries upon its chance-tossed eddies the pattern of something at once transitory and eternal.

Reading transmits the current that keys and charges the mind to this responsiveness. Every class of literature—religion, philosophy, biography, history, science, poetry, fiction— conveys its voltage of inspiration, wisdom, and knowledge. The influences that good reading can shed upon life are no procrustean compulsions, but flow in manifold expression from "the free spirit of mankind." Ideals of courage and endurance and purpose are created for thousands through such biographies as those of Jeanne d'Arc, Lincoln, or Florence Nightingale. Sensitiveness to natural beauty is quickened through poetry, or essay, or vivid word-picture. Sensitiveness to humanity—the ill-used race of man—is deepened through the pages of the great story-tellers and dramatists.

Changing currents of thought and purpose, conflict and turmoil, come to us through books. The present is always tumult and transition. In our immediate present the impact of global war has shattered old stabilities and imposed new compulsions on man's relationship to man. Under the application of modern science everyday life has accelerated and expanded as never before, and the whole form of civilization is changing. The books of today reflect the thoughts, the ideals, the weaknesses, and strength of today; they indicate the paths on which its course be set; they illuminate and interpret its conflicts and its problems. With all its diversity and multiplicity this modern literature is infused with a common purpose—the pursuit of truth: truth in the individual use of the mind, truth in the understanding of man's physical organization, truth in recording the past, truth in recognition of inequalities and shortcomings in the social fabric, truth in the testing and development of human relationships. It is a long pursuit, hampered, contested, deflected by inadequacies and dogmatisms, but stronger and freer today than ever before.

What is good reading? The question is easier to ask than to answer. All reading, any reading, is better than none. Books that have lived long have in that fact proved their power. Books that have given the greatest pleasure to the greatest number of readers are lifted above others by that tidal wave of felicity. Even books born only to die, like the coral insect have left their trace of vital substance in the substructure of the world of literature. It is futile to attempt to specify what are the ten, twenty-five, or fifty "best books." That familiar phrase means only "the books that are the best to me." The choice of books must always be influenced by individual personality. Among any dozen persons who love books, I doubt if there is one who, if honest, would not confess indifference or aversion for some acknowledged masterpiece. Yet the "books that everyone should know" are all worth knowing; from them every reader can draw his own measure of inspiration and wisdom; they are the sources of, the means to, background in understanding and appreciation of literature. As John Mistletoe says: "One of the truisms about books is this: that the things you have heard since childhood were great, really *are* great.

Shakespeare's advice is still sound: "No profit grows where is no pleasure ta'en. In brief, sir, study what you most affect." If you prefer history, or poetry, or biography, or science, or novels, or philosophy, or the discussion of economic and social problems, let your taste have free rein. But though personal taste predominate, it must not wholly rule. Cultivate catholicity, savor the tang of adventure and discovery. There must be a certain rounding out of literature as a whole in reading if breadth of background is to develop. There must be an effort to keep mental elasticity and not let selection settle into a rut, as time goes on and the mind's youthful demand for novelty is blunted. Variety is here both spice and substance of life.

Under the high pressure of present-day living, how is time for reading to be found? This question is often propounded as unanswerable. Its only answer is that those who care for books will somehow, slowly, as years go by, come to know them widely and well. Those protestants who "love reading, but never have a minute for it," in that plea invalidate their claim; for we all find time for the things most vital to us. Even half an hour of daily reading will after six months have brought a rich reward. An hour a day, retrieved perhaps in fragments from the grasp of daily routine, counts for more than would seem possible until its results are seen in perspective. Arnold Bennett wrote in his diary in 1908: "Decided that I must confine reading newspapers to odd moments, and read every day some part of a serious work of instruction and also some verses. So yesterday and today I swallowed the whole of Hayes' *Secret of Herbart.* Now I understand what Herbartianism is." As for reading in bed, that practice long inhibited by traditional family disapproval has received scientific vindication in the researches of Laird and Muller on *Sleep.* Eugene Field discovered long ago that it is the improving and pleasing avocation of all true booklovers; and its justification was put in a sentence by Sir William Osler when he said: "With half an hour's reading in bed every night as a steady practice the busiest man can get a fair education before the plasma sets in the periganglionic spaces of his grey cortex."

It is most useful to keep a record of one's reading. Abbé Dimnet, in *The Art of Thinking,* emphasizes the value of note making—of writing down what has been read or observed and had made an impression on the mind that is felt to be of value. Of course, the fuller the note taking (indicating the subject of the book, the opinion held concerning it, or copying some striking extract), the greater its value in deepening background of book knowledge and developing critical judgment.

Magazines are far more widely read than books; but not by those who know the joys and values of reading. Magazines and newspapers—both dominant factors in American mass culture—are no more than accessories or deterrents to reading; they do not signify that wide ranging and rich adventure in the world of books that is real reading. Magazines have their place, their own usefulness; but no magazine can take the place of standard books. There are periodicals of literary value, of scholarly, technical, or specialized importance, essential to scholars and scientific and technical workers and to men and women in every field. But if more Americans would read good books and cease reading promiscuous popular magazines, we should have a higher level of general education and intelligence.

To bulwark and extend individual reading there must be individual possession of books. The public library, offering its ever renewing supply, is the common reservoir and dispensary of books that otherwise few could know or use. It makes the world of books part of everyday life. But all who care for books will possess some friends and intimates whose companionship cannot be restricted to a formal and limited visit. This may be the simplest and most inexpensive of indulgences, kept closely to low-priced reprint editions or to favorites salvaged from the flotsam of secondhand bookshops. It is not a question of money. Half of what most people spend without demur each month for the movies will bring beauty, wit, gossip, argument, wisdom, and glorious foolishness into any reader's intimate possession. Ownership of books has unending implications and possibilities. It may kindle the thrill of book-hunting and develop into collectorship; it may yield material assurance of investment value; it may reveal unsuspected tastes or stimulate unrealized capabilities; it will surely deepen and stabilize in any household the intangible elements of culture. Immense energies of organized and concentrated publicity are directed toward placing automobiles, radios, electric refrigerators, in every American home; but little attention is given to the value, joy, and pride derivable from the modest private library that ought to be the most indispensable of household utilities. Books are the most interesting and distinguished accessories of any home; merely as furniture, they are cheaper and better decoration than oriental rugs or overstuffed chairs. They give a house character and meaning. The discerning eye looks for them in its first appraisal; their absence is a negative finding upon the cultivation and intelligence of the household; their presence is as illuminating of social, intellectual, and personal status as a merchants's association rating is of material stability and financial integrity.

Librarianship is the only calling that devotes itself to bringing books into the common life of the world. The materials librarians work with are the materials which furnish the understanding, knowledge, and reason that can inform the mind and direct the will to meet the challenge of the time, to fit ourselves to its compulsions, to discern and guide the forces that are shaping the future. The "great trade" of publishing and bookselling, though it is the oldest and most universal agency for bringing together the reader and the printed word, has not the same range of opportunity nor the same variety and intimacy of relationship to readers of all tastes, capacities, needs, habits, and levels of education. The spirit of delight and confidence in books, the receptive and adventurous attitude toward the new and experimental, the catholicity of lifelong friendship and understanding for literature, are attributes of librarianship more than of any other calling. And those attributes must be fused in a dynamic of social consciousness, of confidence and purpose, if librarians are to rise to their potential leadership in welding public understanding and unity for the building of a safer and better world.

Of course, the taste for books is not common to all. It is a spark latent in the individual, most often implanted by heredity, kindled by training or circumstance, and fed and tended by purpose and experience. But only those who possess this spark will draw from librarianship its full measure of inspiration and reward in the interpretation and enrichment of human life through books. For the world of books is the world of man's thought and effort, joy and purpose and inextinguishable hopes, as they pass in heritage from the past to the present and as they are born of each immediate moment. □

THE LIFE OF THE BOOK

Pierce Butler

Books are alive. There are, of course, people who do not believe this. They regard the book as an inanimate object, a mere block of printed paper safely boxed within stiff covers, where a sensible person lets it linger. But, presumably, no one of that persuasion is attending this conference. To all of us, certainly, a statement that the book is alive is neither astonishing or novel. We are accustomed to regard the book as animated by the personality of its author. In it he attains, as it were, terrestrial immortality. Even though his body may have been long since dead and buried, he lives on in his writing and still speaks to the mind's ear of his reader. That is one reason why we may say that books are alive; but there are others. And, properly speaking, this particular metaphor is inaccurate. Books possess an even greater mortality than the metaphor implies. Each one is more than a partial projection of its author. David Copperfield, for example, is not and never was Charles Dickens, despite certain biographical coincidences. David and his friends and acquaintances, their feelings, their deeds, and their words to each other, are present realities of an experience, although historically they never existed. Dickens merely created them, brought them into existence out of nothing. Indeed, once evoked they became independent entities for him also; according to his own

---

Reprinted from *Library Quarterly* 23 (July, 1953):157-163, by permission of the University of Chicago Press.

assertion it was they and not he that controlled his pen when he wrote about them.

Much the same thing, in only slightly different terms, may be said about books that we librarians, so inadequately, call "nonfiction." Factual books are alive also. Though they seem lifeless as they stand on the shelves, these volumes in reality are only dormant. The moment I have one down and open it, it awakens and begins to concern itself about my welfare in a most disinterested and praiseworthy fashion. Many books try to educate me. They are instructive; they tell and explain to me all sorts of things that you can imagine. Some undertake to amuse me with interesting accounts about past events and distant places. Some in lilting words sing to me the joys of life. Some in solemn cadences chant its sorrows. Some plumb the abysses of the unknowable, and some meticulously describe the obvious. And, because thought always leads straight to action, many books undertake to inspire and guide my conduct: some urge me to go out and make this world a different and a better place—by tomorrow morning—and others with equal ardor beg me to raise Belgian hares for a living. And lots of books argue with me in an endeavor—of course, a vain one—to change my religious and political convictions.

But in any case it is the book itself and not the author that speaks to me. However craftily the latter may formulate the message, once he publishes it the book escapes his control and operates on its own and by self-contained powers. Even though, like Frankenstein, he may later come to regret his creative act and attempt to undo it, under modern conditions he will probably be unable to do so, for a book, like a son, has an existence apart from that of its parent and seems to enjoy exercising its freedom.

But the possession of nonbiological life is by no means peculiar to books. All man's more complex artifacts exhibit the same inherent vitality. Every modern machine is alive. Once set going, not its maker's will but the structure he gave it determines its action. It can injure, no less than serve, its master. Indeed, the world of civilization is largely inhabited by such man-made dinosaurs and saber-toothed tigers. Although for this reason it is commonly said that man is the victim of his environment, the statement is nonsense. Exactly the opposite is true. The world is man's slave and obeys him. Man subdues nature by turning nature's powers against herself. He makes his own environment, physically, biologically, and psychologically. If he wants metallic aluminum, which does not occur free under terrestrial conditions, he reduces it from its compounds. In effect, he changes the weather to his liking by heating and cooling devices indoors and by overcoats and umbrellas in the open. With shoes he virtually carpets his pathway with leather across even the roughest country. In effect, he causes the sun to rise and set at his pleasure by his creation of artificial illuminants. The room we now occupy is a cavern in a stone cliff, both made by man and not by geological processes. And, as we Chicagoans are fond of pointing out to strangers, we make our river run backward. In every sense of the word, man makes his own physical environment.

Similarly, man creates his own flora and fauna. In every region where he settles, he kills off noxious species and replaces them with others of his own manufacture. He turns the simple flag plant of the marshes into the opulent garden iris. To the dog of nature, the yellow cur, he adds innumerable artificial species, from the stately mastiff to the ebullient terrier. Empirically, he gives himself a new body and new physical powers. If his own are defective, he can provide himself with a new eye lens to see with and a new eardrum to hear with. Though he is born without fur, he fabricates a textile pelt more effective than that of a seal or a beaver. In effect, he hardens his fist to steel when he makes a hammer. His saw teeth are virtually both a denture and talons such as no natural animal possesses. Man's anatomy forbids him to live under water; yet in a submarine he does so. Though he cannot fly like a bird, in an airplane he scoots through the air faster, and higher and farther, than any naturally winged creature.

Nor are his creative powers limited to modifying other

species and his own body. He makes animals that are wholly artificial. Our grandfathers recognized that the steam locomotive was an iron horse and so named it; but the present generation is more familiar with the automobile, and that is unmistakably a mechanical quadruped. It has skeleton, muscles, and integument, alimentary, circulatory, and neural systems, and in its timing devices and instrument board it performs functions that approximate the conditioned reflexes of physiological psychology.

Yet in all these cultural accomplishments man works only with the materials and forces provided by nature. He does not make something out of nothing. He merely moves things about, takes them apart and puts them together again in new combinations. Furthermore, in every case we have yet mentioned, the basic pattern he follows is also set for him by nature: The purebred dog is no more than an enlarged or a diminished canine. The hammer is a stemmed root burl turned upside down. The microscope and the camera ape the eyeball. The principle of the submarine appears in the nests of certain aquatic spiders. The Wright brothers studied and consciously imitated the flight of sea gulls. And even the genealogy of the automobile can be traced step by step back to the domesticated cattle that nomad barbarians first rode bareback.

Through all these things man merely elaborates patterns already set in nature; but the book belongs to a different order. It is wholly original, for it has no prototype. Though it remembers and speaks, it does so in a different fashion from the human brain and vocal organs. In the book man does not merely improve upon nature—he transcends it. Paper, of course, is a typical artifact. To fabricate it, man takes plants apart and then reassembles their fibers in a thin, smooth, white felt instead of in their original cellular structure. But the text of a book is something entirely different. Indeed, it is probably the most remarkable achievement of culture. In general terms it may be described as a graphic reduction of a mental reduction, of a linguistic reduction, of a specific stream of human consciousness. All these reductions are man-wrought miracles and as such deserve more notice than we ordinarily give them. Consider, first, the linguistic reduction. Language is a most extraordinary thing. I now am using language. By manipulating my vocal cords, I am causing the air of this room to vibrate in modulated frequencies. This atmospheric disturbance makes your eardrums vibrate by resonance at the same wave lengths. All this, of course, is merely physics, a normal and inevitable acoustic phenomenon. But now enters a triple miracle, psychological, mental, and cultural. By the conventions of civilization the sounds that I utter reinduce in my mind the course of thought that I followed when I composed this lecture, and they also induce in your mind the same course of thought as you hear them. In short, I communicate my ideas to you by reducing them to language. Yet the process of communication by language is absolutely artificial and arbitrary. For the sound "book" to stand for the thing that we designate by it depends upon no natural or rational correspondence between them. As a matter of fact, other civilizations have used entirely different sounds for this purpose: the Romans said *liber;* the Greeks, *biblion;* and the Hebrews, *Sefer.*

The second reduction, the mental one, is equally noteworthy. When I reduced my thoughts to words in preparing this paper, I worked in silence. Now, when I read them to you, is the first time they have been actually uttered in this connection. Language itself may be thought instead of spoken—indeed, in our civilization, language seems to be more often silent than vocal. When we think, we turn our thoughts into words, but ordinarily we do not talk to ourselves when we do so. Books are less often read aloud than in silence. In fact, we so habitually reduce language mentally that now, as I read my lecture to you, I am not fully conscious of the sounds I utter, nor are you as you hear them. Our awareness is not of the words themselves but of the ideas they stand for.

We also ordinarily perform the third reduction, the graphic, in the same unconscious manner. When I wrote this paper, it was my hand rather than my mind that did the writing. I did not stop to remember what conventional characters represent the sound "book" any more than in making the linguistic reduction I had to recall explicitly what word represents the idea. In both cases the process was performed unconsciously and automatically. Similarly, when I read the word "book," whether silently or aloud, I do not notice the separate letters of which it is composed but recognize rather its total pattern. Here again our usage is conventional and arbitrary. Indeed, only historical accident is responsible for the fact that we use the character we do to represent sounds instead of something entirely different or, for that matter, for the fact that we write phonetically and not, like the Chinese, ideographically.

Now, as it happens, the lecture to which you are listening illustrates more of our graphic system than the mere process of writing. In the course of time it, together with the other lectures read at this conference, will be published in a printed volume. That is, two thousand identical copies of this lecture, in a more legible form than my manuscript, will be manufactured. Then any person, if he so desires, by buying or borrowing a copy and reading it can reinduce in his own mind the thoughts that occurred to me when I prepared this lecture and which are now present in your consciousness and mine as I read it to you. But at that time I shall probably be thinking of something else or not thinking at all. Therefore, not I but the book will be communicating to you. Furthermore, librarians who are not present today may, by reading the book, obtain approximately the same residual effect that they would if they had heard the lecture. Moreover, some copies of the book will go to parts of this country and to places abroad that I myself shall never visit. And, finally, though the book will undoubtedly be made of inferior paper, a few copies at least will probably outlive me, unless I survive to celebrate another mid-century a hundred years hence, which is somewhat improbable.

Thus, books are alive in a threefold sense: they speak, they travel, and they endure through time. All these characteristics are of the utmost cultural importance and should be

of extreme interest to every bookman. But ordinarily our preoccupation with other matters prevents our thinking much
about them. Only in our poetical moods may we remark that
books have voices; this is rather an intuitive recognition than
a reasoned conclusion. Actually we know very little—far less
than we should—about graphic communication, the cause, the
process, and the effect of reading; as for the movement of
the book in space and time, we commonly dismiss it as beneath our notice. Librarians who concern themselves about
such things we regard as antiquarians and dilettanti who
would be better employed with the bureaucratic intricacies
of administration and professional politics. Such a state of
affairs is most unfortunate. Most of the cultural potency of
the book stems from its mobility and longevity. Only because
books move about and are long-lived can scholarship become
truly cumulative and hereditable. In an oral culture, where
the total knowledge of a people must be contained in living
minds and transmitted by word of mouth, the possibilities of
intellectual development are definitely limited. But in a
graphic civilization, where ideas and facts are put down on
paper, humanity, instead of having to learn and remember,
can utilize the reference process. When one of us wants a
particular intellectual item, he need not go through a series of
experiences or follow a course of systematic instruction to
attain it. Instead, he can find in a book the end-product of
such labors, which other men have performed by proxy for
him. This principle applies not only to such simple factual
questions as "Who is the governor of South Dakota?" but
also to such complex ones as "Why did the people of the
state elect him?" In either case, the proverb denying the
existence of short cuts to learning is refuted. Books are short
cuts to learning because they are substitutes for experience,
thought, and memory. I have never visited Japan, but I know
certain things about it just as well as if my eyes had seen
them. I could not possibly have reasoned out by myself the
properties of the right-angled triangle, yet I am familiar with
the series of inferences that was formerly called "jackass
bridge" because stupid pupils could not traverse it. I do not

remember what the logarithm of 13 is, but that does not matter, for I have a book that remembers it for me.

Now, as we have already remarked, books can do these things for us only because they are long-lived and locomotive. Their normal life-span certainly is longer than that of the men who make and use them. Cicero has been dead these two thousand years, yet Cicero's invective against Cataline still survives to plague schoolboys. And when Cicero as an adolescent was learning to parse Homer, the Homeric poem, still extant, was already approaching its millennium. These, of course, are examples of textual survival through the process of reproduction, first in manuscript and then in printed editions. But books may also be surprisingly durable in an original format. Babylonian tablets four thousand years old exist today in an amazing profusion. Manuscripts of great antiquity on papyrus, vellum, or paper survive in considerable numbers. We have probably several hundred thousand volumes published by the first generation of European printers, and most of these incunabula are still as sound and bright as on the day of their manufacture.

This longevity of books is not only interesting; it is functionally necessary for civilization. No generation can operate culturally with only the literature and editions of its own making. In any library, books by living authors and still in print form only an infinitesimal portion of the total book stock. For this reason the life of the book in time is of the utmost importance to every reader. And librarians in particular should be familiar with bibliographical history in outline and able to refer to particulars concerning any desired period. Moreover, they should know not merely the antecedents of the modern book but the various forms that were developed by other civilizations. Moreover, the study should embrace more than the mere morphology and genetics of the book in every period. It must also include all the functional processes that contribute to book production and use, technical and artistic, industrial and financial, customary and legal, intellectual and educational. Furthermore, bibliographical history should explain as well as describe what is and what has been.

The book exists not in a vacuum, as the librarians used to think, but, as we are now beginning to discover, as an integral element in a cultural organism. And one of the most significant things about that organism is its historical character. Accordingly, bibliographical history is an essential element in the intellectual equipment of the librarian.

The mobility of the book in space is no less culturally necessary. If each community could use only literature of local production, most communities would be bookless. In any library, catalogers record a geographical range of imprints only slightly narrower than the chronological. The locomotive powers of the book are all-important. By means of them, Western scholarship becomes an international enterprise. For example, this conference is not wholly a local activity. The papers read here will be read abroad, and perhaps some of them will produce rejoinders there which, in turn, will come back to American librarians. For us Americans this mobility of books has been especially important. Our geographical and population expansions have been so rapid that only recently has our book production caught up with it. Moreover, when our European forebears came to this country, they had for the most part to leave their inherited book stock behind them. Accordingly, no American librarian or bookseller need feel embarrassed when he outbids Europeans and brings a precious literary heirloom across the ocean. We are cultural descendants of Dante and Shakespeare and Goethe no less than our cousins who remained in the homeland. Only by an accident of history do they live on a normal geological deposit of books while we have to create one artificially. For this reason the flow of books from Europe to America has no parallel in cultural history. The movement of Greek manuscripts to the West during the Renaissance is the only thing comparable, and in that the differences greatly outnumber the parallelisms.

Now, because of the facts that are here mentioned concerning the movement of books and because of others which might be cited, it is obvious that a discipline in bibliographical geography ought to be available to all bookmen and to librarians in particular. This should cover not only the spectacular streams of books through space as a result of historical forces but also the homely peregrinations of the ordinary domestic book under ordinary circumstances. When an edition is published, many of the copies advance in company formation from the warehouse of the publishers to those of jobbers. Thence smaller units deploy to the shelves of retail booksellers. There the books attain, as it were, civilian status and henceforth travel as individuals. Some are immediately recruited by libraries, but many enter the service of private citizens. The latter volumes, when their master no longer needs them or when he dies, pass into the hands of a secondhand dealer and thenceforth may enter upon a long course of frequent movement between a series of domestic bookcases and those of merchants who may be no more than graduate junkmen. But gradually the secondhand book assumes an antiquarian character and henceforth may shuttle back and forth between owners who are collectors rather than readers, and booksellers of superior intelligence and education. But at any moment in its peregrinations a book may be captured by a library. If this happens, the book will enter upon a sojourn of much longer duration, but not necessarily one that is interminable.

Now, in the absence of a developed bibliographical geography, bookmen in general and librarians in particular do not understand the normal orbits of a book in culture. We have numerous apocryphal anecdotes that describe the attitude of old-fashioned librarians who felt that a library book was out of place in the hands of a reader. But, while we laugh at these stories, we often make ourselves equally ridiculous by assuming that the proper destiny of every book is to belong to a library. Actually, a book may perform a more important cultural function by standing in a public market available for private acquisition or by a temporary sojourn in a domestic bookcase than it would in the possession of a public library. And, in the same line of error, many librarians assume that any such library ownership will be permanent. But no one who has handled old books and meditated over their

institutional inscriptions can harbor such a fallacy. Historically, a library is only a temporary local backwater in a tidal
movement of books where certain volumes float together for
a while. For example, the Library of Congress copy of the
forty-two-line Bible was for centuries the chief bibliographical treasure of an Austrian monastery, whose members down
to 1918 would have regarded its alienation unthinkable. But
during the financial collapse of the postwar period they had
to sell it to obtain the bare necessities of food and fuel.
Under conceivable conditions, which all of us in our pessimistic moments have secretly contemplated, it might move
from Washington to a Soviet university in Ceylon, and still
later, after a new barbarian invasion, as a trifle of war plun-
der, become a plaything for the children of a Hottentot
chieftain.

The imaginary instance cited here is obviously exaggerated, but the principle it enunciates is true. The geographical
movement of books under normal conditions is predictable,
but in periods of confusion it is erratic. Accordingly, a discipline in the study of bibliographical geography covering both
forms of travel ought to be included in the training of
librarians.

The present conference is an exercise in bibliographical
history and bibliographical geography, both, however, limited
to the last half-century. Furthermore, it is limited to the case
of scholarly antiquarian literature, because in this the spatial
and temporal movements are most obvious. We propose to
survey recent changes in secular affairs that have produced
the present status of the world of books and presumably will
control the developments of the immediate future. And, because we realize that the library is only one constituent of
culture, we have called in as councilors, scholars and a bookseller, who, we hope, will help us to keep our discussion truly
functional by presenting the needs of the reader and the conditions of book resources.   □

A BOOKMAN'S CREDO

Lawrence Clark Powell

In a paper read at the University of Chicago's Library Institute I indicated some of the deficiencies which I have found in academic librarians. The first and most obvious one is also the greatest: too few librarians suffer from the disease Dibdin called Bibliomania. We are paradoxically not a bookish profession. Too busy to read, is our excuse, and it is a tragic one. To be sure, we do not need more dilettantes who "just love books." Love is not enough. Give us librarians who have a passion for books, who are bookmen by birth and by choice, by education, profession, and hobby. Properly disciplined, this passion for books is the greatest asset a librarian can have.

I expected dissent from this creed and dissent I got. We have had too many librarians who were merely bookmen, the dissenters told me, and who by their bibliomania have retarded the development of their libraries as service institutions. They have accumulated books in vast numbers, it is true, but they have failed to secure well-trained and well-paid staffs to ensure the proper listing and servicing of the hoarded treasure.

What a library needs most, I was told, is a chief whose primary genius and interest are for administration, not for books. If a choice has to be made between a librarian who is

---

Reprinted from *The Alchemy of Books* and Other Essays and Addresses on Books and Writers by Lawrence Clark Powell (Los Angeles: The Ward Ritchie Press, [1954]), pp. 91-96, by permission of the author and the publisher.

an administrator and one who is a bookman, the library will benefit most from the choice of the first. For, the argument ran, the good administrator will recognize the importance of books and will see that his executive hierarchy or staff includes one or more bookmen-librarians.

I left the argument there, for the day was hot and adjournment of the institute was nigh. But on the homeward flight, across the winding Missouri and the rain-veiled Rockies, I pondered this problem of which is more important, the Bookman or the Administrator. My observation has not convinced me that the administrator always recognizes his own bookish deficiency and makes certain that his staff includes some expert bookmen. Like attracts like. The atmosphere and ambience of a library are unconsciously and inevitably conditioned by the man at the head. If he is what he should be, a leader, he will lead the library in the direction to which his compass points. No library, even the largest, can escape its destiny under a vigorous leader. The British Museum Library and the Library of Congress are in great measure what they are today because of two extraordinary leaders—Anthony Panizzi and Herbert Putnam.

The librarian who regards administration as the *summum bonum* will ordinarily not attract or hold bookmen of the highest worth. They will prefer to work in a place where their own ancient language is spoken and not in a library where such servants as cost-accounting and statistical-analysis are enthroned at the chief's right and left.

As a matter of fact no real argument is possible, for we are all agreed that extremism of either kind is undesirable. There have been—and there still are—librarians so blindly bookish as to render their libraries ineffective as places of service. The idea that books are to be used by people has always been suspect. Three hundred years ago John Evelyn noted with mixed emotions the existence of public libraries in Orléans which did not subscribe to the tradition of hoarding. "There are two reasonable fair public libraries," he wrote in his diary on April 21, 1644, "whence one may borrow a book to one's chamber, giving but a note under hand, which is an extra ordinary custom, and a confidence that has cost many libraries dear."

There is not space here to consider at length which is the greater obligation of a library, to serve its readers or to conserve its materials. I say merely that both functions are of equal importance. The good librarian recognizes a threefold obligation—to the past for its heritage, to the present for the support which maintains him and his charges, and to the future which may flower in a Montaigne, a Cervantes, a Goethe, to the ennoblement of mankind.

Libraries should have as few rules as possible, some wise soul once said, and break them all whenever necessary. A good example of such flexibility was noted by Casanova (*amateur* of *lettres* as well as of belles) in the course of a sojourn in Rome. "Two or three weeks after my arrival," he wrote in his *Memoirs,* "the Prince of Santa Croce heard me complaining of the obstacles to research in Roman libraries, and he offered to give me an introduction to the Superior of the Jesuits. I accepted the offer, and was made free of the library; I could not only go and read when I liked, but I could, on writing my name down, take books away with me. The keepers of the library always brought me candles when it grew dark, and their politeness was so great that they gave me the key of a side door, so that I could slip in and out as I pleased."

The other extreme to be avoided is of deifying the modern school-of-public-administration type of librarian to whom the organizational chart and the span of control are what ripeness was to Shakespeare—all. This kind of boss-librarian always seems to me out of place in the book world; he belongs in bureaucracy or big business where he can mingle with those who thrive on the bleak air they breathe.

Let me define the ideal library leader. He will be first of all, I insist, a bookman by choice, education, and experience. He will value the book as artifact and symbol. He will share Milton's belief that books are not dead things, but that they are indeed man's truest immortality, knowing that Shakespeare is more surely the substantial First Folio than he is the shadowy man of Stratford.

The ideal librarian will regard books as teachers *par excellence,* remembering, for example, how they rather than any school or university taught the young Lincoln. He will want to use every good administrative and managerial technique to the end that his library be a place of efficient use and wise conservation.

He will abhor censorship of books and of thought, and from his position of eminence in the community or on the campus he will speak against it whenever its evil appears. He will do his best to increase human liberty and understanding and tolerance.

Thus our ideal librarian will be a bookman-administrator-educator, possessed of a passionate devotion to his stock-in-trade, as well of skill and common sense in managing a complex organization. He will be a public servant aware of man's bookish needs and motivated by a humble desire to help satisfy them.

I have gone back to the seventeenth century for an example of conservatism; now let me return there, to the year 1650 when John Dury published his *Reformed Library Keeper,* and borrow therefrom a capstone definition of a good librarian—a definition whose modernity I hope will prove as acceptable to my dissenters as it is to me.

"The proper charge of the library keeper," Dury wrote, "is to keep the public stock of learning, which is in books and manuscripts; to increase it, and to propose it to others in the way which may be most useful unto all; his work, then, is to be a factor and trader for helps to learning, and a treasurer to keep them, and dispenser to apply them to use, or to see them well used, or at least not abused." □

WHAT IS LIBRARIANSHIP?

Jesse H. Shera

Some twenty years ago, at the University of Chicago conference on the reference function of the library, Pierce Butler deplored the librarian's lack of professional philosophy. The law and librarianship are unique among the professions, he observed, in that, though both have a highly efficient system of practice, neither has developed a corresponding theoretical structure to elucidate, justify, and control that practice. One finds difficulty in understanding his attitude about law, which is an old and highly respected discipline, but he is certainly correct with regard to librarianship. Librarians have always been thorough pragmatists whose ends were immediate and practical. They did not waste their time in idle philosophical speculation, but, confronted with a job that needed to be done, seized whatever tools or techniques were lying around and put them to work.

This intense devotion to immediate ends, not only encouraged disrespect and distrust of theory, but also prompted an attitude toward community service that was most notable for its attempt to be all things to all men. This attitude itself was a deterrent to the formulation of a professional philosophy, and discouraged any analysis of a rationale for the librarians' professional acts. One can commend this devotion

Reprinted from the *Louisiana Library. Association Bulletin* 24 (Fall, 1961):95-97; 117-118, by permission of the author and the Louisiana Library Association.

to service, but its very intensity, its lack of discrimination, has left a heritage of confused professional objectives and indifference to their clarification. However, the revolution now taking place in librarianship, especially as it is exemplified in the increasing interest in automated methods for information retrieval, is forcing librarians to reexamine their professional objectives and formulate a professional philosophy.

Every field of knowledge is a tri-partite unity of an intellectual environment, a methodology, and a body of information, which may be likened to a three-legged stool. Also, like a three-legged stool, if any one leg is missing, or even seriously attenuated, the utility of the whole is lost. Thus the fundamental importance of information to every form of human activity is becoming increasingly apparent.

But information is not only an essential attribute of every branch of human knowledge, every intellectual discipline, it is also essential to sanity itself. The human mind can no more tolerate a vacuum than can nature, for the brain must constantly receive a flow of information upon which it can operate. Every convict who has been compelled to endure solitary confinement knows the threat of becoming "stir crazy." The so-called "coffin experiments," carried out at McGill University have shown that normal intelligent behavior requires a continually varied sensory input (information), and that the brain functions properly only when it is kept "warmed up," like the muscles of an athlete. In these experiments the subjects were confined to small cubicles and isolated as completely as possible from all sensory stimuli. Even such a forty-eight hour deprivation resulted in extreme irritability, headaches, nausea, and in some instances hallucinations. Most important of all, the ability to perform problem-solving tests was measurably lowered; the subjects became more stupid as a result of such isolation. Other experiments have shown that normal young children who have been deprived of intellectual contacts with their elders, become mentally retarded.

Traditionally, and uniquely, the librarian has been the mediator between reader and book, between society and its

graphic records; and the librarian's social objective is to max-
imize the utility of recorded knowledge for the greatest possible benefit to the human race. If one thinks of this function
as a triangle, of which one side represents *readers,* the other
books, or graphic records, and the base, *books and readers* it
is the base that is the focus of all librarianship, whatever the
purpose may be and whomever the clientele.

In a society such as ours, in which literacy is virtually
universal, the act of reading is taken for granted. When reading thus becomes habitual, the intricacies of the complex
process by which ideas are communicated from the symbolism of the printed page to the mind of the reader are often
disregarded. As a result, very little is known about the ways
in which the brain receives the symbolism of the printed
page, interprets these symbols as representing a particular
sensory input, stores this information in the memory, and
subsequently uses it to control behavior. The behavior of
each human being depends upon his knowledge of the world,
and with that knowledge, be it personally experienced or
vicariously derived, rational or irrational, he weaves a pattern
of conduct that is his individual and social life. Thus the reading of a word, or a sequence of words, activates a chain or
complex of brain processes that enables one to live the lives
or share the thoughts of those whom he may have never
seen. As the individual matures the power to extract meaning
from the printed text increases, even though the text itself
undergoes no alteration. This growth is not to be attributed
entirely to intellectual maturation, it is also the result of
accumulated experience stored in the memory and appropri-
ately retrieved at the opportune time. Thus the key to the
true meaning of librarianship is to be found in the power of
the brain to translate the symbolism of the written word into
vicarious experience, assimilate and store this experience in
the memory, and reactivate it on demand. The traditional
metaphor of the library as the memory of a civilization may
have more validity than has been realized, for the brain is also
the library of the individual.

But the brain is much more than a memory that stores

and inventories the stimuli transmitted to it. It can manipulate these stimuli in a variety of ways and as a consequence of these manipulations it can weave new patterns of relationship, fabricate new concepts, and generate new knowledge. From past experience, it can generalize, on the basis of probability, about the future. Francis Bacon said that the mind of man not only recalls and reviews past events, but also it can ruminate upon them or build fanciful images of them. His knowledge of the intellectual processes were psychologically imperfect, but he was on the right track.

Increasingly librarians are becoming aware of the importance of automation to their professional procedures, particularly the relevance that computers may have for facilitating the storage and retrieval of information. But the value of these computers to librarianship, lies not so much in their ability to improve the efficiency of bibliographic searching, though this in itself would signal a great advance; rather, the great contribution that the computer can make to librarianship resides in its power to stimulate the human thought process, and in so doing focus the attention of the librarian upon the central problem of his discipline—the relation between the mind and the printed page. There is a reciprocal relationship between computer technology and neural research, for as we learn more about the design of machines that will stimulate mental processes, we learn more about the operation of the brain itself, and as we learn more about the electronic structuring of the brain we can fabricate improved machines that will simulate thought. From both explorations the librarian will profit, for as research improves our knowledge and understanding of the processes by which the library patron uses the apparatus of the library, the librarian can design better library apparatus for him to use. Admittedly, there are many dark continents in the human mind that remain unexplored, but as we progress in our examination of them new perspectives for librarianship will amost certainly be revealed.

The computer, or more broadly speaking, the machine, then, has brought us sharply back to the question with which we began. What is librarianship? Basically, it derives from two disciplines. Certainly, it is an aspect of communication, and language, or linguistics, is central to it. As our understanding of the processes of the brain improves, it should be possible to increase very greatly the amount of information that can be conveyed by the symbolism of the graphic record. The symbolism of chemistry and mathematics are, today, clearly empirical and of limited value, but they at least suggest the possibility of an improved symbolism for the communication of knowledge. Few would challenge the accuracy of Susanne Langer's assertion that language is man's greatest invention, but this does not imply that we have achieved the ultimate in communication. The possibilities of improving symbolism are very great, and there is no obvious reason why large segments of the population could not learn to read pages of a meta-language by means of which men might more fully explain to each other the complexities of life and thereby become more effective in cooperation. Admittedly research in linguistics is not the responsibility of the librarian, but any important shift in the communication process cannot but have dramatic implications for librarianship.

But librarianship as the management of knowledge is also rooted in epistemology—the knowledge of knowledge it-self—and especially social epistemology, the way in which knowledge is disseminated through a society and influences group behavior. The library as a social invention is concerned with the improvement of the individual, but through the improvement of the individual it seeks the advancement of society. Individuals not only make the society, society con-tinually reshapes the individual; this is perhaps the most im-portant key to dynamics of the library. The basic bond through which individuals achieve unity in a culture is through the communication of information. Thus informa-tion is the cement with which the structure of society is held together. A culture, almost by definition, produces a "tran-script," a record in more or less permanent form that can be transmitted from generation to generation. In primitive non-literate societies this record takes the form of verbal ritual, legends, poems, and ceremonials. The communication of this transcript is one of the most important activities of primitive groups. The invention of writing marked the beginning of the "dissociated transcript," a form of communication independent of the communicator. The growth of this social transcript, in recent years, has proceeded at an increasingly accelerated rate, and the problem of the efficient social utilization of this transcript has become correspondingly more difficult. Yet society finds itself confronted by the paradox that as access to this transcript increases in difficulty its dependence upon it becomes greater. The "paper flood" may threaten to engulf us, but without it we die of intellectual thirst. The growth of the "transcript," is, on the one hand, part and parcel of the growth of knowledge and on the other of the larger growth of organization in society. Which was the result of the other is immaterial. It would be futile to become involved in the hen versus egg controversy. The egg theory of hens is as valid as the hen theory of eggs. The point that concerns us here is that the epistemological foundations of the library tie it ever more closely to its supporting culture, and that as librarians improve their understanding of the sociology of knowledge they enhance their value to society and solidify their indispensability.

For centuries the cultural "transcript" remained relatively small and with respect to its intellectual content, generally lacking in any high degree of complexity. During this long period of stability, when simple bibliographic tools and procedures were adequate for access to library collections, librarians became unconscious of the assumptions that underlay their practice. Now that the profession is confronted by a period of rapid change, both with respect to the demands made upon it and the invention of new mechanisms to meet those demands, librarians must come to terms with an almost totally new vocational environment, or surrender to others the social responsibilities that they have cherished for generations. The once proud empire of philosophy lost by attrition its greatest domains. Scientists annexed the philosophy of science, historians the philosophy of history, mathematicians took over logic, aestheticians the philosophy of art, and psychology seceded. In a somewhat less spectacular, though no less real manner, librarianship is threatened, and I for one have no desire to preside over the liquidation of its empire, modest though it be. □

PUBLIC INTEREST AND THE THEORY OF LIBRARIANSHIP

Joseph Z. Nitecki

The Discussion of the relationship between the public interest and library objectives in this paper rests on the following two premises: (1) The American library constitutes an integral part of the structure of its own society; it originated and grew in response to that society's needs. (2) The structure of American society is a political democracy.

The democracy is here defined in terms of a variety of highly diversified and cross-related individual interests, which together create a pattern of multigroup interests, integrating the similar interests within each group, and segregating between these groups in terms of their conflicting interests. The method of accommodating all of these interests in democracy is political, based on competition between the groups for the sanction of their objectives by society at large. Thus, in a political democracy no individual, nor any group of individuals, is free from these powers of society, nor can it avoid its consequences. Therefore, the library, as a service institution, is the subject of political pressure, but at the same time it becomes a political institution with its own pressures used in the process of implementing its services.

Reprinted from *College and Research Libraries* 25 (July, 1964):269-278, by permission of the author and the American Library Association.

THE NATURE OF THE STIMULUS

The pressures on the library are of varying degrees, coming from various directions and requesting different kinds of services. Thus, the role of the library as a social institution is to provide and to develop the means for a better book-reader relationship, in which different readers, or groups of readers, expect different kinds of books for different purposes.

All of the group-interest pressures imposed on the library may be classed into one of three basic kinds: (1) requests for service, *i.e.*, to provide a given book; (2) requests for education, *i.e.*, to provide a book on a given subject; (3) requests for arbitration, *i.e.*, to provide either (a) controversial books on a given subject, or, (b) books on a controversial subject.

The convergence of these three types of demands is illustrated in Figure 1.

In requesting service, a patron knows what he wants; in demanding education, he wants to know what kind of book he should get; while in asking for arbitration, he expects assistance in choosing between opposing wants.

Each of the above requests constitutes a pressure for service which increases in proportion to the number of such requests made. The pressure may be measured in terms of an aggregate of individual requests, or as a definite demand made collectively by a group in society. In addition, such requests may be positive, *for* a specific kind of book (fulfilling the service), or negative, *against* a particular service offered by the library.

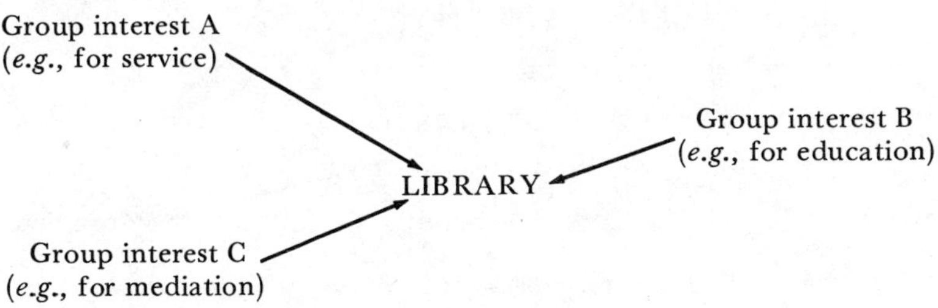

Figure 1 — Differing motivations for demands on the library.

As an example of the way the different pressures might work for or against a particular book in different situations, let us consider a book on birth control. Purely from the standpoint of efficient service, it might be expected in a medical library but would only clutter up the shelves in an engineering library. As an educational instrument, it might be held to have intrinsic value by a population expert but held to be pernicious by a devout Catholic. The subject is at this day controversial, and some segments of the community might approve of its being suggested by a reader's adviser while others might condemn the suggestion. From the standpoint of the public, one form of demand is charged with about as much emotion as another. While the radical right wing group is excessive in its denunciation of books alleged to be communist, probably no bitterness exceeds that of a scholar who finds the library has failed to acquire a book he thinks it ought to have. Those who are devoted to efficiency feel as strongly about it as those who are concerned with education or arbitration.

The library, as an institution of the whole community, can neither ignore nor succumb to any of these group pressures. A kind of response to these interests—which in itself is a *sine qua non* of library existence—constitutes the basis for the theory of librarianship, while its practical application implies an active participation in the affairs of society, not only in responding to, but also in imposing on society a new set of pressures. Thus the library, in fulfilling its obligations, becomes an interest group by itself, with its own political powers in the areas of serving, educating and mediating among the needs of the readers. (Figure 2.)

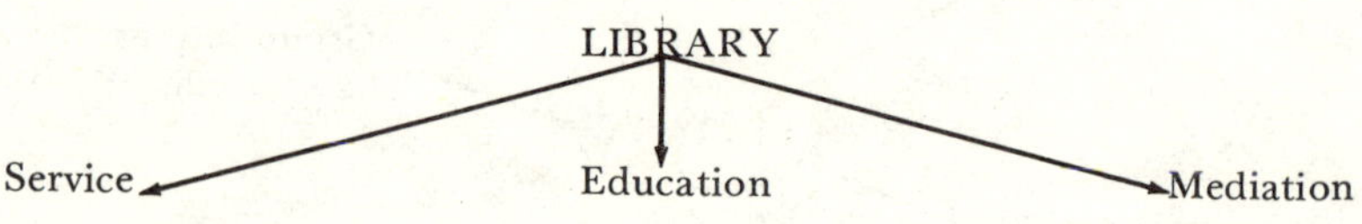

Figure 2 — Differing responses to the demands on the library.

A clear perception of these influences upon society is needed not only for the purpose of defining the role of the librarian, but also in establishing the degree of library involvement. On the other hand, a misconception about these pressures leads to a confusion of goals and to inefficiency in library performance. One of the main reasons for this is a seemingly confusing maze of relationships emerging from the dual position of the library as a recipient and at the same time as a transmitter of different interest-pressures. Juxtaposed, they may be represented by Figure 3.

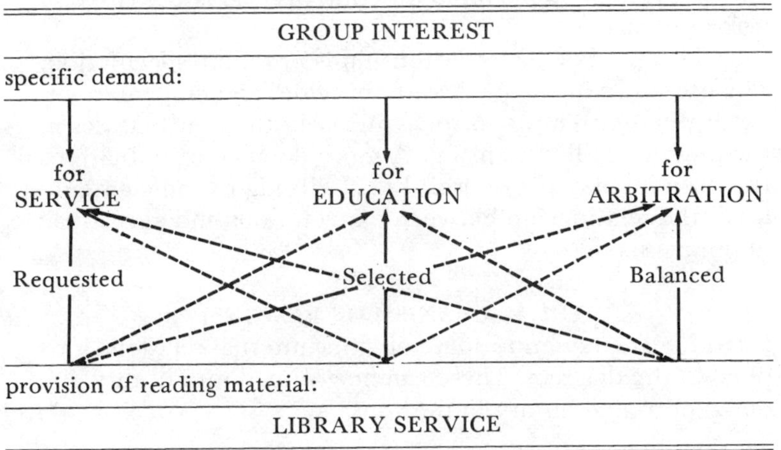

Figure 3
Interrelationship between demands of group interests and library services.

As seen in Figure 3, each of the basic demands made upon the library (for service, education, arbitration) is met by a specific and direct response (provision of requested, selected, or balanced material). However, none of the above functions operates in isolation, and consequently none of the services is limited to a singular effect. Thus, for example, supplying a requested book most probably also affects the educational status of its reader, at the same time strengthening or softening his stand on a given controversial issue. But even more important and significant is the orientation of the

librarian himself. If his conception of library objectives is
limited to, or even merely inclined toward, one of the three
functions indicated in the diagram on page 175, his performance will produce an entirely different result. If, for instance,
the librarian considers himself first and foremost an educator,
he will tend to provide preselected material (determined by
his conception of educational goals) not only in response to
requests for educational materials, but also in fulfilling library
obligations to provide books asked for (by trying to suggest
a "better" book as a substitute), as well as in assisting the
reader to make up his mind on controversial issues (by doing
it for the reader).

This kind of interrelationship is not mere speculation.
The literature of the profession provides an ample number of
examples of attempts to solve precisely these difficulties in
the practice of librarianship. A more detailed examination of
the diagram may prove useful in clarifying to some extent at
least, the relationship between expectations and performance
in library services.

THE MECHANISM OF RESPONSE

First, let us enumerate some obvious internal relations implied in the diagram. These can be grouped into library
obligations and library limitations:

A.   Three library objectives:
    1. To respond to the demand for service
    2. To respond to the demand for education
    3. To respond to the demand for mediation

(These relations are indicated in the diagram as uninterrupted
lines.)

B.   Six library limitations:
    1. Not to provide service only, when asked for education
    2. Not to provide service only, when asked for
      arbitration
    3. Not to provide education only, when asked for service
    4. Not to provide education only, when asked for
      arbitration

5. Not to provide arbitration only, when asked for service.
6. Not to provide arbitration only, when asked for education
(These services are shown in the diagram by interrupted lines.)

In the objectives the stress is on the obligation of the librarian to respond to these requests, *i.e.*, the concept of always trying to satisfy all the needs of a reader. The limitations, on the other hand, constitute an argument against a narrow specialization (*i.e.*, too limited a response) as evident in the two levels of philosophical response in librarianship:

a. The personal philosophy of a librarian who is oriented and dedicated to one of the goals of librarianship exclusively (*e.g.*, a cataloger, a reference librarian, or a library administrator) resulting in a bias, evident in considering the remaining two objectives in terms of the preferred one (*e.g.*, an overstress on classificatory problems, overlooking the practical needs of the library user, etc.).

b. The institutional philosophy, in which the whole library's operations are defined in terms of one of the functions only (*e.g.*, circulation, public and school library), and in resisting demands which formally should be met by other types of libraries.

A comparison of library obligations and limitations yields the following nine library functions:
1. To *store* materials *required* for service
2. To *store* materials *required* for arbitration
3. To *store* materials *required* for education
4. To *aim* at education by *selected* service
5. To *aim* at education by providing *relevant* instruction
6. To *aim* at education by providing *appropriate* data for arbitration
7. To *organize* a *balanced* service
8. To *organize* a *balanced* education
9. To *organize* a *balanced* mediation

This tabulation illustrates an approach suggested in this paper, in which the philosophy of librarianship is formulated in terms of three basic kinds of decision-making processes, diffentiated by the three objectives of librarianship, *i.e.,* to collect, to educate, and to mediate.

It is proposed to show that the shift of emphasis from the goals of librarianship *per se,* into their functional and specific aspects (*i.e.,* limited), may contribute toward the clarification of the relationship discussed. That is, in anticipating readers' requests, the librarian organizes his collection in terms of the nine theorems formulated above, by aiming at storing the material, which is selected and organized in such a way as to provide sufficient assistance in response to the requests for service, education, and arbitration. In consequence of such an approach, when responding to a definite request, the librarian can provide a quick and efficient service by relying on a well-organized collection (*i.e.,* planned, classified, and administered in terms of the three objectives, namely service, education and arbitration). Similarly, in planning the future development of the library or in performing the reference function, the librarian is not biased by one objective, ever-influencing the three functions, but considers each of the objectives in terms of their corresponding functional aspects.

Consequently, each function and its corresponding decision-making process is essential in *any* library. The library specialization, that is, the preferential treatment of any one of these functions, is adjusted to the needs of a specialized reader of the library by changing the *proportions* of the three objectives, but not by eliminating them altogether. Thus, for example, in the specialized medical library, a number of various, unrelated titles and subjects will not be included in the collection, although each of those which are in the library will be used for each of the three purposes, *i.e.,* to provide concrete data, to explain their meaning, or to relate their significance to other facts.

Such a philosophy of librarianship presupposes a theoretical formulation which would relate the objectives of the library to its operations in a consistent, logical pattern.

The view expounded in this paper consists of the differentiation between three philosophical premises:

1. The procedural, concerned with library technology ("storing"), *i.e.*, the arrangement of library resources for determined purposes.
2. The conceptual, concerned with library planning ("aiming at"), *i.e.*, the formulation of specific library objectives or purposes.
3. The contextual, concerned with the administration of library services ("balancing"), *i.e.*, providing required service.

Thus, although in practice the library specialization may be manifold and differentiated by the form and/or the functions performed, the theory of librarianship in its threefold formulation incorporates all of the three functions covering all of the forms of service.

However, it is essential to note that in this theoretical formulation:

> procedure does not imply routinism,
> planning does not imply dogmatism,
> organization does not imply bureaucracy.

That is, the theory proposed is not frozen by conventional, authoritative, or unvarying mechanical interpretations. Each of the three functions singled out is differentiated in terms of different roles called for, but within each of these roles there is leeway in the method of performing these roles.

Furthermore, although all of the three functions are mutually inclusive in the sense that each of them is related to the problem of library goals, book arrangement, and administration, they do not necessarily lead to eclecticism. That is, although individually each approach is in a way incorporated in the other two approaches, none of them alone—in this implied form—determines the goals of decision-making processes but merely participates in them as an organic part of the whole process. However, once the objectives are formulated, the most appropriate decision-making approach is chosen, and then it operates independently, excluding the other two approaches as self-contradictory.

To illustrate this principle, we will use an example of the application of this theory to the roles called for in the activities of technical processes of the library. Although technical processes involve mainly a procedural aspect of librarianship, the other premises are active here, too. The conceptual approach is involved in planning and the contexual in the organization of the work.

TABLE 1
Different Philosophical Premises Illustrated in Library Technical Processes

Internal Motive		External Manifestation	End Result
Premise	Device		
Procedural Conceptual	Classification system Code for consistency of application	Efficiency	Functional Collection
Contextual	Manual of operation		

In Table 1 we notice that the main manifestation of technical processing is the provision of efficient and smooth operation which in turn will increase the functional aspects of the collection. Yet this over-all procedural approach consists of a number of internal objectives of varied character. The efficiency of operation is conceived in terms of a systematic classification (procedural aspect), its consistency (which is a conceptual goal aimed at), and a set of arbitrary decisions needed in controversial or conflicting situations (*e.g.*, formulated in the library's manual of operation, which is to be consulted in cases of conflict between the accepted procedure and exceptional situations—a contextual mediating device).

In this example we can see the distinction between the internal motives and the resulting external process. If in this scheme the internal stimulae were not subjugated to the over-all objectives, the process shown in Table 2 would result.

TABLE 2
Effects of Failure to Consider Overall Objectives

Decisions Based Exclusively on	Effects on the Process
Procedural system	Over classification
Conceptual consistency	Inflexibility
Contextual manual	Artificiality

That is, if each of the internal motives were independently responsible for the initiation of the process of operation, the collection would reflect the evils of not-so-unreal exaggerations, for example: the use of long and minutely subdivided call numbers in a relatively small library; lack of flexibility in not accommodating for new subjects not provided for in the printed classification schedule; and the artificiality created by rules made to fit the needs of day-to-day operations.

The illustration of the relationship between the relative roles of the different approaches can be extended to the library situation in general. Although each of these philosophies operates autonomously within the library organization they do not destroy the unity of the library.

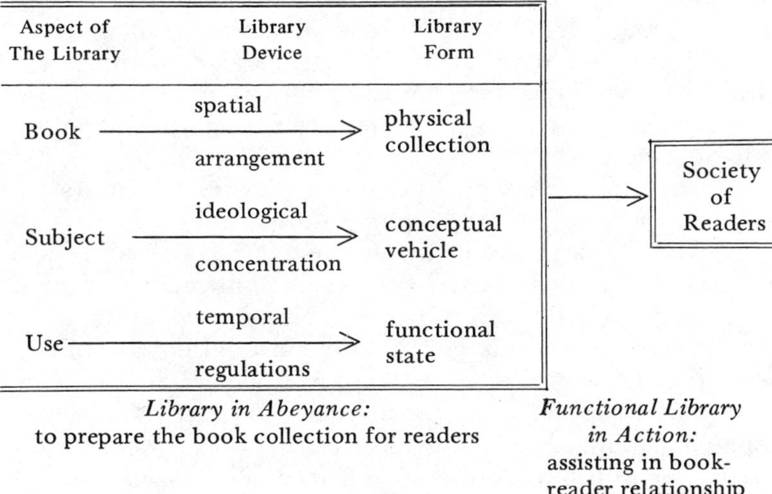

Library in Abeyance:
to prepare the book collection for readers

Functional Library in Action:
assisting in book-reader relationship

Figure 4
The contribution of three functional philosophies to library unity.

In Figure 4 we can see the analogy to the situation of a specific aspect of library operations, illustrated by the previous diagram, by distinguishing between the library form, which is a set-up, a kind of organizational blueprint, and the functional library, conceived in terms of its operations.

And again, in considering the library's dormant characteristics, we distinguish the internal differentiation between its physical, conceptual, and functional characteristics. That is, in each library organization we have to make a distinction between the problems related to the physical book itself, to its subject, and to its use, each posing different problems and objectives. Consequently, different theories are needed to formulate these different operations. None of the definitions of a part of the library would sufficiently define the whole library (*i.e.,* the library defined as a storage of books, as a conceptual vehicle, or as a functional unit, exclusively). Only if combined in cooperative functioning can these aspects fulfill library expectations. Thus we conclude with a restatement of what was the opening assumption of this paper. The role of the library in a society implies an interplay of different factors in an overall effort of the library to sustain its existence. In other words, the library as an institution is not taken for granted, and its place in society is not sanctioned by external reasons, independent of itself. On the contrary, its constitution is determined by the rights and obligations which emerge out of the competitive situation among all the social institutions striving for their rights to participate in the life of society.

The supreme justification for such existence and the relative importance of the library in the society are determined by the degree of its involvement in the affairs of the society. The means of participation are political in nature, measured in relative terms by pressures imposed on the library by the group interests and the power of library influence over these group interests. Library achievement is determined by the procedural, conceptual, and contextual development simultaneously; the more efficient the procedure, the better the possibilities of achieving its objectives, and the more respected the mediative character of the library, the more powerful its influence upon society.

THE CRITERIA IN DIFFERENTIATING
AMONG THE THREE PHILOSOPHICAL APPROACHES

The next step, after defining the mechanism of the library structure in dealing with various pressures, is to analyze the pressures themselves. As we have already noted, these pressures are used in a democratic society in order to promote the specific interests of various groups in society. A given group interest, when approved by the consensus of the majority of the members of the community involved, receives a public sanction which entitles it to be considered as an interest of the society at large, *i.e.*, a "public" interest—thus, in turn, becoming a legitimate concern of the social institutions which are responsible for meeting such public demands.

As we have already noted, the social institutions approach the problem of fulfilling these needs by developing three different kinds of attitudes, attempting to meet the three basic characteristics inherent in these public interests—namely, to provide the proper conditions needed to (a) satisfy the needs which are already formulated, (b) to assist in the expression of needs which are not fully understood by the reader, and finally (c) to mediate among conflicting needs. We have argued that each of these requirements is generically autonomous, calling for an independent theory of its own, and we concluded that only the three approaches combined together in a cooperative interaction can do justice to the variety of public interests in a political democracy.

The problem we are facing in this section is to establish a set of principles by which we could differentiate these services in librarianship.

We propose to use three kinds of threads unifying the theory of librarianship: the role of the librarianship, its goals, and the kind of decision-making process developed. Each of these aspects should be considered in terms of the concept of public interest as it is interpreted by the three theories of public interest. This will be attempted by comparing the

meaning of "public" and of "interest," and the relationship
between them, as represented by the definition of public
interest proposed by each of these theories.

Figure 5 is the tabulation of the criteria as an illustration
of each of the theories of public interest.[1]

	Interpretations		
Public Interest:	Procedural	Conceptual	Contextual
"Public"	Traditional	Durable	Aggregate
"Interest"	Legal	Collective	Individual
Defined as	Norms	Forms	Attitudes
Philosophy of Librarianship:			
Goal	Preservation	Interpretation	Assistance
Role	Custodianship	Education	Mediation
Process	Technical	Moral	Political

Figure 5
**The philosophy of librarianship compared
to the theories of public interest.***

The characteristics defining the procedural, conceptual,
and contextual theories of public interest can be briefly sum-
marized as follows:

a. Proceduralism defines the public interest as a means,
i.e., the norms which determine the ways of achieving the

---

* For the bibliography concerning the themes of public interest
discussed in this essay, see the author's original paper, pp. 131-40, and
especially:

a. Glendon Schubert, *The Public Interest: A Critique of the Theory
of a Political Concept* (Glencoe, Ill.: The Free Press, 1960), for his
threefold classification of theories of the public interest;

b. Oliver Garceau, *The Public Library in the Political Process: A
Report of the Public Library Inquiry* (New York: Columbia University
Press, 1949), for the historical generalization of library goals;

c. Howard R. Smith, *Democracy and the Public Interest.* University
of Georgia Monographs, No. 5 (Athens: University of Georgia Press,
1960), for the analysis of the role of the public interest in a political
democracy.

overall goals of the society. In this definition, the "public" is considered as an active manifestation of the values established in the span of its historical development. It is therefore viewed in the framework of traditions, which not only formulated the "public" itself, but also its mores, *i.e.,* the basic values which are accepted and embodied in the fundamental moral fiber of the society. And finally, the proceduralist is not concerned with the search for these values. They are already stated for him in the legal code, regulating the coexistence of the group interests within the society. Thus, any group interest which is legal becomes also "public" by contributing to the development of traditionally established values. The role of the proceduralist is therefore to assist the realization of these values by providing the best possible means of their attainment.

This formulation parallels the procedural philosophy of librarianship, stressing the importance of technical processes in preserving the cultural heritage of the society. The procedural librarian is therefore a custodian of the past; his goal is best fulfilled by protecting the collection in such a way that it will be simultaneously accessible for use by the contemporary public and preserved for public use in the future. His attitude toward public interest is best defined in terms of the procedural theory of public interest.

b. The conceptual philosophy of public interest rests on the acceptance of an ideal, "durable" conception of the public, which becomes a model or "form" for the aspirations of society. For this reason, the conceptualist rejects the significance of any specific public interest, if it leads to a preferential treatment of the interests of one group in society. To him, all the conflicts between segments of society should be resolved in terms of the interests of the whole society. Consequently, his goal is to contribute toward the unification of society by redirecting and re-interpreting group interests in terms of the ultimate interests of a society. In short, his function is to educate.

A corresponding role of the librarian is expressed in the educational aspect of librarianship, which is aimed at interpretation of the cultural values of society. The process involved in this conceptual function of the library calls for a selection of suitable reading materials for the library collection and its actual use. The selection is based on a value concept of "suitable" and "proper" material, and therefore it is ethical in essence. The conceptual librarian is a planner in the sense that he is concerned about the "ideal" kind of library collection and services. His role is to determine the goals of librarianship, transcending the immediate interests of any segment of the public.

c. The contextual interpretation of public interest is exclusively concerned with the specific group interests as they emerge in actual conflicting situations. The goal of the contextualist is to assist in resolving the conflict, and not to suppress the interest. In other words, he conceives the public as an aggregate of individual group interests, each striving toward the achievement of its specific interests, while the society, as conceived by him, is the aggregate of these interests at any particular moment. The public interest should be attended to, not because it is a common good, but because it leads toward it. It formulates the attitudes which in turn determine the co-existence of multiple interests. The role of a contextualist is to encourage the expression of these interests and to assist in resolving the ensuing conflicts. In librarianship, this is precisely the function of the library administrator who strives to establish library resources which are open to all group interests and which are sufficiently varied to meet a variety of conflicting demands.

In achieving his objectives, the contextualist relies on a political process determining the proper course of action in terms, not of efficiency (proceduralism) or moral values (conceptualism), but of the consensus of the majority of the library public. Since consensus has to be won, the librarian has to lead the fight for library approval and consequently is concerned with problems of promotion, public relations, etc.

QUEST FOR PARTICIPATION

The concept of involvement is a prerequisite of the notion of public interest. The organization which does not actively participate in solving the contemporary problems of its society, such as, for example, the Museum of Natural History, is relatively free from the direct influence of public interest pressures upon its activities. Such was also the case of the library in the beginning period of its development. In the pre-modern stage of librarianship, the librarian combined the roles of a scholar and a custodian together with that of a bibliophile, and the library collection was a result of the demands made on him for books and their content. In the modern period the trend is reversed, since it is the librarian who imposes his activities upon the society by developing different kinds of services in *anticipation* of a variety of expected demands for his services.

The following outline summarizes the development of the library's objectives in the last four centuries. In Table 3 we may notice the emerging over-all pattern of modern librarianship, beginning with the stress on book content, through attempts to enlarge the scope of its influence into an integrative role of the library as a cultural unit, constituting an organic part of the society.

TABLE 3
The Evolving Objectives of The Library

Approximate Time Sequence	17-18 Centuries	18-19 Centuries	19-20 Centuries
Ultimate goals	*To read*	*To educate*	*To mediate*
Policies	Book *availability*	Book *usefulness*	Book *availability & usefulness* for diversified purposes
Areas of achievement	*Storage*	*Internal library* organization	*Cooperation* between libraries
Public reaction	*Toleration* of the library	*Acceptance* of the library	*Participation* in the activities of the library
Library image	*Ornament*	*Utility*	*Tool*

The growth of the modern theory of librarianship may be characterized as a gradually emerging concept of library involvement in the affairs of its community. It began with the emphasis on the value of reading in itself which was a belief closely related to the dominant philosophy of that period, stressing the importance of the humanistic notion of self-improvement of individual members of the community, which together would strengthen the general will of the society. It was the period of enlightenment in both political and library philosophies.

The second library period, characterized by the progress made in the improvement of library techniques, was again in accord with the common belief in the precepts of natural law, which by the nature of their "inevitability" imposed a harmony of all interests in the uniformly organized society. In librarianship, this was a period in which an effort was made to propagate reading as a cure for social maladies, on the assumption that all such maladjustments are the result of unintentional violation of the laws of nature.

In contemporary political theory, the stress is on the relativism of goals demanding a correspondingly relativistic method of achieving them. In both the political and library theories of public interest, it means the maximization of the participation of social institutions in the actual life of society, aiming at the minimization of conflicts. This is achieved by searching for a common ground of understanding. In both cases, it is a period of complete involvement in the affairs of society, rejecting any evaluation of its problems from the position of an outsider.

The stress on the ideals of conceptualism was developed in a historical period of great optimism and faith in human potentialities, the approach of proceduralism reflected the age of scientific preoccupation in improving the physical aspects of human conditions, while the contextual stress on the problem-solving method of today is formulated in the contemporary language of relativism. Therefore, both the political theory of public interest and the philosophy of library science were, and are, the semantic expressions of concurrent ideas. Both expressed the general philosophy of their time.

PRACTICAL IMPLICATIONS

Concluding this essay, we are faced with the perennial question which arises in connection with any theoretical work, especially in a predominantly practical field such as library science—the question of relevance: "So what?"

The basic approach of this paper consists in a search for a unifying principle—for consistency—to prevent internal contradiction between various specialized activities within the library. We have considered in this paper the peculiar nature of library operations, characterized by both an internal diversification of roles and at the same time a unification of these library activities into a general library service to society. Thus, the specialist must apply his specific approach within the context of a general library operation, while a general theory of librarianship must both include a formulation of the basic postulates of the discipline itself, which distinguish it from other disciplines and at the same time account for the existence of a number of subtheories, reflecting the diversified objectives of library specializations.

An awareness of unity is expressed in the over-all functioning of the library in society, while competition between the various specialized approaches enriches the dynamic growth of the discipline, resulting in an efficient, valuable, and useful service to the reader.

This view of the library can be applied by the librarian in his dual role as both recipient and initiator of social pressures. The library will not only serve the interests of its own community but also contribute to the development of new interests. Thus, although the library is primarily an institution designed to serve the reader, its contemporary position in society suggests an active initiation of ideas rather than a passive providing of books.

In short, there is a need for the development of a philosophy of librarianship which will probe into the complexities of its nature, discussing, enlarging, or refuting syntheses similar to the one presented in this paper.

Such a philosophy may clarify the interpretation of our purposes, thus solving the practical difficulties diagnosed sometime ago by C. O. Houle: ". . . librarians speak at cross purposes. . . . They fail to understand one another because they do not appreciate in what different ways they approach a common problem. Often they do not even know how to ask one another the question which will make their differences clear, much less resolve them."[2]   □

[1] For the sake of clarity, we abstract each of the three approaches from the totality of library functions, describing each in isolation and in terms of its own primary characteristics. Thus, by discussing proceduralism, for example, we refer to these aspects which differentiate it *internally* from the other two approaches. A person who in a given decision-making process utilizes the procedural criteria, is, at that time, called a proceduralist in a positive sense; if however, he extends proceural principles to situations warranting conceptual or contextual considerations, then he becomes a proceduralist in a negative sense.

[2] Cyril O. Houle, "Basic Philosophy of Library Service for Adult Education," *Library Journal*, LXXI (November 1, 1946), 1513.

OLD WINE IN NEW BOTTLES

Guy A. Marco

On my first day in my first class in library school, the professor tried to stir up a discussion of "the philosophy of librarianship." The discussion never picked up momentum, for the elementary reason that none of us students knew what philosophy of librarianship meant. The professor might have told us, but teaching via the discussion method hardly allows for such direct statements from the podium. Long afterward I found a simple definition of that awesome phrase; J. Periam Danton wrote that a philosophy of librarianship was a view of the profession's "aims, functions, purpose and meaning." It might be practical to simplify aims, functions, purpose and meaning still further, into the single concept of "objectives." For a profession, as well as for an individual, a set of clear objectives constitutes the essence of a philosophy. What we are planning and hoping to accomplish is, in a real sense, what we are.

It follows that the 1966 conference theme of the Ohio Library Association, "Reshaping Library Objectives," is a philosophical theme. This is very refreshing to me, since I have always thought that we librarians as a group tend to be reticent about dealing with our philosophy. We spend too little time and thought on objectives, and, I think, too much

Reprinted from the *Ohio Library Association Bulletin* 36 (October, 1966):8-14, by permission of the author and the Ohio Library Association.

time and thought on means and methods. You can demonstrate the accuracy of this observation for yourselves by looking at the kinds of professional questions which most frequently concern you. Philosophical questions, dealing with objectives, begin with "why"; another kind of philosophical question, dealing with definition, begins with "what is." Technical and administrative questions, dealing with means and methods, begin with "how." By asking ourselves, for example, how we can adequately present in our book collections all sides of controversial issues, we are concerned with a methodological problem. It is a difficult problem, to be sure, but not nearly as challenging as the philosophical problem which underlies it, and which asks the question: *why* try to present all sides of controversial issues? Another specimen of a methodological problem is: how can we increase the percent of library users in a certain community? Obviously a philosophical question which looks over the shoulder of that one is: *why* try to increase the percent of library users? As you know, both of these sample "why" questions—about balanced collections and about seeking more library users— have been answered pro and con by responsible and respected writers of library literature. Your answers will depend on your view of the proper objectives of the library. There will always be contrasting answers to the "why" and "what-is" questions, since they represent philosophical problems, and philosophical solutions. On the other hand, "how" questions tend to be answered definitely, after technology and experience have worked on them long enough. I don't mean to say that they solve themselves, but that their solutions may be anticipated with some confidence even as we address ourselves to them, although such solutions may not arrive in that interesting interval we call our own lifetime.

THE "HOWS" AND THE "WHYS"

As a check of this statement, we might look back on that pioneer conference of librarians held in New York in 1853 —said to be the first formal gathering of librarians anywhere in the world. The questions raised, explicitly or implicitly, by that earnest conclave, can be classified as "hows" or "whys." The "hows" have all been answered by now, while the "whys" remain as disturbing as ever. Some of their "how" questions dealt with establishment of a national library, exchange of materials among libraries, standarization in cataloging, preparation of recommended booklists for public libraries, extension of popular and research library services to persons without such service. As methodological problems, all these look simple enough to us 113 years later. But the fundamental philosophical issues at stake in such problems are not really much clearer to us than to the 82 good men who assembled in the chapel of New York University in 1853. What is the purpose of promoting a highly organized, cooperative, standardized, smoothly functioning system of libraries? What are the ideal objectives of libraries in a nation which fosters hundreds of institutions working simultaneously along paths that sometimes parallel and sometimes cross our own? We are still trying to find out. At that 1853 Conference, there was at least one attempt to put library functions into a framework of definite objectives. In his opening address to the Conference, Charles Coffin Jewett stated that "Our object is of a more manifestly and eminently practical and utilitarian character. We meet to provide for the diffusion of a knowledge of good books, and for enlarging the means of public access to them. Our wishes are for the public, not for ourselves." In the same address, Jewett set forth an interesting justification for the need to enlarge access to good books saying that:

> *Another demand of our peculiar civilization is, for the means of thorough and independent investigation. We wish to own no men as masters. We intend to re-examine all history from our own American stand point, and we must rewrite it, where we find its facts have been tortured to teach the doctrines of injustice and oppression. The mental activity of this country is surveying every field of research, literary, scientific, aesthetic, industrial, and philanthropic. It requires to know what others have done and thought, that it may itself press farther out-*

ward. This country, therefore, demands the means of the amplest research, and this demand must and will be met.

OUT OF TUNE

This statement of a library philosophy constructed as a corollary to American political philosophy seems very provocative; yet I do not know of any subsequent elaboration of Jewett's thought into a systemized statement of library objectives growing from the "peculiar civilization" that is the United States. Of course library development in America has, in general, paralleled the development of national ideals and goals. But there are still some disjunctions, some fine points where library policy seems out of tune with our national character. Let me cite just one example of such a disjunction. We are firmly committed as a nation to the concept of innocence until guilt is proved beyond any reasonable doubt; and our legal system continually builds new safeguards for the benefit of a citizen who is accused of wrongdoing. In your public library, however, you may have to prove your innocence of evil intent before you can lay hands on a book which teaches how to make a home-made bomb, or how to pick a lock. Indeed, many libraries will not even acquire books which they judge to have some potential use to the detriment of society, which is a way of passing negative judgment on the moral character of an entire community. Whether the library objective of serving directly and positively the purposes of a democratic society is a good one or not, it is an idea, publicly expressed 113 years ago, which deserves fuller consideration. My point is that this thought of Jewett's, a philosophical thought if you will, remains disturbing and intriguing for us, while the methodological questions which were rightfully demanding to him and his conferees have only historical interest to our generation.

The fact is that all the big "why/what" questions appear to have been asked already, for librarianship as well as for ethics, metaphysics, esthetics and similar branches of inquiry. Furthermore, answers to these questions have been offered by reflective persons in every field. As we direct our attention to "reshaping library objectives," it may be fruitful to review the thinking of two library philosophers, two men who represent opposite positions on the question of library aims and purposes. They are Pierce Butler, who sees libraries as agents of society and considers the library profession to be one of the social sciences; and A. Broadfield, who sees libraries as most directly concerned with individuals, and consequently thinks of library science as one of the humanities. Actually this polarity, between social sciences and humanities, encompasses all possible responses to the question of library objectives; if we think clearly about it we will recognize that while both answers are abstractly possible, each one of us must necessarily select one of them only: because they cancel each other out.

Here then are two bottles of old wine, one red and the other white. Let us pour out a glass of each, swirl it, hold it to the light, sample the aroma and flavor. Then let us try, each privately for himself, to select the one that suits his own palate—remembering that we cannot have both, since red and white wines are not compatible. Finally we will be ready to transfer our chosen wine into the new bottles created by the special nature of our own time and place, but we will do so in full awareness of the fact that decanting the wine will not change its characteristics, and that whatever name happens to be on the new bottle will not affect the merit of its contents.

THE CULTURAL ARCHIVE

One purpose which libraries serve is the archival; any library's holdings may be viewed as aspects of the history of a civilization, if only as records of a particular phase in publishing history. To some library philosophers, this is the natural and primary goal of libraries, and preservation is the key objective which the library ought to keep foremost. Elements of this line of thought can be traced back to the Assyrians and Egyptians, the Greeks, the Romans and the medieval monasteries. But the classic elucidation of the principle, broadened to take in preservation of all the elements in a civilization—

rather than special interests only—was written in 1933 by Pierce Butler of the University of Chicago Graduate Library School. Butler identified books as the "collective social memory" and the library as the preserver of scholarship and the intellectual content of a culture. The librarian, according to Butler, is "society's custodian of its cultural archives." The librarian's responsibility, however, *does* extend beyond acting as a passive keeper of documents; Butler says he must find ways to "exploit those archives for communal advantage." Whatever means you may wish to follow in working toward "communal advantage," if you are going to utilize the cultural archives you must first of all be very familiar with those archives; in other words you need to know bibliography. We may note in passing that a well-defined professional philosophy tends to foster well-defined programs of professional education. The conception of library science as bibliographical history leads to a certain kind of library school curriculum, which we see today more prominently in England than in this country, a curriculum grounded in history of printing, publishing and the so-called book arts.

One outcome of Butler's ideas, and of the ideas of his Chicago colleagues in the thirties, has pervaded library thinking so thoroughly that we are hardly aware of it. If you think of library problems from a social scientist's viewpoint, you will tend to apply the methods of social science in solving them. Hence our familiar apparatus of surveys, questionnaires, quantifications and statistical analyses. By the way, Butler is careful to point out that not every individual librarian need concern himself directly with preservation of the cultural memory, or in developing a body of principles and methods for librarianship. Indeed it will be the lot of relatively few librarians to be so involved, for most of us still have to occupy ourselves with the mundane but essential tasks inherent in the daily operation of our libraries. But he did hope, and I trust we all echo his hope, that every librarian will have a sympathetic understanding for this effort to establish principles, objectives, and a sound body of knowledge necessary to act on such principles. Furthermore we may hope that every librarian will receive with interest statements of a philosophical nature which may emerge from colleagues who are blessed with time and insight enough to create them.

SOCIETY'S INSTRUMENT

Another thought of Butler's will serve as a transition to our second bottle of old wine. It is that "a major phase of the library's service to any individual reader will be to assist him to an effective method for achieving his own private purpose, so long as this is not anti-social . . ." The other library philosopher I want to talk about today would agree with the beginning of that remark and dispute the finish. He is the British public librarian. A. Broadfield, who wrote a stimulating little volume on library philosophy in 1949. The tenor of Broadfield's thinking is in vivid contrast to Butler's although their views do overlap in places. For while Butler sees libraries as an instrument of society, that is to say of the group, Broadfield sees libraries as servants of the individual. In the last quote I drew from Butler, it was evident that his concern with individuals is a real one, but that his concern is limited by the ethical framework imposed by the community; Butler wants libraries to assist individuals in self-achievement, "as long as this is not anti-social." Broadfield wants libraries to assist individuals in self achievement with whatever results may follow, social or anti-social. We could say that to him librarianship is humanistic in its essence, while to Butler it is primarily a social science.

To our basic philosophical question "why have libraries?" Broadfield answers "for the sake of freedom of thought." To him "the existence of society is justified by the welfare of the human being, and this consists in or is impossible without freedom. A philosophy of librarianship should affirm that the part of the life of society which is librarianship has for its purpose the maintenance of the part of the life of the individual which is the activity of thinking freely." Obviously there is in the Broadfield flask a measure of 18th century French wine, but as I said earlier the great questions of philosophy were asked long ago. Broadfield does not pretend to be inventing individualism—he is seeking to apply it consistently in the consideration of library objectives. He cannot accept the idea of putting any boundaries on the freedom of choice in reading matter, whether these boundaries are keyed to social mores, literary quality or political expediency. "The final judge of what is necessary is to be the prospective user, not society nor the librarian." As librarians we are not, according to Broadfield, in the business of implanting truth and eradicating falsehood. Instead we ought "to create the conditions in which truth can prevail." We do this by providing the necessary tools for the kind of judgments which will tend toward truth; we may "help a man to form his judgment by giving him access, through catalogues, bibliographies and shelves, to unsuspected interrelations of knowledge. Although the first responsibility for judgment rests with the individual he could not judge wisely without the library, which places before him unexpected truths."

It is instructive to try formulating, from Broadfield's answers to the "why/what" questions answers to the "how" questions which follow from them. Should public libraries buy low-quality fiction? Yes, so that the reader, exposed to both good and bad literature, has the "opportunity to form his own judgment by comparing the two." Should libraries follow Herbert Putnam's advice and avoid books which teach "restless, irreverent or revolutionary doctrines?" Most definitely not; "deliberate exclusion of any description of literature is not part of librarianship. The doctrine implied in systematic exclusion is as pernicious as any of those mentioned, since it throws into jeopardy values as great as the values supposed to be threatened by them."

THE INDIVIDUAL ABILITY

Broadfield is telling us here of his faith in the individual's ability to distinguish between good and bad, in literature as in other spheres of existence, so long as the individual has total access to every possible choice. In time he will reject the pernicious, subversive books—but they may not be the same books which the librarians of the country, or the Supreme Court, would have identified as pernicious or subversive.

I must assure you, if you have any doubts, that Broadfield is talking about adult reading only. What children read
obviously must be supervised and directed, just as their other
activities are. We should beware of the library thinking which
pretends that a twelve-year old is an adult, ready to form his
own standards and judgments in literature; this is probably
more of an administrative convenience among certain librarians than the sign of systemized philosophy.

Possibly I have not given you enough of the hallmarks of
Butler and Broadfield to enable you to grasp the differences
in library practice which result from taking one or the other
as a guide. Here is a situation set forth by Butler which we
can put into the terminology of a book selection policy; it
gives us a glimpse of the abstract thinker confronting a tangible issue. "The knowledge that comes from reading has no
social significance unless it is acquired by such persons as can
inject it into the vital stream of communal life. For an American banker to know Sanskrit may be a source of great satisfaction to himself and to his friends, but it will probably add
nothing to his vocational skill or to his more general qualification as a citizen. For the teacher of language teachers it is,
however, almost essential if he is to impart a valid understanding of the fundamentals of comparative philology. On
the other hand, the welfare of the whole community may be
indirectly affected if this same banker possesses a general
knowledge of Hindu religion; this might, under conceivable
circumstances, tend to liberalize his mind and determine
where the weight of his influence will be placed when the
people are in danger of making a short-sighted decision of
permanent consequences."

For Sanskrit we can as well substitute any sort of hobby
or avocation which is unrelated on the surface to a person's
social role. Building a harpsichord will not make you a better
lawyer, according to this line of thought, and studying
Romanesque architecture will not make you a better dentist,
or a better children's librarian. Nor will any such studies produce a better citizen, in the sense of the word used by Butler
—that is, as a social being best equipped to give efficient

service to his community, to vote with full knowledge of
political facts, etc.

To this, Broadfield has an answer (though I should note
that he never refers to Butler specifically in his book):

"The aim of education and of librarianship, whose purpose is educational although its methods and assumptions are
different from those of education as commonly understood,
ought not to be to produce the "exemplary citizen", since
this by definition makes men copyists."

THE IDEAL MAN

It is evident that Butler's apparent ideal man, the citizen fully
assimilated into functioning of his community, cannot have
universal qualities, since communities differ in purpose and
belief. The ideal citizen in classical Athens was quite a different man from the ideal citizen of Augustan Rome, and the
exemplary social being in Leningrad today could readily be
distinguished from the perfectly adapted member of British
aristocracy. Broadfield believes that teaching men to be citizens only serves to divide them, while letting them think in
perfect freedom and make uninfluenced decisions, about
their community and everything else, will eventually bring
them together in peace.

Sanskrit, harpsichords and eleventh century churches
are good for the individual human being, as aids in the development of what Aristotle calls the unique human capacity:
reasoning. The arts and other esoteric studies of limited
"social value" have the cardinal function of providing models
for comparison, and sets of factors with implications in which
we are not personally involved—and which we can therefore
judge and study abstractly, without the interference of our
own desires and interests.

And a library plays somewhat the same role as an art
work in shaping our mind, taste and judgment. On its shelves
there are the subtleties, the contrasts, the sequential relations, the "unexpected truths" which we find in great poetry
or music. Exposure to the expressiveness of the past and
present in the form of an untrammeled library book collec-

tion will enlarge our potential for understanding ourselves and one another.

We have probably had enough old wine for today. I hope it has been neither too sharp nor too sweet. And I hope that we can all carry some of those venerable flavors with us as we turn back to the more simple beverages of library routine and daily decision, and as the occasion arises I hope we will each take the bottle of our preference, pour out a glass, swirl it, and hold it to the light.   □

FIELD THEORY AND THE CURRICULUM, A UNIFIED APPROACH

Neal Harlow

This is a proposal to adopt a theoretical (some may say a verbal) approach to the formulation of curricula. There is today no single definition of "librarianship" with which all who are active in the field will agree. Within the range of possibility will be found such varied interests as accounting systems for book funds, the problems of dates in bibliographic citations, criteria for selecting and evaluating information, systems analysis, and the creation of computer input. Only in very limited areas has a theoretical or structural approach been made. And like other fields which have not yet "achieved a state of synthesis,"[1] the lack of a theoretical base tends to encourage practioners (librarians and teachers) to accept tradition and practice because "some arbitrary status authority" has declared in favor of it. We are not now, therefore, in a position as educators to organize a curriculum around a stated body of theory or usage, nor can we afford to postpone change indefinitely while seeking a seemingly illusive consensus.

Clearly, much of present day curriculum is an accident of history, harking back to Melvil Dewey and nineteenth century technical education with its objective to produce

Reprinted, with minor changes by the author, from "Changing the Curriculum," *Journal of Education for Librarianship* 10 (Fall, 1969): 78-85, by permission of the author and the publisher.

good workmen. Teaching "how to do the job" in time gave way to teaching the elements of each operation, and by around 1900 library schools had divided their studies into "reference," "bibliography," and the "selection of books." To these staples were added before 1920 most of the rest of the now familiar core: cataloging, classification and subject heading work, and library administration. "It is a principle underlying all schools of practical instruction," an early educator stated, "that they must follow and not lead the profession"; and in order to keep training timely and practical (*i.e.,* operationally oriented), courses were added representing newly evolving specialties: "county libraries," "small libraries," "large libraries," and bibliographic cataloging. Keeping up-to-date continued to produce such course titles as "government publications," "special libraries" and "school libraries," and eventually "systems analysis," "information science," and "computer programming." Changes in curriculum have been characteristically by accretion, with the approach to existing courses remaining very much the same, and a minimum of loss by attrition taking place at the other end. Little inclination has been shown among library schools to analyze the *structure* of the curriculum theoretically and critically (in spite of contributions by C. C. Williamson in 1923, Joseph Wheeler in 1946, and E. J. Reece in 1949) or to provide the initiative and control to bring basic change about. The schools, too, have been *operationally* oriented—graduates do after all "continue to be in great demand by employers."

There exists today a persuasive strategy for analysis and control which may have useful implications for librarians; it is known as "field theory" and is derived from the study of physics. It presents a generalized notion of a "field" within which all occurrences take place—all events in "nature" occur within some field, large or small—and the properties and structure of the *field* (rahter than any limited or intrinsic forces) explain local phenomena. The solar system and living organisms and instances of such integration and of the regulation of reactions by the total structure. Field theory is consciously opposed to "atomism" (wherein reality can be broken down eventually into indivisible parts) and is disposed toward larger, more complex, and "natural" rather than artificial units. Study of such a field is primarily directed toward identifying and arranging its elements into "interbehaving" systems which interact with each other as "wholes" rather than "bit-by-bit."[2] All events are considered to be organized or structured in ways which are not (simply) serial, that is, taking place solely in a time sequence. A truly organic view of behavior requires that all activities within a system be not only relative to each other but that they be special instances of the same underlying continuity.

The following characteristics of field theory seem to be important: analysis which starts with the situation as a whole; the use of a constructive rather than a classificatory method (emphasizing organization rather than parts); a dynamic (not a static) approach; a distinction between relationships within a system and in a sequence (systematic vs. historical influences); and the use of a mathematical representation of the field.[3]

In adapting field theory to librarianship, we might start with the system or frame of reference within which knowledge and information are created, communicated, and utilized; this would imply the existence of other related systems of equal or larger size: the social structure, politics, education, business, etc. Next we could construct sub-systems of interacting influences and activities related to sources of information, communication processes, and people (instead of subdividing functions and operations into distinct types and parts, for example, not viewing "bibliography" from one outlook and "cataloging" from another, both being means for organizing information for transmission and use). We would take a consistently active role (as involved participants) rather than a passive one. We would distrust the appearance of simple one-way relationships (librarian to user, cataloger to bookshelf), seeking causation in a "whole," multidimensional view. And insofar as possible, we would frame these complex interacting structures in graphic, quantifiable terms for more precise study and understanding.

Applying the concepts suggested by physics, the "field" of librarianship could then be tentatively described as embracing the whole range of existing knowledge and information, embedded in a larger field of action involving the production of new knowledge, learning, decision making, etc. The *structure* of the field is the *process of communication*—generating, organizing, and storing information, establishing the interface between the information file and user, retrieving, analyzing, and validating information, transfering it to the user, and obtaining feedback. And the physicist's concepts of "particles" and "waves" can be usefully interpreted in this context by identifying "particles" with separate "bits," "items," "facts," and "data"; and "waves" with the propagation of "ideas," "concepts," and "subject matter" which are made up of but are not limited to the sum of the meanings of their individual parts. A "general theory" must also take irrational elements into account (likened to anti-matter in physics); and the phenomena of serendipity, free association, and perhaps some of the chance combinations made possible by the computerized manipulation of large stores of data illustrate this avenue of relief (and of potential innovation) from an otherwise highly organized and complex system. The physicist's concept of "entropy" is observable in the tendency toward disorganization in information systems, in the degrading of meaning during transfer, and in the margin of error implicit in all of our methods.

It is not the objective of this paper to develop a valid general theory of librarianship but to argue the necessity of taking a unified approach to the field in respect both to its scope and activity. Although librarianship is a process (and a part of other processes), most teachers and librarians seem to see it otherwise: viewing "the library" as an agency separated from other agencies; seeing the field fragmented into "information science" and "library science," into "type-of-library" and "type-of-activity," processing and public service, acquisitions, cataloging, reference, and administration. The curriculum was initially established on this model, which has steadfastly persisted to the present day. Thus the library tends to exist as a separate and highly localized institution, made up of distinct "divisions" or departments, held together largely by an organizational hierarchy; it is not seen (and it does not therefore function) as part of a continuous, dynamic social activity for organizing and transmitting knowledge. It cannot take a relevant role or become truly involved in a system of which it is unaware. Its development is along bureaucratic lines (new budget lines, new expenditures) and not in relation to the process of communication. It may react "bit-by-bit" to individual "demands" placed upon it but not in response to the needs of the system as a whole.

If the field of librarianship is indeed the whole range of knowledge and information (within the larger system of new knowledge, learning, and decision making), structured by the process of communication, how do we construct appropriate sub-systems as a framework for our now fragmented concepts? This is a theoretical area requiring much exploration, but the following tentative sub-systems are advanced: (1) the generation, organization, and storage of the record (collection building, bibliographic organization, creating the appropriate "file" or "store"); (2) the interface between the record and user (mediation, question negotiation, identifying the character and level of information needed); (3) the retrieval of information (search strategy, finding, analyzing, and evaluating data) and its transmission; and (4) the evaluation of output in terms of satisfying users' needs in learning, decision making, and human behavior, and as feed-back for systems adjustment.

These sub-systems of the librarian's field of communication, if they are viable, are governed more by forces flowing *from the field* than from the sub-systems themselves. Among these forces are the "literatures" of the subject areas (which vary in their organization as well as in form and content, some being cumulative, others additive, with varying amounts of access built in, etc.); and the characteristics and needs of people (which depend upon individual interests and responsibilities, acquired behavior patterns, levels of sophistication, education, motivation, and other factors). Working with information and people necessitates taking into account pertinent insights, principles, and constraints which derive from a number of disciplines, among them information science, systems analysis, public administration, political sci science, behavioral science, the humanities, and the "content" of these subject areas (their body of knowledge as differentiated from what is useful in them to the communication process).

The relationships with the field and among the sub-systems can be described graphically as in the following diagram, the central ellipse symbolizing the field of librarianship set in a larger field and surrounded by still other fields and disciplines; the sub-systems within the library field are represented by numbers (1) to (4): and the double-headed arrows indicate the reciprocal influences obtaining among all the "parts" and the "whole."[4]

According to this theory, the actions and functions of librarianship will be ineffectual if carried on in isolation; for real, pervasive, reciprocal energies constitute the field, and the attributes and behavior of the parts—if they are relevant—are determined by them.

Within this theoretical organization of the field of communication, what are the gravitational effects upon librarianship and consequently upon library school curricula? Is "cataloging" to be taught as a branch of bibliography, of information science, systems analysis, administration, and behavioral science? Is it influenced by the nature of the "literatures" and the needs of people? If it is a part of the sub-system (1) Acquisitions/Organization, is it also deeply affected by (2) Interface between the record and people, (3) Retrieval/Transmission, and (4) Evaluation/Feedback? Can cataloging be taught as a "separate" course in this context?

Identical questions can be asked about "book selection," "administration," "school libraries," and "information science." And where do we deal with the formulation of objectives, "question negotiation," "users" (and non-users), "levels of need," "collegial" vs. "hierarchical" relationships, "acquiry" and "inquiry" in learning, and automation? If the "core" program is to cover what all librarians need to know

The Librarian's Field of Communication

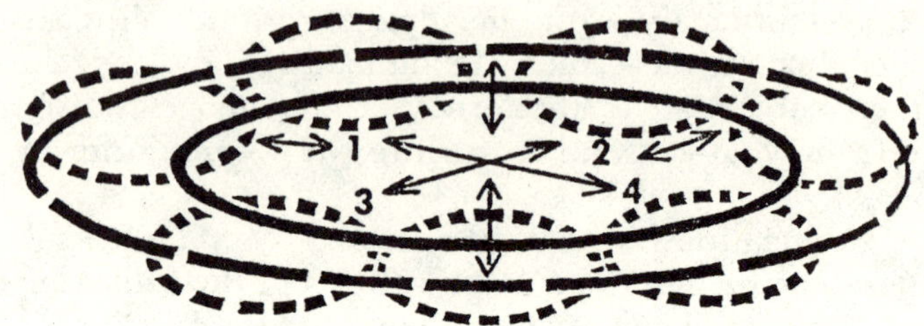

Sub-Systems of the librarian's field of
communication:

> 1 - Acquisitions-organization
> 2 - Interface between record-user
> 3 - Retrieval-transmission
> 4 - Evaluation-feedback

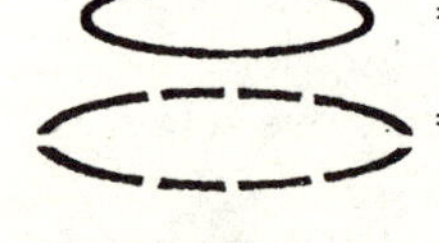 = The librarian's field of communication

= The larger field of learning, decision-making,
and new knowledge

 = Related disciplines and influences (the "litera-
tures," people, and the disciplines of infor-
mation science, systems analysis, public
administration, sociology, behavioral science,
the humanities, education, etc.

$\longleftrightarrow$ = Reciprocal influences

Each of the subsystems in the field of librarianship impinges upon the
others:

(1)   -Acquisitions/Organization

> (2)-Interface
> (3)-Retrieval/Transmission
> (4)-Evaluation/Feedback

(2)   -Interface

> (1)-Acquisition/Organization
> (3)-Retrieval/Transmission
> (4)-Evaluation

(3)   -Retrieval/Transmission

> (1)-Acquisition/Organization
> (2)-Interface
> (4)-Evaluation/Feedback

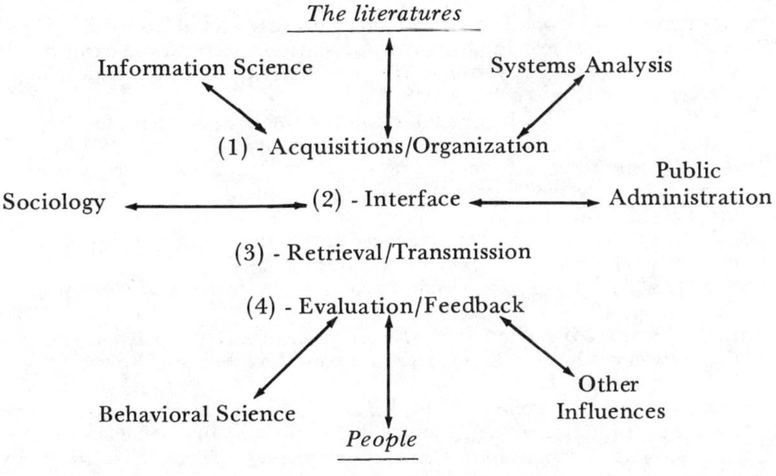

in common (in contrast to what may be required in special situations), can "reference," "book selection," and "cataloging/classification" truly fill this prescription? How do we build research, leadership, motivation, and inspiration into graduate professional study?

Our *field* is out there somewhere, bearing down upon us powerfully from all directions, and "field theory" provides a relevant contemporary setting in which to make a clean break, *if this is desired,* with present educational practice.   □

References
[1]   Fagan, Edward R.: English Field Theory and General Systems. *The Record: The Teachers College Record.* 69:733-742, May 1968.
[2]   Hartman G. W.: The Field Theory of Learning and Its Educational Consequence. *In:* National Society for the Study of Education, Forty-first Year Book, Part II, *The Psychology of Learning,* Chicago, University of Chicago Press, 1942, p. 166.
[3]   Lewin, Kurt: Field Theory of Learning. *Ibid,* p. 215.
[4]   Hartman, *op. cit.*

MATERIALS TO BE STUDIED
(In order of reading)

Hughes, Everett C.: Education for a Profession. *Library Quarterly*, 31: 336-343, Oct. 1961.

McGlothlin, William J.: *The Professional Schools*. New York, Center for Applied Research in Education, Inc., 1964.

McConnell, T. R., *et al.* The University and Professional Education (*In:* National Society for the Study of Education. Sixty-first Yearbook, *Education for the Professions*, Chapter XII, pp. 254-278. Chicago, University of Chicago Press, 1962.)

McGrath, Earl J.: "The Ideal Education for the Professional Man." (*In: Education for the Professions, op. cit.*, Chapter XIII, pp. 281-301.)

Bruner, Jerome S.: *The Process of Education*. Harvard University Press, 1961, particularly Chapter II, The Importance of Structure, pp. 17-32.

Lee, Calvin B. T.: Knowledge Structure and Curriculum Development. *Educational Record*, 47:347-360, Summer 1966.

Young, J. A.: Restructuring chemistry curricula. *Journal of Chemical Education*, 49:564, Oct. 1967.

Hutchins, Robert N.: The University Law School. (Paper read at the dedication of the building for the Rutgers Law School, Newark, N.J., September 9, 1966.)

Taube, Mortimer. Documentation, Information Retrieval, and Other New Techniques. *Library Quarterly*, 31:90-103, Jan. 1961.

Taylor, Robert. *Curriculum for the Information Sciences: Final Report: Recommended courses and curriculum*. Bethlehem, Pa., Lehigh University, Center for the Information Sciences, Sept. 1967, Report No. 12.

"Model for the Evaluation of Curriculum in Information Science Programs." (Prepared for a workshop of the American Society for Information Science, ASIS-EIS Curriculum Committee, 1968.)

White, Carl M.: *The Origins of the American Library School*. New York, Scarecrow Press, 1961.

Reece, Ernest J.: *The Task and Training of Librarians*. New York, King's Crown Press, 1949, particularly chapters II-VI.

Horn, Andrew H.: "Implications . . . of Greater Awareness by Librarians of the Social Responsibilities of Libraries and Librarians." (Working Paper for a departmental conference, U.C.L.A. School of Library Service, Feb. 26, 1969.)

Ginsberg, Eli, and Brown, Carol A.: *Manpower for Library Services*. New York, Conservation of Human Resources Project, Columbia University, 1967 (published 1969).

A PHILOSOPHY OF LIBRARIANSHIP

Louis Shores

I

If love of wisdom is the etymological beginning of a definition of *Philosophy,* then I contend there is more philosophy
in our library literature of the world than it has been fash-
ionable, in the past, to admit.

After more than half a century of practice in, what I
have called many times in my writings, our *Profession of
Destiny,*[a] I am convinced there is hardly a librarian I have
had an opportunity to converse with for longer than passing
who has not revealed to me some professional beliefs, often
keenly and feelingly. Perhaps in terms of depth and profun-
dity the professional philosopher might discount many of our
practitioners' reflections. But it would not be becoming to
one who claims to be a "lover of wisdom" to dismiss arro-
gantly the beliefs of any one, no matter how naive and
proximate.

Nor would it be fair to accuse librarians of total commitment to *pragmatism.* If the professional literature has tended
to espouse *value in use* as the real test of truth that tendency
deserves some compassion, at least, in the face of many ad-
verse cultures, throughout history, that have exaggerated the
material in their quests for the ultimate. Admittedly, there

Reprinted from *Library and Information Science* (Mita Society for
Library and Information Science, Keio University, Tokyo), No. 9, 1971,
pp. 40-48, by permission of the author and the publisher.

has been a disproportionate attention to technic, especially in the "how to" literature, and in the commitment to *survey* which has dominated practice in recent decades. But tucked away in even such practical writings there have been snatches of beliefs and hunches, of conjectures and futures, of suggested innovations and experimentations, that have suggested philosophy.

There is more than a chance that we overlooked, or underestimated, professional beliefs in our literature. Perhaps this is part of our general climate of protest, of forever identifying problems, of finding relief in the excoriation of scapegoats, of celebrating what's wrong with something. Our own professional specimen of the general negativism that affects the current intellectual and spiritual climate of the world is what I have often referred to as the *Librarian's Ancillary Complex.*

In composite, the Ancillary Complex, relished by even some of our leaders, insists Librarianship has no discipline of its own. Our education for the profession has been so frequently and vehemently denounced in "letters to the editor" that, at times, it has appeared that all one needed to allay *campus unrest,* generally, was to reform *library school,* specifically. A key point in the *ancillary* stance is that the literature of Librarianship is of such *low* quality that, to borrow from the earlier American evangelist Billy Sunday's bombastic diatribes, the library author would have to fly an airplane to enter hell. And as for philosophy, declares the *ancillarian,* librarianship has had almost none. Perhaps so.

But I dissent. Because I agree with the late novelist Jan Struther that librarianship is one of the few professions for which one can, today, have intellectual and spiritual regard. I begin with a declaration of faith in Librarianship as "the profession of destiny." I base this on my acceptance of Paul Tillich's definition of *faith* as "concern with the ultimate." It is my belief that the profession of *Librarianship,* the *Library Art,* come closer to concern with the ultimate than most of the professions and disciplines to which so many librarians feel ancillary.

In what follows are some extracts from the developing philosophy of one librarian, who has written and published thousands of words of library philosophy, despite the lack of recognition, by some, as related to a philosophy of librarianship. A fuller statement is in preparation for a book.

II

Librarianship has had no lack of definition. Our several professional dictionaries and glossaries, in many languages, have gone beyond the identifications found in general dictionaries and encyclopedias. Not entirely satisfied, some of us have augmented these definitions with declarations of belief about the profession, as a whole, and about such major divisions as *classification and cataloging, selection and acquisition, circulation and dissemination, reference and its modulation to information science,* to cite what we have sometimes designated as the four major divisions of library service. Furthermore, we have supplemented with philosophies for each of the four library types: *academic, public, school, special.* The literature of *library education for use and of education for librarianship* abounds with philosophical concerns for the preparation of the next generation. And if further evidence is needed that librarianship is deeply concerned with philosophy, especially non-pragmatic, review the growing literature in two of the newest library school concentrations; *library history,* and *comparative librarianship.*

I have spoken with hundreds of librarians all over the world, in my professional life time. With almost all who have conversed on our profession for even a few minutes, uninterruptedly, philosophy has interposed. I dare not even begin a directory of library philosophers, because the list would be so long, but I will try an experiment. As I think back over my last "Around the Library World in 76 Days,"[b] on a philosophical quest for what I call, "The Quiet Force," I begin in Tokyo, at Keio University's School of Library and Information Science. Perhaps Professor Sawamoto will recall our animated dialogues on a philosophy of *Library education.*

Retracing the route, in Manila, we compared our beliefs,

Potenciana David, librarian of the Far Eastern University, and
I, on the ultimate place of the library in higher education.
From there, back to Canberra, Australia, where Sir Harold
Leslie White, then National Librarian, expressed an ultimate
about library relations to government. Back across the Indian
Ocean, some 26 hours away by air, Rene Immelman at the
University of Cape Town deliberated with me on the relation
of freedom to responsibility in a library philosophy of book
selection. There was an all-African library congress at the
University or Rhodesia and Nyasaland, and diverging library
philosophies expressed especially by some representatives of
"new nations" would have disturbed confirmed ancillarians.

Almost with nostalgia, I recall the evenings on *reference*
philosophy with Olga Pinto, in Rome. Then back to Marcel
Thomas, intellectual director of the Bibliothèque Nationale's
Manuscript Division. How much library-literary philosophical
conversation hovered around his work on the Dreyfus case
and Emile Zola's *J'Accuse!* Had the library a role in communicating the truth about a false charge? To London, and
to several of those philosophical dialogues, that had begun as
long ago as my Fulbright exchange in 1951, on national librarianship, on organization librarian, and, above all, on en-
cyclopedism and its relation to librarianship's mission of information. Back home, philosophically deep-thinking Jesse
Shera and I philosophized history from the standpoint of
some new dimensions library history might contribute. There
are other parts of the world I have visited previously and
since where library philosophy has dominated conversation.
Perhaps near the top of philosophical memories were my
efforts to meet with Ranganathan during my two years as a
soldier in India. Subsequently, rewards came in London
meetings and in his visit to our Florida home, where I sat
cross-legged on our carpet as he conversed from his lotus-leaf
position. One of his disciples, A. K. Mukherjee has written
thoughtfully about philosophy in his book on *Librarianship.*[1]

If I have resorted to a librarian directory, after all, it is
to clinch with only one example per nation the point that librarians think, speak, and write philosophy, all over the

world, far more frequently than ancillarians recognize. And so to the philosophy of librarianship of one librarian.

III

For me, *Librarianship is the profession dedicated to the preservation, dissemination, investigation, interpretation of the knowledge most SIGNIFICANT TO MANKIND.*

Generally, libraries aim to acquire, organize, and disseminate the records of this knowledge most significant to the community served. This Record of Civilization I have described as the GENERIC BOOK. Compactly, I have defined the GENERIC BOOK as the *sum total of man's communication possibilities.* It comprises all *subjects, levels,* and *formats.* In an essay for the US *Saturday Review,*[c] which the editors chose to make the editorial for the first National Library Week, I philosophically suggested that the profession of librarianship, almost alone among all of the professions; and Library Art, almost alone among all of the disciplines, dealt with the only evidence we have of life.

During World War I, it is reported, after a battle in which the toll of French soldiers had been especially heavy, one soldier asked, tragically, upon the loss of his closest friend, "General, *What is Death?*" Any one who has served in the armed forces and experienced the death of a comrade, who one moment is beside him talking and the next moment is struck silent, will appreciate the General's spontaneous response to the question.

"Death," said the French General, *"Death is sudden incommunicability."*

Concerned as this librarian has been for as long as he can remember with *the meaning of death,* he has never found a more meaningful definition; not even in Herman Feifel's monumental symposium[2] on the subject by 18 of the world's leading thinkers. But more importantly, this incident helped to define the meaning of LIFE for him.

For if Death is *incommunicability,* as he believes it basically is, then LIFE must be the opposite. All of a sudden, the evidence of LIFE became to this librarian *communicability.*

From this philosophical starting point, the librarian

proceeded to the question how does man now prove that he is alive, and not dead? How has man in the past given evidence of being alive and not dead? The inevitable answer: through his *communication.* Which led to the next question: in what form or forms has man communicated? In a range of forms involving all of the known five senses, and, who knows, even in those extrasenses which persist in disturbing science's comfortable faith in its "method," as investigation continues in the parapsychological and psychical laboratories of some of the great universities of the world. The sensory forms communicate with man's gustatory, olfactory, and tactile senses, through such formats, for examples, as food, perfume, and cloths, respectively. Perhaps even more importantly communication is effected orally and visually through speech and graphics.

As this librarian pondered the evidences of life in man's communicability, and considered the range of forms in which man had communicated, from the beginning of, at least, the record of civilization, it became apparent that the *sum total of man's communication* equalled the evidence of life as distinguished from death. He was excited. This sum total also equalled the GENERIC BOOK.

IV

As this librarian reviewed the history of the book, he placed the printed page in its proper historical perspective. The contention by some librarians, especially in the United States, that there was something coming into libraries that had to be designated "non-book materials" was historically, at least, inaccurate. The stubborn insistence in the library literature on an artificial separation of print and other media formats into "book" and "non-book" materials was the underlying cause for a long and painful crusade this librarian had undertaken to bridge the gap that had developed between librarians and audiovisualists. His book *Instructional Materials,*[d] in 1960, was the culmination of a series of shorter writings advocating unity among all who worked with the GENERIC BOOK. Included in these shorter writing were debates with separatists among not only librarians and audiovisualists, but among educational administrators as can be read in the million-circulation *NEA Journal,*[e)] for example.

As one philosophical part of the GENERIC BOOK concept, this librarian formulated, in preliminary form, his *format classification* of the GENERIC BOOK. Historically, he first pointed out that long before the invention of printing there had been a recognized library book. In the libraries of Babylon and Nineveh, perhaps nearly six thousand years ago, the book was a baked clay tablet covered with symbols that had been pressed into the wet surface. Later, also perhaps, the Egyptians found a better way to produce a book. They used the *papyrus* plant which grew wild along the banks of the Nile, stripping the bark, and pasting the layers into a kind of paper. Several of these sheets were formed into long strips, sometimes as long as over 100 feet, rolled into a papyrus roll which could be unrolled a little at a time to reveal hieroglyphic writing, done in narrow columns, with a reed pen. To be consistent, would the spearatist insist that because they were not printed these papyrus rolls, or the vellum parchment formats that followed were "non-book" materials? On the contrary, there was a 15th century librarian, in a monastery, who insisted that only the manuscripts were books fit for a library, and that the print coming from some new-fangled machine called a printing press, were "non-book."

The *format classification* this librarian proposed aimed to classify the physical makeups of the GENERIC BOOK—to reveal the range of physical formats through which man has given evidence of life, representative examples of which can be found in the libraries of the world. In the basic summary of the format classification, library media are divided into six major divisions: (See the table on page 218).

This summary of the GENERIC BOOK formats was only a beginning to a system of media classification which assumed that the physical makeup of the medium may influence communication. This assumption, introduced perhaps as early as 1935, when the first audiovisual course for librarians was developed at George Peabody Library School, anticipated

Format Classification of Library Media

Division	Subdivisions
Print	Textbook; Reference Book; Reading Book; Serial
Graphic	Picture; Maps; Charts; Objects; Exhibits. . .
Projection	Still (slide, filmstrip. . .); Motion (16 mm . . .); Micro (film, fiche, card, print; bio . . .)
Transmission	Disc; Tape; Radio (transcription); Television (kinescope, videotape . . .)
Resource	Natural (mine, forest . . .); Social (museum, airport, hospital . . .); Human (inventor, traveller, poet . . .)
Programmed	Print (catechismal); Machine; Computer.

the current attention to the thinking of Marshall McLuhan.[3] As subsequently developed in the Florida State University crusade for "unity of materials," the GENERIC BOOK concept advanced the theory that communication and learning might be affected not only by *subject* interest, and maturity *level* of the communicant, but by the *format* of the medium.

Again and again it was demonstrated that a pupil who had difficulty understanding a print communication could easily pick up a thought through a 16 mm time-lapse motion picture, or from a transparency overlay, or with a field trip to a natural resource. When the "listening Post" was introduced into the *Materials Center* idea for a school library, it was found that secondary school pupils who had difficulty appreciating a Shakespeare play from the visual reading of it were revealingly aided by the set ear phones that transmitted an audial reading by a distinguished Shakespearian actor. But *vice versa* was also true, despite the growing tendency of some media philosophers like Duhamel[4] and McLuhan to fear for the future of print. Many teachers have discovered with surprise that there are still many children in our schools who learn better from the printed page than from audiovisual or computer-assisted instructional materials.

The theory of the GENERIC BOOK opened many philosophical avenues to education, to librarianship, and perhaps even to that branch of philosophy known as epistemology.

For example, the GENERIC BOOK suggested that for the first time in the history of education it might at last be possible to do something about "individual differences." The range and variety of media are now so considerable that it is possible to match individual differences in learners with individual differences in media. Out of this theory developed the augmented Carlylian movement of the 20th century, spearheaded by the LIBRARY-COLLEGE[f] concept for higher education and the MEDIUM SCHOOL[g] concept for elementary and secondary education.

The theory of the GENERIC BOOK could have implications for librarianship at many points in its statement of aims and purposes. Take for example the critical aspect of *book selection.* Heretofore book selection in libraries had been based largely on *subject* selection. To a lesser degree, and more usually in young peoples' libraries, attention had been given to maturity *level* selection. But if any attention was given to *format* as a basis for selection, it was to admit audio-visuals as "non-book" supplementaries. GENERIC BOOK selection is three-prong. Selection is not only by *subject* and by maturity *level,* but by *format,* with commitment to the principal that physical makeup of a medium may affect communicability as much as either of the two criteria formerly dominating selection.

V

As much as any other component of this librarian's philosophy of librarianship, the GENERIC BOOK concept has shaped his growing conviction that the Library Art has relations with other branches of knowledge quite unique. Unless it is philosophy itself, which has sometime been defined that way, the Library Art has the best claim of any discipline to being "the sum of all knowledge." Because librarianship serves all of the disciplines and has traditionally prided itself on its impartiality toward all, it is in a peculiarly strategic position to contribute that generalism for which an over specialized world of scholarship has covertly yearned.

To begin with, we must once and for all remove any

lingering ancillary doubts that the profession of librarianship is based on a discipline. Under the simpler dictionary definition of discipline as "1. instruction; 2. a subject that is taught; a field of study . . ." (*Webster's New Collegiate Dictionary,* 1963, p. 237), what constitutes the library school curriculum qualifies our claim. There is now a field of study, on which librarianship is based, so worthy of university instruction that no fewer than 50 graduate schools in the United States alone boast of an accredited program in library education.

A few comparisons with other disciplines will fortify our belief in the discipline on which our profession is based. If we agree with Sir Charles Percy Snow that there are "Two Cultures,"[5] and that Humanists have not yet taken the "Scientific Revolution" seriously, we will have to recognize what the library discipline has done to bring these two cultures together. Despite the fact that librarians have been accused of leaning toward the Humanist position in the quest for reality, there has been no greater commitment to the scientific method in the last three decades than is found in the library literature. Ever since this librarian's own orientation in the new Graduate Library School of the University of Chicago, dating back to 1929, he has almost frighteningly, at times, tended to recognize but one culture.

Aware of the near-monopolistic position of the scientific method in our mid-20th century thought, this librarian has, in recent years, developed a growing concern for the near-abdication of librarianship's Humanistic tradition. He has, on rereading, indeed, questioned Snow's assumption that the Scientist knows more about the Humanities than the Humanist knows about the sciences.

As we look at the disciplines in our universities today, those championed by the various learned societies, it is frightening to contemplate how many have committed themselves to the scientific method as an approach to reality. The study of society, has for some time now imitated the natural sciences almost unquestioningly. It is with concern that this library historian has watched historiography tending toward a so-called scientific method in history. But even more discouraging is the increasing amount of computerized investigation in the Humanities. Word counts of various kinds, proliferations of questionnaires in literature and music, in the visual and auditory arts, and even in theology and philosophy, attest to the fact that the two cultures, daily, are tending to become one.

There is no intention here to underestimate Science and its method. Admiration and wonder underwrite the accomplishments of science for mankind. But as librarians, it behooves us, from our traditional position of tolerance toward all of the specialisms, to offer some balance, as between the "two cultures," and among the many disciplines. From our generalist perspective, we should be able to exert some of the caution that concerned contemporary philosophy expresses.

In the article on the "Scientific Method" which philosopher William Werkmeister wrote for *Collier's Encyclopedia*[6] (20:500-8) he refers to the "Bias and the Limitations of Science" in a concluding section. Commenting on the "physicalism" of an "unified science," Professor Werkmeister amplifies

> "This is the view that, in principle at least, all knowledge must be statable exclusively in terms of physical objects and that whatever is not so statable cannot be knowledge."

There is a second form of science bias, in Dr. Werkmeister's opinion: ". . . that only the methods of science can yield knowledge and that there is no approach to reality except through science."

With Dr. Werkmeister, every student of the library discipline must reject both biases. As he points out

> ". . . there are methods of investigation which are the proper procedure of philosophy, rather than of science, and which are foundational even to the sciences. Logical analyses, the dialectical clarification of meaning and of the cognitive situation as a whole, the analysis of categories and their interrelations, the quest for first premises of the whole of human experience—for valuations no less than for knowledge—are some of the activities which, though indispensable to the advancement of knowledge, do not depent upon the method of science."

What the philosopher is challenging us with is to join him in restoring a balance between the two cultures; to reintroduce a *gestalt* among the frustrated specialisms; to protect the possibility that the "riddle of the universe" cannot be solved exclusively in terms of physical objects. Who, more than the librarian, has through the centuries aimed to disseminate, impartially, all of the approaches to truth and beauty man has dared to attempt?

That is the relation of the library discipline to the other disciplines, in this librarian's opinion: side by side with the philosopher, to provide a *gestalt* for all of the specialisms; to point to the inevitable unity of knowledge, the wholeness of the universe.

VI

How deeply the Library discipline is involved in what Dr. Werkmeister refers to as the quest for valuations in the current "information crisis." Adorers of the cliché as our activists are, we tend to celebrate an exaggerated "information *explosion*." What they are really saying is that the effort to "retrieve" the proliferation of separated bits of fact have begun to tax human memory. To some extent, the electronic means of retrieval have almost kept pace with the cascade of minutiae being exhibited as evidence that contemporary man must be wiser than ever before. The protesters and their increasing protests, in most parts of the world should raise questions as to whether all of these bits and pieces of information we are now so passionately committed to "retrieving" have really increased man's wisdom at all, certainly on ultimates. More than ever before, it would seem, mankind is in need of a value *implosion*.

This librarian has mediated and reflected about the philosophy of information at least as far back as 1929, when he began work on what some of his colleagues have considered his major work—*Basic Reference*. The three books in the series[i) and the nearly 100 shorter essays in *Reference* and in what he has referred to as the *modulation* to Information Science have represented an Information Philosophy of one librarian, however inadequate. This Information Philosophy is here briefly recapitulated. Because space compels extracts only, this section concentrates on four aspects of the *Basic Reference* concept: 1) *Redefinition;* 2) *Literature;* 3) *Encyclopedics;* 4) *Modulation.*

In the Annual Lecture for the Library Association in Bournemouth England, May 1951,[h)] this librarian redefined *Reference* as *promotion of free inquiry,* thus departing from the passive role of reference service which had dominated all three previous philosophies of Reference, before, identified by James Ingersoll Wyer[7] as "conservative," or "moderate," or "liberal." In the first the librarian did nothing for the inquirer that he could not do for himself. The second philosophy suggested a half-way relationship between the patron and the librarian in which the latter did some of the things the inquirer could do for himself, but less quickly and perhaps less expertly. The "liberal" went all out for the inquirer, doing everything possible, voluntarily.

But to this reference librarian all three schools of thought appeared to be dominated by the ancillary complex of passivity—waiting for the inquirer to ask the question before undertaking to assist him to any degree at all, from conservative to liberal. From years of reference experience I was convinced that answering inquirers' inquiries would always be a significant aim and purpose in reference service for all types of libraries. But over and above the inquirer-initiated inquiries there was a professional obligation on our part to promote inquiry, not only by the lethargic part of our world mind, but even among those who are currently referred to as "activist." In every community served by libraries—academic, public, school, special—there was a creative obligation by our profession to promote the strengthening of the community mind, of the national mind, of the world mind by encouraging not only inquiry, but correct documentation of answers. By teaching correct documentation reference librarianship would guard against totalitarian brainwashing.

In this documentation a wider and better knowledge of the literature of reference was needed, not only by the librarian but by the patron he served. Concerned because the vast and rich literature of information had been comparatively neglected not only by fellow instructors in literature, a field in which I myself was then teaching, but by librarians, I set about in 1930 to arrive at a selection of the "basic titles" that librarians should master, and a smaller selection that laymen, based on age, interest, etc., should make a part of their life. Although I approached my initial selection quantitatively, by the overworked questionnaire method, described in the preface to the first edition of *Basic Reference Books*[i) (1937), the text of the book was qualitatively accented. It represented my inclination in the instructional dualism between *method* and *material* that has always confronted the reference teacher. My belief in the *literature of reference* as a discipline "for study" is perhaps another evidence that not all librarians favor the pragmatic. As a concomitant, I proceeded to augment the classification of types and subtypes of reference books, establishing some new categories like "how-to" manuals, audiovisual sources, etc.

This categorization of types led to a concentration on the "queen" of reference types, on what the late, great Isadore Gilbert Mudge called the "backbone of reference"— the *encyclopedia.* From educational use with some new dimensions for myself and for my students I moved first to evaluation and review, and then to designing and editing major English language works in the United States, for world wide use. So began what I have called my *Encyclopedics*—the gateway to my information implosion. The essence of *Encyclopedics* is the principle that regardless of the proliferation of separate facts the information problem is still the same— selection, evaluation, and *gestalt.* Of all the traditional *Reference* and contemporary *Information Science* struggles with the so-called "explosion" the encyclopedist, over the centuries, back as far, at least as Pliny the Elder, has been closest to a solution. I have defined *encyclopedia* as a *summary or synthesis of the knowledge most significant to mankind.* It is this definition that has underlined my three decades of designing and editing several encyclopedias, including *Collier's,* to which I have devoted 25 years of my professional life. I have an increasing belief that both Reference and Information Science must restudy the encyclopedia from the standpoint of the information quest in which both aspects of librarianship are now engaged, often in isolation from each other.

VII

Which brings us to the *modulation*. Inherent in the librarianship I have practiced and principled for a half century is an evangelistic complex to reconcile. It accounts for my dissent with much of the current dissent; my contention that in the history of protests few have been more sterile, more lacking in positive solutions than the current marching brand; my belief that no liberal can ally himself with the hypocritical "non-violence" of the contemporary hi-jackings, kidnapings, forceful occupations of premises, demands for all of the "listening" time and the right to heckle or walk out when the other side has its turn. I believe a more significant protest can be accomplished by a positive attempt to reconcile inherent imperfections in man. On a small scale I tried to bridge the gap between librarians and audiovisualists. After my return from some involvement in the growing schism between the documentalists (forerunners of the Information Scientists) both during my Fulbright year in the United Kingdom and on the Europe continent, I resolved to forestall another such schism as I had experienced with the audiovisualists. I introduced into my basic Reference class, as early as 1953, a comparative unit on Information Science. I included an early week at the University computer center, key punching, KWIC indexing, and comparing counterparts and differences in subject headings and thesauri; heads and descriptors, Dewey divisions and sections with groups and fields, etc. It was my good fortune to recruit a topnotch Information Scientist to our Florida State University faculty—Dr. Gerald Jahoda, a distinguished chemist, before he went on to supplement with library science education. A deep thinker on the problems of information generally, and on indexing in particular,

Dr. Jahoda readily entered into the dialogue on Reference and Information Science, with a mutual aim to reconcile.

When I undertook to essay this modulation for the British yearbook *Progress in Library Science,*[j] Dr. Jahoda critically read the manuscript. My thesis was that both needed to look at each other more continuously than they have. Traditional Reference had much to learn from such concepts as "interest profiles" and "selective dissemination of information" as well as from certain indexing techniques, and from "Systems Design." But Information Science needed to look back, also, at systems design, for example, in basic reference books to rediscover examples that anticipated such things as "citation frequency" and inverted entry. Indeed, the good encyclopedia might be worthy of restudy from the standpoint of its monumental indexing, alone. These are only telegraphic messages about the implications in the modulation concept.

VIII

Within the limitations of an essay, only extracts of a developing philosophy of librarianship can be indicated. Were there more pages they would be devoted to beliefs in the high role of librarianship in education as the trend to independent study mounts. Some indication of this can be found in the shorter published writings on the *Medium School,* and in the two books on the *Library-College.* If still more space were available, the philosophy behind the crusades for *Library History,* as begun with the doctoral dissertation and book, *Origins of the American College Library,*[k] and continued with the founding of the *Journal of Library History,* the American Library History Round Table, and the Florida Library History Seminars, would be unfolded. There would be pages, if not chapters, for the evangelisms on COMPARATIVE LIBRARIANSHIP and the belief that world librarianship must serve as the causeway to world understanding and peace; for tolerance by removal of such artificial barriers among humans as coloration differences, as witnessed by long involvement in what the United States used to call "Negro

Library Service;" for using the public libraries of the world as positive forces for reform through dialogue to replace the current negative activism of protest; to unite all in the common cause of strengthening the world mind.

But, within this limited space, all that I have been able to essay is that this librarian, like most of my colleagues in world librarianship have been much more philosophically concerned with our calling than our library literature, generally, recognizes.   □

REFERENCES

General
1   Mukerjee, A. K. *Librarianship:* Its philosophy and history. N.Y., Asia Publishing House, 1966.
2   Feifel, Herman, ed., *The Meaning of Death*. N.Y., McGraw-Hill, 1965.
3   McLuhan, Marshall, *Understanding Media:* The Extensions of Man, 1964.
4   Duhamel, Maurice, *In Defence of Letters*. 1939.
5   Snow, C. P. *The Two Cultures and the Scientific Revolution*. 1959.
6   Werkmeister, William, "Scientific Method." *Collier's Encyclopedia,* 1969. V. 20, p. 500-8.
7   Wyer, J. I. *Reference Work*. American Library Association. 1930.

by Louis Shores
a)   *A Profession of Faith:* First annual Mary C. Richardson Lecture, March 27, 1958. Genesio, N. Y. State University.
b)   *Around the Library World in 76 Days*, Berkeley, Calif. Peacock Press, 1966.
c)   "Books: Continuous Communicability." *Saturday Review,* March 22, 1958. V. 41, p. 26 (Editorial)
d)   *Instructional Materials*. N. Y., Ronald Press, 1960.
e)   "Library and AV Center: Combined or Separate?" *N.E.A. Journal,* May 1958, V. 47, p. 342-3.
f)   *Library-College USA*. Tallahassee, South Pass Press, 1970.
g)   "The Medium School." *Phi Delta Kappa*, 1966.
h)   "A Frame of Reference." London, The Library Association, 1952 (The Annual Lecture, p. 98-105)
i)   *Basic Reference Books*. American Library Association, 1937; 1939; *Basic Reference Sources*. 1954.
j)   "Encyclopedias and Information Systems Design." *Progress in Library Science*. Ed. by Robert L. Collison. London, Butterworths, 1967.

[k] *Origins of the American College Library*. N.Y., Barnes & Noble, 1935; Hamden, Conn. Shoe String Press, 1966.

[l] *The Journal of Library History, Philosophy, and Comparative Librarianship*, 1966- V. 1- (quarterly)

THE PREMISE OF MEANING

Archibald MacLeish

What is a collection of books? Which can be reversed to read: what is a book in a collection?—a book to a library?—to a librarian? Is it merely the unit of collection, a more or less fungible (as the lawyers put it) object made of paper, print and protective covering that fulfills its bibliographical destiny by being classified as to subject and catalogued by author and title and properly shelved? Or is it something very different? Is it still a book? Is it, indeed, something more now than a book, being a book selected to compose with other books a library? But, if so, what has it become?

When he was seventy-four years old the Cretan novelist Nikos Kazantzakis began a book. He called it *Report to Greco,* Greco being, of course, the older and even more famous Cretan who painted the *Burial of Count Orgaz* and other canvases. *Report* is the operative word in this title: Kazantzakis thought of himself as a soldier reporting to his commanding officer on a mortal mission—his life. "I collect my tools: sight, smell, touch, taste, hearing, intellect . . . I call upon my memory to remember, I assembly my life from the air, place myself soldier-like before the general and make my report . . . For Greco is kneaded from the same Cretan soil as I and is able to understand me better than all the strivers of

---

Reprinted from the *American Scholar* 41 (Summer, 1972):357-362, by permission of the publisher and of Houghton Mifflin Company, agents of the author.

past and present. Did he not leave the same red track upon the stones?"

Well, there is only one *Report to Greco,* but no true book—no book truly part of a true library—was ever anything else than a report. Shakespeare used a different—and, being Shakespeare, a better—metaphor but it comes to the same thing. Lear speaks it to Cordelia at that sunshine moment toward the play's end before the deluge of the dark. They will go off, says Lear, the two of them, to their prison cell and "take upon's the mystery of things/As though we were God's spies." All poems worthy to be preserved as poems are written so—by God's spies beneath the burden of the mystery— and so are all other gathered writings of whatever kind however we may classify them, whether as fictions or as science, as history or philosophy or whatever. A true book is a report upon the mystery of existence; it tells what has been seen in a man's life in the world—touched there, thought of, tasted.

But it does more, too, as Kazantzakis' *Report* does more: it interprets the signs, brings word back from the frontiers, from the distances. Whether it offers its news in a live voice or is left, like Emily Dickinson's snippets of paper tied up with loops of thread, to be found by an astonished sister afterward in a little drawer, it speaks of the world, of our life in the world. Everything we have in the books on which our libraries are founded—Euclid's figures, Leonardo's notes, Newton's explanations, Cervantes' myth, Sappho's broken songs, even the vast surge of Homer—everything is a report of one kind or another and the sum of all of them together is our little knowledge of our world and of ourselves. Call a book Das Kapital or The Voyage of the Beagle or Theory of Relativity or Alice in Wonderland or Moby Dick, it is still what Kazantzakis called his book—what Shakespeare intended by that immortal metaphor—it is still a "report"— upon the "mystery of things."

But if this is what a book is in a library, then a library, considered not as a collection of objects that happen to be books but as a number of books that have been chosen to constitute a library, is an extraordinary thing. It is not at all what it is commonly supposed to be even by men who describe themselves as intellectuals—perhaps I should say particularly by men who describe themselves as intellectuals. It is not a sort of scholarly filling station where students of all ages can repair to get themselves supplied with a tankful of titles; not an academic facility to be judged by the quantity of its resources and the promptness of its services. On the contrary it is an achievement in and of itself—one of the greatest of human achievements because it combines and justifies so many others. That its card catalogues and bibliographical machinery are useful no one doubts: modern scholarship would be impossible without them. That its housing and safekeeping arrangements are vital, essential, necessary goes without saying. But what is more important in a library than anything else—than everything else—is the fact that it exists.

For the existence of a library, the fact of its existence, is, in itself and of itself, an assertion—a proposition nailed like Luther's to the door of time. By standing where it does at the center of the university—which is to say at the center of our intellectual lives—with its books in a certain order on its shelves and its cards in a certain structure in their cases, the true library asserts that there is indeed a "mystery of things." Or, more precisely, it asserts that the reason why the "things" compose a mystery is that they seem to mean: that they fall, when gathered together, into a kind of relationship, a kind of wholeness, as though all these different and dissimilar reports, these bits and pieces of experience, manuscripts in bottles, messages from long before, from deep within, from miles beyond, belonged together and might, if understood together, spell out the meaning which the mystery implies.

For the point is that without the implication of meaning, which is to say the premise of meaning, there can be no mystery anywhere. The dark is not mysterious: it is merely dark. Even the greatest of physicists, even Einstein himself, when he wished to speak of the universe as science observes it, spoke of it as standing before us "like a great, eternal riddle." And a riddle, needless to say, even a scientist's riddle,

even a scientist's eternal riddle, even a scientist's eternal riddle of the dimensions of the universe, is something which, by
hypothesis, exists to be solved.

It is this fact—the fact of the library's implicit assertion
of the possibility of meaning—which provides the drama of
the dedication of a new library in a world like ours. Whatever
the opening of a library may have been back in the days of
Mr. Carnegie's kindness when all good Scots believed that
reading resulted in understanding and the rest of the world
believed the Scots—whatever the opening of a new library
may have been in those days there is a taste of irony about it
now and more than a stir of drama. Our world—at least that
part of our world which we call the West—no longer hopes for
meanings. Even the philosophers, whose goal was once what
they called A Final Explanation, concern themselves these
days with something less—with a process. And as for the
intellectuals, more numerous as confidence in the intellect
declines, their shuttling caravan has almost come to rest at
the last oasis on the road to Prester John—the sandy spring of
the absurd. Their leaders may desert them. Ionesco himself,
author of *The Bald Soprano,* may regret the disappearance of
meaning from the world. But the caravan holds firm beneath
the dying date trees. "There was a time, long, long ago," says
Ionesco, "when the world seemed to man to be so charged
with meaning that he didn't have time to ask himself questions . . . The whole world was like a theater in which the
elements, the forests, the oceans, the rivers, the mountains
and the plains, the bushes and each plant played an incom-
prehensible role that man tried to understand, tried to explain to himself . . . Exactly when," says Ionesco, "was the
world emptied of substance, exactly when were the signs no
longer signs?" To which the caravan responds with a single
voice that there was a time long, long ago when Ionesco's
answer to all those draughty questions would have been
"Who cares?" Certainly the caravan doesn't care. Meanings
went out for it with Hiroshima. All that's left us is absurdity.
Unless you count despair.

But if Ionesco's complaint is out of fashion, what shall

we say of the Great Affirmation spelled out in almost visible letters above the door of a new library? Those Reports to Greco on its shelves exist in a relationship which implies that the library's business is relationship. But the generation the library is to serve has been raised in the belief that what matters is not the relationships which compose our lives but something very different—something called relevance—the relevance of each aspect of existence to ourselves. Not the weft and weave that surrounds us, the mystery of things, the riddle of the universe, the implicitness of meaning, but an immediate identification of each thing with each self on the assumption that there is no meaning and that only self is real. Love, for example, which is all relationship, total relationship, infinite connection, is made relevant by turning it to sex which is connection and nothing more. Death, which was once, in the old world of relationship, the perspective of everything, the distance that turns the mountains blue, becomes relevant by becoming conclusion: not even exit—just an end.

And life itself, once that infinite possibility, that prison cell where the defeated king could take upon himself and his mild daughter the vastness of our human wonder, is made a prison cell and nothing more—the ultimate relevance—in a solitary and absurd confinement where nothing, not even Godot, ever comes and nothing answers but the idiot whimper of self-pity.

Oh, there is drama enough on this occasion, irony enough, but which way truly does the irony cut? Is it the library's implicit assertion of the immanence of meaning that has become ridiculous in our fuddled time, or is it the tired caravan of intellectual fashion stumbling toward the Mountains of the Moon? I do not know the answer but I know something that can learn the answer. I know that meaninglessness is just as much a matter of belief as meaning. The caravan of the intellectuals would have you think that someone has discovered meaninglessness out there beyond us in the desert—in the infinities of space—and brought it home like a phoenix egg to prove the world is void. Nothing could be more childish. Meaninglessness, like meaning, is a conclusion in the mind, a reading, an interpretation.

And science—honest science—knows it. Jacques Monod, the French biochemist who sees living beings as chemical machines that construct themselves out of chemical chance, concludes that the process of life is blind and man an accident. But he reaches this conclusion, as he himself acknowledges, by way of his belief in theories of quantum mechanics in which other scientists, Einstein among the lot, are unable to believe. "A mutation," writes M. Monod, "is in itself a microscopic event, a quantum event, to which the principle of uncertainty consequently applies." But to Einstein the consequence does not apply because the assumption is unsound. Einstein, as Gerald Holton puts it, was a scientist "fighting for a causal physics" who assumed "a rational God of causal laws who would not play dice with the universe." Whether Einstein's assumption is right or M. Monrod's, is not, perhaps, for us, and certainly not for me, to say, but one thing is clear even to a scientific illiterate like myself: the issue between M. Monrod and Einstein, or between their positions, is an issue of belief. Einstein makes that clear enough. Quantum physics was to him a "false religion." And he said so. In so many words.

It would be helpful to us, with a library to open and a question to answer, if there were an Einstein of the world of letters to match that explicit Einstein in the world of science. For it is in the world of letters that the contemporary taste for meaninglessness has presented itself most flagrantly as something more than a taste, more than an opinion: as an established fact to be accepted with despair. And it is in the world of letters that this masquerade can do most damage. Critics may pursue the meaningless relentlessly, as they may pursue anything else that moves, without damage to their reputations or themselves. And playwrights, ambiguous reporters, may make their fortunes by it—they have. But the poor devil of a poet lives by meanings if he lives at all. Relationship is all he has to work with: that *analogie universelle* which Baudelaire discovered in the poems of two thousand

years and which the poems not yet written still must seek.
For the poet, the novelist—the artist in letters—to assert the
meaninglessness of the world is the ultimate act of human
folly, the act that ridicules itself. Even if the "principle of uncertainty" were established to the satisfaction of all science
and M. Monod were right in his finding that no "master plan"
exists for the construction of his "chemical machines," man
would still exist. And it is precisely man who, through his
arts, through his thought, through his Reports to Greco, has
constructed meanings over millennia of time, whether the
universe has confirmed them or not. Job's demand for justice
was shouted down by the voice from the whirlwind but Job,
because he was a man, took back his life and lived it not-
withstanding.

No, it is not the library, I think, that has become ridiculous by standing there against the dark with its books in order
on its shelves. On the contrary the library, almost alone of
the great monuments of civilization, stands taller now than it
ever did before. The city—our American city at least—decays.
The nation loses it grandeur, becomes what we call a "power," a Pentagon, a store of missiles. The university is no
longer always certain what it is. But the library remains: a
silent and enduring affirmation that the great Reports still
speak, and not alone but somehow all together—that, whatever else is chance and accident, the human mind, that
mystery, still seems to mean.   □

MELVIL DEWEY devised his Decimal Classification while working in the library of Amherst College. In 1876 he helped found the American Library Association, acting as its secretary for the first fifteen years and being twice elected president. He also began *Library Journal* and edited it from 1876 to 1881. In 1883 he was made Chief Librarian of Columbia College in New York and he started there a training class which became the first library school. In 1888 he moved to Albany as director of the New York State Library, taking his students with him. He directed the library and the school until 1906, when he retired.

JOHN COTTON DANA graduated from Dartmouth in 1878 and studied law, but ill-health sent him to Colorado, where he taught in the public schools, and in 1889 he was made librarian of the new Denver Public Library. He was a radical who gave free access to the shelves, opened a children's room, and advertised the library around the city. In 1898 he went to the Springfield, Massachusetts, City Library, and in 1902 to the Newark, New Jersey, Public Library, remaining there until 1929. He was president of the American Library Association in 1895 and founder and first president of the Special Libraries Association in 1909.

ARTHUR E. BOSTWICK took a Ph.D. at Yale and worked on *Forum, Literary Digest,* and the *Funk and Wagnalls Standard Dictionary* before beginning his library career as librarian of the New York Free Circulating Library in 1895. After three years in the Brooklyn Public Library, he became Chief of Circulation for the New York Public Library in 1902. In 1909 he moved to St. Louis and directed the public library there until 1938. He was president of the American Library Association in 1907-08 and was its delegate to survey the libraries of China in 1925. His book, *The American Public Library* was published in four editions from 1910 to 1929.

SAM WALTER FOSS was a graduate of Brown University, class of 1882. For the next five years he edited a weekly newspaper in Lynn, Massachusetts, and wrote a humorous column for that and other weekly newspapers, including the New York *Sun*. In 1887 he became the editor of a newspaper in Boston and an editorial writer for the *Globe*. Between 1892 and 1907 he published four volumes of light verse, in the last of which appeared his still-popular "Song of the Library Staff." His most widely known poem is "The House By the Side of the Road." From 1898 to 1911 he was librarian of the Somerville, Massachusetts, Public Library, and from 1904 to 1906 chairman of the finance committee of the American Library Association.

HERBERT PUTNAM, a son of the New York publishing family, was a graduate of Harvard College and the Columbia University Law School when he want to Minneapolis as librarian of the Athenaeum. In 1887 he became head of the public library there, but in 1891 he left to practice law for four years in Boston. At the end of that time he was made librarian of the Boston Public Library. In 1899 he was called to Washington to be Librarian of Congress and served until 1939. He was president of the American Library Association in 1898 and 1904.

ERNEST CUSHING RICHARDSON was Assistant Librarian at Amherst while studying there and went on to be librarian and professor of bibliography at Hartford Theological Seminary from 1884 to 1890, receiving a Ph.D. in 1887. In 1890 he went to Princeton as librarian and in 1920 was given the title of Director. He retired in 1923 and two years later was named consultant in bibliography and research at the Library of Congress and was general director of the Union Catalog at his death in 1939. He was president of the American Library Association in 1905 and wrote a classic book on *Classification* (1901).

J. PERIAM DANTON was educated in Germany as well as at three American colleges before taking his Ph.D. at the University of Chicago Graduate Library School. Upon graduation in 1935 he went to Colby College as librarian and in 1936 to Temple University, where he was librarian for the next ten years. He then became Dean of the School of Librarianship at the University of California, Berkeley, retiring in 1961. Since then he has been involved in counseling and international library affairs. Among his special interests are library education and book selection. His most recent book is *The Dimensions of Comparative Librarianship* (1973).

LOWELL MARTIN worked in libraries and taught while studying for his master's degree and then his doctorate at the University of Chicago Graduate Library School. In 1946 he became professor at the School of Library Service at Columbia University and the following year associate dean. He moved to Rutgers as dean in 1953 and in 1959 became vice-president and editorial director of the Grolier Society. In 1969 he returned to Columbia as professor. He has published *Public Administration and the Library* (1940), *Personnel Administration in Libraries* (1946), and *Library Response to Urban Change* (1969).

HERBERT GOLDHOR took his Bachelor's degree at Columbia and his Ph.D. at the Chicago Graduate Library School in 1942. In 1946 he joined the faculty of the University of Illinois as professor in the Graduate School of Library Science. In 1952 he became librarian of the Evansville, Indiana, Public Library and in 1961 returned to the University of Illinois as Assistant Director of the Graduate School of Library Science, becoming Director in 1963. He wrote *Practical Administration of Public Libraries* with Joseph L. Wheeler (1962) and is an energetic promoter of library research.

FRANCES CLARKE SAYERS was trained in library science at the Carnegie Institute of Technology. She was in charge of children's librarianship at the New York Public Library from 1918 to 1923 and again from 1941 to 1952. Between 1925 and 1932 she was with the American Library Association working in adult education. From 1934 to 1941 she was Lecturer in Children's Librarianship at the University of California, Berkeley, and from 1954 to 1965 held a similar position in Los Angeles. She has written five books for children and edited an anthology of children's literature. Her *Anne Carroll Moore: A Biography* was published in 1972.

HELEN E. HAINES started her career as an editor for the R. R. Bowker Company in 1892 and worked on *Publishers' Weekly*, *Library Journal*, and the *American Catalog*, among other tasks. From 1897 to 1907 she was recorder of the American Library Association and she edited the Proceedings of the annual meetings of the Association. In 1908 she moved to California for her health and in 1914 began to teach book selection at the University of California, Los Angeles, at the University of Southern California, and, during summer sessions, at Columbia University. Besides her immensely popular *Living With Books* she wrote *What's in a Novel?* (1942). She died in 1961.

PIERCE BUTLER attended Dickinson College and both Union and Hartford Theological Seminaries. He had the B.D., M.A. and Ph.D. degrees and was a priest of the Episcopal Church. He found work in the Newberry Library in 1916, stayed there until 1931, and then joined the faculty of the Graduate Library School at the University of Chicago, where he taught until 1952. He was a founder of *Library Quarterly* and a member of its editorial board as long as he lived. His best known publication is *An Introduction to Library Science* (1933), which is revered as a classic philosophic overview of the profession.

LAWRENCE CLARK POWELL majored in English literature and took his Ph.D. in France. He was employed in rare book stores and publishing houses until 1937, when he completed library training at the University of California, Berkeley. He began his library career at the Los Angeles Public Library and then the library of the University of California, Los Angeles, where he rose rapidly to be Chief Librarian and Director of the William Andrews Clark Memorial Library. In 1960 he became Dean of the School of Library Service in addition to his other positions. He retired in 1966 and in 1971 went to the University of Arizona as Professor in Residence. He is widely known as an essayist.

JESSE SHERA went to the Chicago Graduate Library School from Miami University and Yale. After finishing his doctorate in 1944, he was Assistant Director of the University of Chicago Library for three years, then Professor at the Graduate Library School for four, becoming Dean of the School of Library Science at Western Reserve University in 1952. In 1960 he was made Director of the Center for Documentation and Communication Research at Western Reserve and retained both positions until his retirement in 1970. He has published on the organization of knowledge, library history, library education, and the theory of librarianship.

JOSEPH Z. NITECKI, with an M.A. in philosophy from Roosevelt University, received his second Master's in library science at the University of Chicago Graduate Library School and was cataloger at the Law School Library there from then until 1963. He was Branch Librarian of the Wilson Junior College from 1962 to 1966 and became Director for Technical Services at the University of Wisconsin—Milwaukee in 1968. In 1972 he went to Temple University where he has been made Associate Director for Technical Services at the Samuel Paley Library. He has published two other articles on the philosophy of librarianship.

GUY A. MARCO studied at the American Conservatory of Music and took Master's degrees in both music and library science at the University of Chicago. He received a Ph.D. in musicology in 1956, having been Assistant Librarian and instructor in music at Wright Junior College for two years. He held the same positions at Amundsen Junior College from 1957 to 1960 and then went to Kent State University as Chairman of the Department of Library Science. In 1966 he was made dean of the School of Library Science there. He has published on music, music bibliography, and book reviewing.

NEAL HARLOW's training concentrated on English, History, and Fine Arts before he took his degrees in librarianship at the University of California, Berkeley. He served in the California State Library and headed two library departments at the University of California, Los Angeles, from 1945 to 1950. He was University Librarian at the University of British Columbia from 1951 to 1961 and Dean of the Graduate School of Library Service at Rutgers from 1961 to 1969, when he retired. He has served on numerous national bibliographic and professional committees, boards, and councils.

LOUIS SHORES received his Master's degree in library science from Columbia University and went to Fisk University as librarian in 1928. He spent a year at the Chicago Graduate Library School, but took his Ph.D. at Peabody College, where he was made librarian and director of the library school in 1933. In 1946 he became Dean of the Library School at Florida State University, retiring in 1967. During these years he was associate editor and then editor-in-chief of *Collier's Encyclopedia*, and founded the *Journal of Library History*. He has published widely on librarianship and education.

ARCHIBALD MacLEISH went from Yale to the Harvard Law School and practiced law in Boston after World War I. He published his first book of poems in 1924 and eight years later he was awarded the Pulitzer Prize for poetry. He received his second Pulitzer Prize for drama in 1959 and has several other distinguished awards, as well as more than twenty honorary degrees. In 1939 he left his position as curator of the Niemann Foundation at Harvard to be Librarian of Congress, serving until 1944. Subsequently he was one of the founders of UNESCO. His writings on librarianship were gathered in *Champion of a Cause* (1971).

ABOUT THE COMPILER

BARBARA McCRIMMON has a B.A. degree from the University of Minnesota, a Master's in Library Science from the University of Illinois, and a Ph.D. from Florida State University. She has been Assistant Librarian of the Illinois State Natural History Survey, Librarian of the Illinois State Water Survey, and Librarian at the American Meteorological Society Headquarters Library, Boston, Massachusetts, as well as Editorial Assistant and Acting Managing Editor of the *Journal of Library History*. She has published articles on Antonio Panizzi as administrator, the Libri case, and Prosper Mérimée as library reformer, and wrote her dissertation on the printing of the British Museum's *General Catalogue of Printed Books* 1881-1900. A collector of autographs of librarians and others in the book world, she is a director of the Manuscript Society and is a member of the American Library Association, the Bibliographical Society, the Bibliographical Society of America, and the Private Libraries Association.

Asheim, Lester. "New Problems in Plotting the Future of the Book." *Library Quarterly* 25 (October, 1955):281-292.

Berelson, Bernard. "The Myth of Library Impartiality," *Wilson Library Bulletin* 13 (October, 1938):87-90.

Bishop, William Warner. "Changing Ideals in Librarianship," *Library Journal* 44 (January, 1919):5-10.

Broderick, Dorothy. "The Librarian in Today's Society." *Library Journal* 92 (April 1, 1967):1413-1416.

_______________. "I May, I Might, I Must; Some Philosophical Observations on Book Selection Policies and Practices and the Freedom to Read," *Library Journal* 88 (February 1, 1963):507-510.

Bundy, Mary Lee, and Paul Wasserman. "Professionalism Reconsidered," *College and Research Libraries* 29 (January, 1968):5-26.

Burke, Reverend Redmond A. "Philosophy of Librarianship," *Catholic Library World* 19 (October, 1947):12-15.

Butler, Pierce. "Survey of the Reference Field," in Pierce Butler, ed., *The Reference Function of the Library:* Papers Presented Before the Library Institute at the University of Chicago, June 29 to July 10, 1942 (Chicago: University of Chicago Press, [1943]), pp. 1-15.

Carnovsky, Leon. "The State and the Community Library," in Leon Carnovsky and Lowell Martin, eds., *The Library in the Community* (Chicago: University of Chicago Press, 1944), pp. 1-11.

Christ, John M. "A Theory of Educational Librarianship," in his *Toward a Philosophy of Educational Librarianship* (Littleton, Colo.: Libraries Unlimited, 1972), pp. 70-84.

Crunden, Frederick M. "The Library: A Plea for its Recognition," in Arthur E. Bostwick, ed., *The Library and Society:* Reprints of Papers and Addresses (New York: H. W. Wilson, 1920), pp. 333-342.

Faison, Georgia H. "Growth of a philosophy of reference service," *Southeastern Librarian* II (Winter, 1961):285-292, 312.

Fletcher, William I. "The Public Library and the Community," in his
    Public Libraries in America (Boston: Roberts Bros., 1894), pp. 31-38.
Haines, Helen E. "Technics or humanization in Librarianship?" *Library
    Journal* 63 (September 1, 1938):619-624.
Harris, Michael H. "The Purpose of the American Public Library: A
    Revisionist Interpretation of History," *Library Journal* 98
    (September 15, 1973):2509-2514.
Heiliger, Edward M., and Paul B. Henderson, Jr. "Concepts," in their
    Library Automation: Experience, Methodology, and Technology of
    the Library as an Information System (New York: McGraw-Hill,
    [1971]), pp. 215-232.
Henry, W. E. "Librarianship as a Profession," *Library Journal* 42 (May,
    1917):350-355.
Kaser, David. "The Ptolemaic Theory of Librarianship," *The Oklahoma
    Librarian* 21 (July, 1971):10-13.
Kerr, Willis H. "A Working Philosophy for Librarians," *Public Libraries*
    26 (February, 1921):59-62.
——————————. "Philosophy—Thirty Years Later," *Library Journal*
    72 (February 1, 1947):187-190.
Kilgour, Frederick G. "Systems Concepts and Libraries," *College and
    Research Libraries* 28 (May, 1967):167-170.
Kolitsch, Myra. "Toward a Philosophy of Librarianship," *Library
    Quarterly* 15 (January, 1945):25-31.
Lydenberg, Harry Miller. "Librarians and Educators; a Librarian's View
    of Both," *Journal of Adult Education* 5 (June, 1933) 260-264.
MacLeish, Archibald. "The Librarian and the Democratic Process."
    A.L.A. Bulletin 34 (June, 1940):355-358.
——————————. "Of the Librarian's Profession," *Atlantic Monthly*
    165 (June, 1940):786-790.
Martin, Laura K. "About Recruiting and a Philosophy of Librarian-
    ship," *Journal of Education for Librarianship* 4 (Winter, 1964):
    163-168.
McCrum, Blanche Prichard. "Idols of Librarianship," *Wilson Library
    Bulletin* 21 (September, 1946):41-47.
McMullen, Haynes. "Research in Backgrounds in Librarianship."
    Library Trends 6 (October, 1957):110-119.
Molz, Kathleen. "Education for Sensibility in the House of Facts,"
    American Libraries 1 (January, 1970):29-32.
Nitecki, Joseph Z. "Reflections on the Nature and Limits of Library
    Science," *Journal of Library History* 3 (April, 1968):103-119.
——————————. "Towards a Conceptual Pattern in Librarianship: A
    Model," *General Systems Bulletin* 2 (June, 1970):2-16.
Powell, Lawrence Clark. "The Elements of a Good Librarian," *Wilson
    Library Bulletin* 34 (September, 1959):42-46.
——————————. "The Gift to Be Simple," *Library Journal* 82
    (February 1, 1957):311-317.

Shera, Jesse H. "An Epistemological Foundation for Library Science,"
in Edward B. Montgomery, ed., *The Foundations of Access to
Knowledge:* A Symposium (Syracuse, N. Y.: Syracuse University,
Division of Summer Sessions, 1968), pp. 7-25
_______________ . "Isis and the Librarian's Quest for Unity," *Ohio
Library Association Bulletin* 29 (April, 1959):19, 21.
_______________ . "The Quiet Stir of Thought or, What the Computer
Cannot Do," *Library Journal* 94 (September 1, 1969):2875-2880.
_______________ . "Toward a Theory of Librarianship and Information
Science," in his *Knowing Books and Men; Knowing Computers, Too*
(Littleton, Colo.: Libraries Unlimited, 1973), pp. 93-110.
Shores, Louis. "A Frame of Reference," in John David Marshall,
Wayne Shirley, and Louis Shores, comps., *Books, Libraries, Librar-
ians:* Contributions to Library Literature (Hamden, Conn.: Shoe
String Press, 1955), pp. 362-377.
_______________ . "Our Quiet Force: A Changing Role," *Catholic
Library World* 38 (May-June, 1967):587-592.
_______________ . "A Profession of Faith": First Annual Mary C.
Richardson Lecture, March 27, 1958 (Geniseo, N. Y.: State Univer-
sity of New York at Geniseo, [1958].
Temple, Phillips. "Library Responsibility," *Catholic Library World* 21
(November, 1949):35-38.
Vincent, George E. "The Library and the Social Memory," *Library
Journal* 29 (November, 1904):577-584.